Israel's Wisdom Literature

A LIBERATION-CRITICAL READING OF THE OLD TESTAMENT
Alice L. Laffey, Series Editor

Israel's Wisdom Literature: A Liberation-Critical Reading
Dianne Bergant

Forthcoming Volumes:
The Pentateuch
Alice L. Laffey

The Deuteronomic History
Sharon Pace Jeansonne

The Prophets
Carol Dempsey

Israel's Wisdom Literature

A Liberation-Critical Reading

Dianne Bergant

Fortress Press
Minneapolis

ISRAEL'S WISDOM LITERATURE
A Liberation-Critical Reading

Cover and book design by Joseph Bonyata.
Cover art by Sandra Bowden. Used by permission.

Library of Congress Cataloging-in-Publication Data

Bergant, Dianne.
    Israel's wisdom literature: a liberation-critical reading/
    Dianne Bergant.
        p. cm.—(A liberation-critical reading)
        Includes bibliographical references and index.
        ISBN 0-8006-2875-6 (alk. paper)
    1. Wisdom literature—Criticism, interpretation, etc.
2. Liberation theology. I. Title. II. Series.
BS1455.B38 1997
223'.06—dc21   97-203
                                                                   CIP

The paper used in this publication meets the minimum requirements of the American National Standard for Information Sciences—Permanence of Paper for Printed Library Materials, ANSI Z329.48-1984.

Manufactured in the U.S.A.   AF 1-2875

01   00   99   98   97   1   2   3   4   5   6   7   8   9

Contents

Editor's Foreword

THIS SERIES AROSE OUT OF FEMINIST CONCERNS, INCLUDING THE conviction that the biblical texts were produced by men in a patriarchal culture and that the ways in which the texts depict women and men are consequently conditioned by the assumptions associated with patriarchy. But such concerns lead essentially to other concerns. If the culture depicted in the texts is patriarchal, then it is also hierarchical; its way of organizing society is not only to place men over women but also to place free men over slaves, rich over poor, Hebrew over foreigner, as if persons could be appropriately relegated to one or another rung of a ladder depending on their sex, status, or prestige in society.

According to ladderlike or triangular models of social organization, even the lowest-runged humans rank higher than nonhumans, with those living nonhumans commonly identified as animals ranking higher than those living nonhumans commonly identified as plants. According to this scheme, all living beings rank higher than the matter commonly identified as nonliving which inhabits the universe. Although the applications of patriarchy-hierarchy find different expressions at different times in history and in different ethnic cultures, and although the ancient Israelites as hunting and agricultural societies were likely more conscious of their dependence on the nonhuman and therefore less likely to exploit with abandon than contemporary industrialized peoples, nevertheless, the principle of the legitimating of domination is inherent in the patriarchal-hierarchical worldview.

Such a patriarchal-hierarchical paradigm legitimates the domination of others considered of lesser value and depicts as normal an envy of those considered greater, while defining the desire to "climb the ladder" as "healthy ambition," a quality to be cultivated. This attitude stands in stark contrast to forms of social organization that assume the interdependence of the cosmos and posture themselves respectfully before the fragile ecosystem of which human beings are only a part, and certainly not the pinnacle. *A Liberation-Critical Reading* struggles with interpreting the biblical texts in ways that do not legitimate the patriarchal-hierarchical paradigm that permeated the culture that produced the biblical texts. These volumes seek to approach these texts from the perspective of a respectfully interdependent worldview.

I wish here to express my gratitude to Helen and Bill King from whose farm I came to understand the difference between my former very narrow version of feminism and the ecofeminism to which I now aspire, and the women who have agreed to participate in the series and shared my struggle, to Sharon, Carol, and Dianne. I am especially grateful to Marshall Johnson, my editor at Fortress Press, whose patience and faithful encouragement have been invaluable.

ALICE L. LAFFEY

Preface

THE FOLLOWING EXAMINATION OF THE WISDOM TRADITION of ancient Israel claims several characteristics that may set it apart from other studies of the same biblical material. First, it includes all of the books found in the Roman Catholic canon, and it treats these books in the order in which they appear there. Second, it is interested in the final canonical form of each book rather than the various stages of its development and redaction, and it interprets the book from that point of view. Third, it maintains that "integrity of creation" is the architectonic interpretive perspective, and it understands the biblical message from within that context. Fourth, it critiques the biblical material through a lens that is sensitive to the issues of race or ethnic origin, class, and gender, and it reflexively considers these three issues from the standpoint of the revelatory message of each biblical book.

This book is not a line-by-line or section-by-section commentary, nor is it a comprehensive analysis of the biblical books. It is, instead, a selective examination of the material from a liberationist point of view with an eye to contemporary resignification. It deliberately avoids questions of a historical nature and proceeds from a reader-centered approach.

1

Introduction

The Integrity of Creation

I N 1988, THE WORLD COUNCIL OF CHURCHES SPONSORED a consultation at Annecy, France, which attracted scholars who espoused various liberation and other political theologies. All of the participants came to realize that the theme of liberation can be applied to questions dealing not only with the human family but also with all life forms and, indeed, with the earth itself. The report of this consultation, delivered to the World Council, was remarkable for its "emphasis on linking concerns of ecological sustainability with concerns of social justice; on moving beyond oppressive understandings of God; on recognizing the deleterious effects of exclusively Western understandings of development on the peoples of Asia, Africa, Latin America, and Oceania; on recognizing the importance of science for contemporary Christian thought; on recognizing biblical resources for affirming what the World Council has called the integrity of creation" (Birch et al., 1990:290).

The points in this statement lend themselves to the following prioritization: (1) Basic to everything is recognition of and commitment to the fact of the intrinsic integrity of all of creation. (2) From this follows an appreciation of the importance of science for contemporary Christian thought. (3) Next, the need to move beyond oppressive theological understandings will become evident. (4) Only then can concerns for social justice be linked with those of ecological sustainability. (5) Finally, the importance of biblical approaches that originate from within diverse cultural settings will be recognized. The components from this statement of the World Council of Churches constitute the parameters of the world of understanding and concern out of which this study of the wisdom literature of ancient Israel grows. For this reason, a brief explanation of each component is in order here.

The Intrinsic Integrity of All Creation

We are natural creatures, and everything about us is a part of the natural world or mediated to us through it. For this reason, the concept of "the integrity of creation" is here considered the architectonic category of all experience and understanding. "The value of all creatures in and for themselves, for one another, and for God, and their interconnectedness in a diverse whole that has unique value for God, together constitute the integrity of creation" (Annecy Report, quoted by Birch et al., 1990:277). Recognition of the fundamental integrity of all of creation may be commonplace in the domains of the physical and life sciences, but it is relatively new to most branches of theology, with the exception of process theology (Cobb, 1982:111–34; Daly and Cobb, 1989:190–203) and some forms of ecofeminism (L. Daly, 1990:88–108; Merchant, 1980; Primavesi, 1991; Ruether, 1975:186–211). Should such a concept be universally accepted, its ramifications would be felt in all branches of theology.

Technology has sometimes led us to believe that we can step outside of our environment to examine and control it. It is important to remember that we do not merely live within our environment as we live within a building. We may be a unique dimension of the natural world, but we are not separate from it. We are part of it, and it is part of us. Humankind is embedded in nature, in the creative matrix that has given and continues to give life (Peters, 1991:9). Nature is also embedded in human beings. "We are truly children of the universe, made of the same stuff as the mountains and the rain, the sand and the stars. We are governed by the laws of life and growth and death as are the birds and the fish and the grass of the field. We thrive in the warmth of and through the agency of the sun as does every other living thing. We come from the earth as from a mother, and we are nourished from this same source of life" (Bergant, 1992:28). The intrinsic integrity of all creation is the fundamental presupposition of this study and will also be one of the lenses through which the wisdom literature will be examined.

Science and Theology

The second point from the Annecy Report admits the relationship between science and theology. "A religious tradition is not just a set of religious beliefs or abstract ideas. It is a way of life for its members" (Barbour, 1990:xiii). This way of life is embedded in a culture and reflects an implied cosmology or vision of the universe, which, in turn, will be made manifest through cultural patterns of behavior. Any significant cultural change will result in a shift in society's worldview. Some of the breakthroughs in contemporary science have been revolutionary and have contributed to a paradigm shift (Kuhn, 1970).

Since the biblical tradition is situated within the cosmology of the society that produced it, a shift in scientific paradigms will require a comprehensive reexamination of theology and, possibly, a reinterpretation of the biblical testimonies (Küng and Tracy, 1989). This reexamination and reinterpretation have not always been forthcoming. While accepting the fruits of contemporary science and technology, some people read the Bible in a very literalist way and, consequently, continue to espouse the prescientific cosmology that they perceive there. Believing that one can neither call on science to prove the truth of biblical testimonies (such as the report that heavenly bodies in direct line provided Joshua a victory over Gibeon [Josh 10:12-14]), nor fit biblical symbols into scientific patterns (for example, interpreting the six days of creation as a telescoping of evolutionary ages [Gen 1—2:4a]), interpretation faces a significant challenge in this regard. One might ask: Can religious testimonies embedded in the cosmology of one culture claim universal normativity and, subsequently, have meaning in a second culture that espouses a significantly different cosmology? One of the goals of this study is to provide examples of such recontextualization and resignification.

The Bible and Ecology

Despite the present failure of theology generally to embrace an ecological perspective, the Annecy Report maintains that biblical narratives do in fact provide a distinct understanding of creation's intrinsic integrity. If this claim is true, then perhaps what in the Bible appears to be an anthropocentric (human-centered) type of worldview has been imposed by the biblical reader rather than implied by the biblical author (Bergant, 1991:5), thus allowing the biblical material to be interpreted in more ecologically sensitive ways. Such an optimistic understanding of the biblical tradition is a direct challenge to any view that lays primary blame for our ecological difficulties at the doorstep of the Scriptures themselves (White, 1967:1203–7). It is also opposed to various anthropocentric biases brought to biblical interpretation by readers, be they androcentric (male-centered) or gynocentric (female-centered).

Most interpreters contend that the Bible displays a fundamentally theocentric (God-centered) perspective within which the principal value of creation lies less in its usefulness to humans (instrumental value) than in the fact of its existence from God (intrinsic value). Although creaturely limitations do make it impossible for us to measure reality from anything but a human point of view, it is quite another thing to maintain that humankind is itself the actual measure of everything. The intrinsic value of creatures is presupposed in biblical passages such as the creation narratives (Gen 1—3), the account of the Noachic covenant (Gen 9), the YHWH Speeches (Job 38–41), and various other poetic sections (such as Ps 104, Eccl 3:1-8, among others). They contend that the world has not been created merely for human use. The Bible is very clear on this point. The original couple may have been told "to subdue and have dominion" (Gen 1:26, 28), "to serve it and to guard it" (Gen 2:15), but humankind's primary relationship with the rest of creation is less mechanistic than it is organic (Merchant, 1980).

The affinity of creation theology to the wisdom tradition of Israel has long been recognized. In most studies, however, creation has usually been considered one theme among many, rather than the basis of all theology as is proposed here. This study will be distinctive in that the lens through which the wisdom literature will be examined and the standard against which it will be evaluated will not be the bias and tyranny of unyielding anthropocentrism, which has held sway for so long, but a perspective sensitive to the integrity of creation and its intrinsic value.

Ecojustice and Liberation

Ecological sustainability and social justice are not alternative human concerns and should not be pitted against each other. In fact, there can be no justice without sustainability and no sustainability without justice. Linking ecojustice and liberation helps us to think anew of the relationship between independent subjects and dependent objects. Science and technology have enabled us to isolate aspects of nature in order to examine them critically. We have been enriched by this capacity to scrutinize, but we have also been desensitized by its frequent objectification of the natural world. When human beings consider themselves the only subjects, it becomes easy to regard other creatures as objects with no intrinsic value, created merely to serve human agendas. This is anthropocentrism at its worst.

Human oppression, whether material, racial, sexual, or other, includes some degree of this same objectification, but in these situations the oppressed people are being objectified. They are treated not as subjects with powers of self-identification and self-determination but as objects expected to conform to the will of those who have power. In many ways they are perceived as the rest of the natural world has been perceived, merely as resources for the projects of those in control (Johnson, 1993:65f.). Such has been the situation of enslaved or indentured peoples throughout history. Human liberation demands both self-determination and economic justice for all. However, neither self-determination nor economic justice will long endure without a healthy ecosystem to sustain us. Conscious of the fact of the integrity of creation, we have come to see that real human liberation can only be sought within the context of ecojustice.

Cultural Interpretation

Liberationist approaches to the Bible insist that people who are ordinarily not heard must be partners in the interpretive process from the outset and not merely recipients of the work of the critical commentators. In fact, they must be the ones who direct the reflection of the community if biblical interpretation is to be deemed adequate. Everyone else must enter into the process in terms of solidarity with and accountability to those who were previously voiceless.

Much of what has come to be considered legitimate, even objective, biblical interpretation has been done from the perspective of the dominant "North Atlantic" worldview. Only recently have culturally specific interpretations been gaining wide acceptance. Much of this work is being done by commentators who are committed to their own cultural distinctiveness, but who are also schooled in prevailing critical methods. The specific character of their worldview provides them insight into contemporary implications of the biblical tradition not available to interpreters of the dominant culture.

Popular versions of the biblical tradition have probably been produced and handed down within various cultural groups for generations. They have not usually been known to outsiders, however, either because they have been considered too sacred to be exposed to strangers or because outsiders have not considered them of value. Today this same traditional religion is the object of investigation by scholars interested in popular religious intuition not dependent on the dominant culture's interests or interpretive methods.

While no interpreter can uncritically assume the social location of another, insights from various cultural perspectives can significantly modify one's worldview and sensitize one to issues that might otherwise go unnoticed. Three aspects of human identity that significantly influence the construction of one's social reality are race or ethnic origin, class, and gender. Human domination of one group over another is usually founded on some bias related to one of these aspects. More often than not it is a combination of the three. Liberationist interpretation must take these aspects and their combination into consideration. Therefore, while the fundamental presupposition and a major concern of this study is the integrity of creation, the critique itself will primarily focus on issues of race or ethnic origin, class, and gender.

Interpretive Method

Theory of Interpretation

In recent years, interpreters have acknowledged the difficulty of translating the theology of the biblical tradition for contemporary believers. Concerns and challenges differ from culture to culture, from generation to generation, from world to world. The ancient world is not the same as the contemporary world, and so its theology cannot easily be transported across the ages. The limitations of historical approaches have led interpreters to employ new methods for analyzing the Bible. New critical approaches examine literary characteristics as ways of discovering meaning in the text. These approaches maintain that once a piece of literature (or any form of art, for that matter) is completed, its meaning is intrinsic to itself and does not need the artist to interpret it. Some insist on the "semantic autonomy" of the text (Ricoeur, 1976:25, 43–44) to the exclusion of any historical reference (Polzin, 1977). Others highly value insights gained from historical-critical analysis that can throw light on the poetic function of the work (Habel, 1985).

Biblical interpretation is indebted to theorists such as Hans-Georg Gadamer and Paul Ricoeur, who have provided ways of understanding the dynamics of communication and interpretation. Gadamer believed that there is a fundamental connection between a work of art (a text) and the one experiencing it (the reader). He insisted that a work of art is truly a work of art, not in isolation but only when it transforms the one who experiences it. In itself, its artistic essence resides as potential truth, ready to be recognized by the one experiencing it. When the subject who is recognizing this truth belongs to a particular historical moment with its own tradition and understanding different from that of the historical moment of the artist, tension develops between familiarity and strangeness, between continuity and discontinuity. Gadamer resolved this tension by introducing the notion of dialogue or conversation between the text and the reader.

In his analysis of interpretation itself, Gadamer distinguished between three different worlds: the world *behind* the text (the world from which the text arose and the subject of historical approaches), the world *of* the text (the creation of the author and the subject of many literary approaches), and the world *in front of* the text (the new world of meaning made possible by interpretation) (Gadamer, 1975:254–64). According to him, understanding takes place when the horizon of the world projected by the text meets and interacts with the horizon of the reader. This results in a "fusion of horizons" (Gadamer, 1975:341–74). For him, understanding is never merely a mastery of objective data. It is a subjective interaction with the work of art.

Building on Gadamer's theory of interpretation, Ricoeur believed that "hermeneutics begins where dialogue ends" (Ricoeur, 1976:32). Although in his theory of discourse (dialogue) he explains how experience is expressed in language, he goes on to show how language becomes the vehicle of new experience. Thus he points out differences between oral conversation and the interpretation of texts. In oral speech there is an immediacy between the speaker and the hearer. This enables the speaker to make certain that the hearer not only grasps the *sense* of the communication but is aware of the *reference* intended.

On the other hand, a written text is removed from such immediacy in three ways: (1) Once it is written, it exists by itself, without the author to throw light on its meaning. (2) It is also removed from the original audience and is available to a limitless number of readers. (3) It can be carried beyond cultural and generational boundaries and convey its message in very diverse contexts. This distantiation or distancing makes interpretation necessary, for, while the text may still make sense, it has no specific reference and is open to a variety of referents. Ricoeur identifies this as the "surplus of meaning" (Ricoeur 1976:45–46). This "surplus" explains why a text can yield an array of different meanings without compromising its literary integrity.

Where Gadamer opposes explanation and understanding, Ricoeur relates them. He sees explanation as the unfolding of the potential range of meanings that the text can yield, and understanding, in one sense of the term, as a grasp of meaning. Actually, the whole process of interpretation begins with a kind of guess, an intuition about the subject matter. It moves through a complex dialectic of explanation and developing understanding and finally rests with a subjective experience of meaning which is really a level of appropriation (Gadamer's "fusion of horizons"). Interpretation is precisely the dialectic between explanation and understanding (Ricoeur, 1976:71–88).

Gadamer has been criticized for his uncritical presumption of the benign character of the tradition received. He did not consider the biases that it contains and projects. Ricoeur, on the other hand, agreed with Freud that the force and meaning of language can conceal a false consciousness (Ricoeur, 1970). Refining Freud's "hermeneutics of suspicion," he went on to develop a way of constructing meaning that is open to the possibilities of the future while aware of the limitations of the past.

Three very important insights from these theorists inform the way the wisdom literature will be interpreted in this study. They are Gadamer's "fusion of horizons" and Ricoeur's "hermeneutics of suspicion" and "surplus of meaning."

Critical Approach

A new critical method lends itself to this kind of interpretive theory. Called canonical hermeneutics, it examines the reinterpretations done by communities of faith as they brought the religious tradition of the past to bear on their own experience. To uncover the interpretive techniques used by ancient biblical communities it employs both literary and historical methods, believing that a similar interpretive process can be used for understanding the Bible's message in the present. It contends that in the formative process of the past, just as in the interpretive process of the present, a believing community resignifies (gives new meaning to) a religious message born of another time and of other circumstances. In other words, the community living in a new context understands a biblical message in a manner different from the way it was originally understood (Ricoeur's "surplus of meaning"). Canonical critics are not satisfied merely with meaning as such, however; they are interested in discovering how the biblical message functioned in the past and might function in the present.

Evidence of recontextualization can be found throughout the Bible itself (for example, Matt 1:23 uses Isa 7:14; Mark 1:2-3 uses Mal 3:1 and Isa 40:3). A careful literary comparison uncovers clues suggesting that the earlier material was resignified to address new historical situations. This is precisely the interpretive method that canonical critics seek to develop for contemporary use.

Canonical critics recognize three components to this interpretive method: (1) the biblical text; (2) the new context within which the text is read; and (3) the process of resignification (Sanders, 1984:77–78). Each one of these components plays an important role in the process of resignification. With regard to the first component, historical-critical, literary-critical, structuralist, linguistic, or any number of other analytical approaches can be used to discover whatever possible meanings the biblical passage might yield (Ricoeur's explanation). This task may appear to be quite technical, but most people today have some experience in, or at least knowledge of, biblical analysis.

A large portion of the present study will be an explanation of the text. The analysis is done, however, not merely to determine what the text says and what it meant but to discover its *rhetorical function*. Canonical critics insist that there is a dimension of ambiguity in the biblical texts that makes them versatile. This versatility is not the same as "surplus of meaning," it is more a kind of rhetorical adaptability. The versatility of a text facilitates such adaptation.

The second component of canonical hermeneutics calls for insight into the new context that receives the tradition. This requires knowledge of the contemporary community and its local and global contexts. Such knowledge includes: some understanding of present-day social systems and the way they operate in our lives; an informed appreciation of the economic and political realities that shape our local, national, and international societies; insight into the respective community's *mythos* and *ethos*. Society is a multiracial, multicultural, multilingual, multiclass, and multigenerational community of women and men. These dynamics constitute the social location of the reader and, consequently, shape the lens through which interpretation is done. The complexity of contemporary reality begets ambiguity. Even the slightest circumstance can change things. What seems appropriate in one situation may be unfit in another; a message that consoles in one circumstance can denounce elsewhere. Social location, with all of its particularity, can be neither ignored nor minimized.

Once both the biblical text and the contemporary situation of the community have been analyzed, the real reinterpretation or resignification can take place. This third component of canonical hermeneutics probably poses the greatest challenge for interpretation. What technique should one employ in this process?

Interpretive Techniques

Canonical critics claim that an unrecorded interpretive method exists just beneath the surface of the biblical text and serves as the best approach for resignification. They have uncovered clues to the identity of this hidden method which has been called comparative midrash (Sanders, 1984:46–60). Examining how some passages use earlier biblical material, they have been able to discover evidence of historical analogy, typology, and a form of rabbinic argument similar to *argumentum a fortiori* (a conclusion that follows with greater necessity than a previous conclusion, for instance, "If these things are done when the wood is green, what will happen when it is dry?" [Luke 23:31]).

Some contemporary interpreters find these particular techniques inadequate for today. Nonetheless, interpretive techniques are always present, consciously or not, and so the interpreter must be aware of which techniques to employ and how to do so critically. Faced with this challenge, many people choose a kind of concordism that seeks correspondences between real-life situations and similar events described in the Scriptures. This approach limits the message of revelation to current situations that seem to have parallels in biblical history. It also tends to confuse *what* happens in the story with the *meaning* of what happens (Croatto, 1987:6–7). Reading the books of Joshua and Judges in this way has frequently been used to justify the occupation of land already inhabited by other people. On the other hand, this kind of reading can also produce noble aspirations. The story of Israel's flight from Egypt has both inspired and encouraged believers who live under oppressive systems.

Other people seek to resignify by using some type of correlation that is less concerned with similar historical occurrences than with common human experience. An uncritical type of correlation has led some to conclude that the timeless biblical message can answer questions that have plagued people over the ages regardless of the difference in the social location of the hearer. Following this approach, biblical prescriptions for living in the land are merely repeated, not reinterpreted. A more critical method of correlation insists that the biblical message can be opened to us through the use of critical analogy (Tracy, 1975:43–63, 79–81). Interpreters who use this approach would suggest that the homelessness experienced by so many people today prepares them for understanding Israel's attachment to the promised land at every time in its history.

Whichever technique is employed, certain principles must be kept in mind during the entire process of interpretation. First, recognition of the ambiguity of reality cautions against any readings that claim to be incontrovertible. Second, the biblical passage acts more as a mirror for identity than as a model for morality. Third, the focus of interpretation is the action of God and not the action of human beings. Finally, God's action offers the reader a new mode-of-being-in-the-world (Sanders, 1979:1–27, 132–40) that can be transformative (Ricoeur's appropriation).

This book will use a form of critical correlation similar to a contemporary adaptation of a medieval Jewish rabbinic allegorical approach, which "involves the determination of significance by means of factors independent of, and external to, the textual surface" (Fishbane, 1989:116). The code used to explain the text or translate it into a new context of meaning will be an advocacy posture sensitive to the three issues of race or ethnic origin, class, and gender. This code will serve as a lens through which the biblical material is read (titled in the subsections "Unmasking the Powers"). It will then set the parameters for the challenge of the biblical message (in the subsections "Into the Looking Glass"). In other words, the advocacy stand and the biblical message will interpret each other. Finally, the end of the entire interpretive endeavor is rhetorical, in the sense of constituting a persuasion, and not merely explanatory (Wuellner, 1987). The Bible, if it is to be authentically the word of God, must transform the minds and hearts of those who hear it. That is the final and true goal of interpretation.

Social Location

It is a truism that the world is known only through the particular perspective of the knower. In reading, the world of the text is perceived and understood according to the social location of the reader. Until recently readers have not always been self-conscious about their social location. Those who enjoy positions of power have often accepted their perspective as normative for all. This perspective has usually been that of the white, middle-class, North Atlantic male. Although groups within society that enjoy limited or no power at all are still socialized into this dominant worldview, their social location as marginal within the dominant culture provides them with a significantly different perception of its values and standards.

Every interpretation of the Bible has rhetorical force. To claim that a reading is neutral is to support the perspective of the dominant status quo. On the other hand, a reading can be liberative in one of two ways: either the major theological questions arise and are answered from within the actual experience of oppression, or a stand in solidarity with the oppressed is taken and theology developed out of that stand. As stated above, the approach followed here is an advocacy stand sensitive to issues of race or ethnic origin, class, and gender. In this regard, my social location as a white, middle-class, North Atlantic female enables me to speak from situations both of privilege and of marginalization.

The Wisdom Literature of Ancient Israel

The narrative character of the Bible has led most people to presume that it contains some kind of history. God had chosen this people, guided them, revealed the law to them, and rewarded and punished them according to their fidelity to that law. In effect, God was perceived as the principal actor in the drama of this people's history. Although historical-critical analyses have enabled interpreters to distinguish between actual events and the religious interpretation that Israel gave to them, the characterization "salvation history" still enjoys great prominence. The national epic of Israel, beginning with the call of the ancestors and concluding with the Roman occupation, is considered by many the basic literary framework of the entire First Testament and the primary theological category of Israel's theology.

A rigid linear perspective of Western interpretation recognized its own preference for history in the biblical narrative and concluded that the ancient worldview was not much different from its own. Using a developmental model of interpretation, it judged earlier customs and theology to be inferior to those that followed. In addition, it frequently dismissed as borrowed from heathen sources anything that did not in some way fit into the pattern of Israel's story. This, coupled with the wisdom tradition's lack of specific Israelite religious concern, has caused many to relegate this material to a minor place in the tradition, some biblical theologies even placing it as an addendum at the end of the book.

The wisdom tradition of ancient Israel was not unlike that of the rest of the Near Eastern world. It was both awed by the wonders of nature and concerned with human behavior, human accomplishment, and human misfortune. Observation of nature and reflection on life led the sages of Israel to conclude that there was some kind of order inherent in the world. They believed that if they could discern how this order operated and harmonize their lives with it, they would live peacefully and successfully. Failure to recognize and conform to this order would result in misfortune and misery. A primary function of this tradition seems to have been instruction in a style of living that would assure well-being and prosperity.

Captivated by the wonders of nature, the Israelites believed that their God was the great Creator responsible for the world, its organization, and everything within it. They maintained that the splendor of creation could have come only from one who was both powerful and wise. This creator was not only the primeval architect of the universe and provident sustainer of reality but also the demanding judge who preserved established order. Since Israel believed that social order was but a reflection of the natural order of the universe, creation ideology quite possibly played a more significant role in its worldview than was previously thought.

A careful study of the texts that have come to be known as the wisdom literature shows how difficult defining this diversified and elusive concept is. Wisdom has been variously referred to as: the meaning *in* life, the meaning *of* life, ancient humanism, a way of coping, the way to success, the discovery of the orders of creation and conformity to them, and so on.

Although there may be significant resemblance in these various definitions, each one focuses on the phenomenon from a slightly different standpoint and thereby provides distinctive perspective. Although the sages maintained that certain natural laws could be perceived and followed, they never taught that life would ever be completely understood or controlled. In fact, they believed that the dimension of wisdom most desired, the wisdom that alone explains the universe and the inner workings of life, is beyond human reach and resides with God alone.

Works Consulted

Barbour, Ian G. 1990. *Religion in an Age of Science.* San Francisco: Harper & Row.

Bergant, Dianne 1987/1992. *The World Is a Prayerful Place.* Reprint. Michael Glazier, Inc. Collegeville, Minn.: Liturgical Press,

_____. 1991. "Is the Biblical Worldview Anthropocentric?" *New Theology Review* 4:5–14.

Birch, Charles, William Eakin, and Jay B. McDaniel, eds. 1990. *Liberating Life.* Maryknoll: Orbis Books.

Cobb, John B., Jr. 1982. *Process Theology as Political Theology.* Manchester: Manchester University Press.

Croatto, Severino 1984. *Biblical Hermeneutics: Toward a Theory of Reading as the Production of Meaning.* Maryknoll: Orbis Books.

Daly, Herman E., and John B. Cobb, Jr. 1989. *For the Common Good: Redirecting the Economy toward Community, the Environment, and a Sustainable Future.* Boston: Beacon Press.

Daly, Lois K. 1990. "Ecofeminism, Reverence for Life, and Feminist Theology." In *Liberating Life,* edited by Charles Birch, William Eakin, and Jay B. McDaniel. Maryknoll: Orbis Books.

Fishbane, Michael. 1989. *The Garments of Torah.* Bloomington: Indiana University Press.

Gadamer, Hans-Georg. 1975. *Truth and Method.* New York: Seabury Press.

Habel, Norman C. 1985. *The Book of Job.* Philadelphia: Westminster Press.

Johnson, Elizabeth A. 1993. *Women, Earth, and Creator Spirit.* New York: Paulist Press.

Kuhn, Thomas S. 1970. *The Structure of Scientific Revolutions.* 2d ed. Chicago: University of Chicago Press.

Küng, Hans, and David Tracy, eds. 1989. *Paradigm Change in Theology.* New York: Crossroad.

Merchant, Carolyn. 1980. *The Death of Nature: Women, Ecology and the Scientific Revolution.* San Francisco: Harper & Row.

Peters, Karl E. 1991. "Interrelating Nature, Humanity, and the Work of God: Some Issues for Future Reflection." Unpublished paper, Templeton Foundation Symposium.

Polzin, Robert M. 1977. *Biblical Structuralism: Method and Subjectivity in the Study of Ancient Texts.* Philadelphia: Fortress Press.

Primavesi, Anne. 1991. *From Apocalypse to Genesis: Ecology, Feminism and Christianity.* Philadelphia: Fortress Press.

Ricoeur, Paul. 1970. *Freud and Philosophy: An Essay on Interpretation.* Translated by Denis Savage. New Haven: Yale University Press.

_____. 1976. *Interpretation Theory: Discourse and the Surplus of Meaning.* Fort Worth: Texas Christian University Press.

Ruether, Rosemary Radford. 1975. *New Woman/New Earth.* New York: Seabury Press.

Sanders, James A. 1979. *God Has a Story Too.* Philadelphia: Fortress Press.

_____. 1984. *Canon and Community: A Guide to Canonical Criticism.* Philadelphia: Fortress Press.

Tracy, David. 1975. *Blessed Rage for Order: The New Pluralism in Theology.* Minneapolis: Winston/Seabury Press.

White, Lynn. 1967. "The Religious Roots of Our Ecological Crisis." *Science* 155:1203–7.

Wuellner, Wilhelm. 1987. "Where Is Rhetorical Criticism Taking Us? *Catholic Biblical Quarterly* 49:448–63.

2

Job

Introduction

LITERARY STUDIES OF THE BOOK OF JOB GENERALLY HAVE DEALT with issues such as imagery, genre, structure, and the history of composition, all with an eye to the reconstruction of historical referents. They have sought to uncover the identity of the biblical author and the original audiences, to identify the issues facing these people and the theology that informed their lives (Habel, 1985:13–19). More recently, some scholars have been persuaded by the New Criticism to look at the literary integrity of the book. They insist that, despite its obvious composite nature (a prose prologue [1:1—2:13] and epilogue [42:7-17] framing a collection of seemingly disparate poetic dialogues [3:1—42:6]), the book of Job is a literary unity (Habel, 1985). In this they agree with canonical critics who also insist that it is the final product that should be considered (Childs, 1979).

When Paul Ricoeur's theory of language is applied to the book of Job, we discover that on one level the narrative framework is itself the message. Whatever the chronological development of the prose framework and the poetic dialogues of Job may have been, the significance of the final literary pattern cannot be ignored (Dornisch, 1981:13); on the contrary, it is the fundamental narrative form of the book (Seitz, 1989:10). The basic structure itself suggests a kind of rite of passage (cf. van Gennep, 1960). In the prose prologue, Job lives an ordered life of righteousness and prosperity. Without his understanding why, his entire life is turned upside down (separation). The poetic dialogues show him in the chaotic throes of affliction and confusion (liminality). The speeches of YHWH open to him a newly ordered life into which he steps. The prose epilogue portrays him as reinstated in society, a transformed man (reappropriation).

Despite the obvious literary breaks, the plot itself moves from section to section with very little difficulty, and the character portrayal can be easily traced. Although the prose narrative relates the actions essential to the unfolding of the plot, the book is a perfect example of narration-through-dialogue (Alter, 1981:63–87).

I aim at a close, critical reading of the book of Job (literary approach). I will concentrate on the points of view of the characters, for it is the conflict of these points of view that constitute the drama of the book. I show how, by means of this characterization, the author intends to arouse feelings of empathy, sympathy, or antipathy, and thus to persuade the reader to embrace a particular point of view (Booth, 1982). It is at this point that the "hermeneutic of suspicion" will be set in motion, in order to see who benefits from the rhetorical intent of the author (advocacy stand). The biblical material will then be reread in an attempt to open the reader to the new liberative revelatory possibilities of the text.

Reading the Story
The Appearance of God

I begin with a look at the characterization of God (Gutiérrez, 1988:xi–xix; Habel, 1992:21–38; Mettinger, 1992:39–49). I do this for two reasons: first, what God says and does determines the flow of the narrative (Polzin, 1977:120–21); second, the religious stature of the other characters can be judged only in terms of the nature and quality of their response to God's activity. God first appears in the heavenly council (1:6-12; 2:1-6), a place from which God issues decrees and sends forth messengers (Ps 82:1; Zech 6:5). Here God enters into dialogue with the Satan, and God's first words are questions (vv. 7-8). Does this suggest that God is ignorant of the Satan's activities, or is God asking for an account of the Satan's responsibilities? God presumes that while performing the responsibilities of roaming and patrolling the earth, the Satan certainly observed God's servant Job. God's interest here is not so much in Job as in the Satan's observation of Job's integrity, an integrity that God takes for granted (see Crenshaw, 1984: 57–75).

God is accused of protecting Job from circumstances that would severely test the extent of his devotion (v. 10). As a simple present-day poem states:

> It's easy enough to be happy,
>   when life flows along like a
>   song.
> But the one worthwhile,
>   is the one who can smile,
>   when everything goes dead wrong.

The Satan then challenges God: stretch forth your hand, this time to afflict Job rather than to protect or to bless him (v. 11). The twofold presupposition here is: God is the source of both blessing and affliction and if God can cause even the righteous to suffer, then there is no necessary correspondence between misfortune and the lack of moral rectitude. This may all sound absurd to people who cannot imagine that God would not be governed by principles of strict justice, but God refutes neither the Satan's assertion nor any implications that might flow from it. Instead, God delivers Job into the ready hands of the Satan, to be dispossessed of his children and his possessions but spared personal bodily torment (v. 12). There is no wrath here; this is not punishment. God permits this because the Satan has issued the challenge. The text provides no motives. Although it is not God's hand that strikes Job, God cannot be absolved of responsibility. God is, after all, the source of blessing and affliction, and it is only with God's permission that Job can be stricken.

In a second episode in the presence of the heavenly council God questions the Satan and receives the same response as before (2:2). Again God presumes that the Satan has observed the righteous Job. This time, however, God attests to Job's initial innocence, assumes full responsibility for Job's distress, and points out the steadfastness of Job's piety despite his adversity (v. 3). A second time the wager is put forward and God acquiesces to the Satan's proposal to afflict Job. This time God gives permission to assault the man himself but without taking his life (vv. 5-6).

The prologue provides a very interesting representation of God. This God lives removed from human beings and deals with them through intermediaries. This God seems to be proud of the moral integrity of Job and yet, at Job's expense, succumbs to the outrageous wagers of the Satan. The God of this prologue has the power to bless or to afflict and does so irrespective of any customary principle of retribution. Finally, nothing in this account suggests that the author passes any kind of judgment on a God who acts in this manner.

God is silent until the dialogues between Job and his visitors have concluded. Then from the midst of a whirlwind, God speaks with majesty directly to Job. The reader does not get the sense here that God is far off, as was the case in the prologue, but neither does the text say that God left the heavenly council in order to confront Job. This encounter between God and Job takes place in the midst of the natural world, the home that women and men share with the rest of creation. Might the chasm that many claim exists between the divine council and the stage of human drama actually be one of a lack of perception and insight? Is God closer than we think, perhaps even the matrix and the marrow of all that is?

The divine speeches (38:1—40:2; 40:6—41:34), while in poetic form, consist of a barrage of questions about Job's knowledge of or control over aspects of the natural world. God's first words, "Who is this?" (38:2), indicate that this theophany is really a response to the challenges that Job has flung at heaven. The query taunts Job as one whose words presume knowledge and status that he does not possess. The questioning of Job that follows will point this out. However, clearly God believes that Job can withstand this confrontation, for God bids him gird his loins like a *geber*, a strong or valiant man. This desolate and disfigured man, who has already survived the torment of God's silence, is now ordered to face the force of God's speech. While this directive is certainly a challenge to Job, it also acknowledges God's confidence in Job's ability to withstand the rigors of the encounter. There is a mocking tone to the interrogation: "Tell me, if you have understanding" (v. 4); "surely you know!" (v. 5); "Declare, if you know all this" (v. 18); "Surely you know, for you were born then, and the number of your days is great!" (v. 21). The God who earlier spoke with pride of Job's moral integrity and steadfastness (1:8; 2:3), and who trusts in Job's strength and endurance, here tests his intellectual acumen and his capacity to rule the universe.

The first divine speech directs Job's attention to the design of the world and to some of its inhabitants: the earth and the sea (38:4-11); dawn, darkness, and the netherworld (vv. 12-21); the heavens (vv. 22-38); wild creatures (38:39—39:12); and a few unusual animals (vv. 13-30; Habel, 1985:517–20). God does not seem to address any of the concerns of Job's extensive complaints. Instead, God unfolds the grandeur and mystery of much of the universe but does this, daring Job to claim a prominence within it that belongs only to a creator or to a partner in creation. Although God is questioning Job and his competence, it is God's creative imagination and comprehensive providence in creation that are revealed. Behind God's interrogation is one fundamental question: How do you measure up to my majesty?

The speech ends as it began, with a reference to Job. God initially described Job as one who "darkens counsel by words without knowledge" (38:2). Here God calls him a "a faultfinder . . . who argues with God" (40:2). This framework of accusation indicates that God's concentration on the wonders of creation is not an avoidance of the issues raised earlier by Job, specifically the issue of the character of human life. Rather, in a way that at first appears oblique, it is a response to his concern. God is teaching Job that humans are not the center of the universe (Perdue, 1994:168–81, 191); it is, however, precisely in the grandeur of the natural world that Job will gain the insight he seeks.

The second speech also begins with a summons to prepare for an ordeal, followed by a denunciation of Job's complaints. God inquires whether Job condemns God in order to justify himself. The reader knows, as of course God also knows, that Job has no need to be justified; he never lost his integrity. To what does God allude here? In what way has Job put God in the wrong? (These questions will be answered later in the study.) The summons continues with an elaboration of the way that Job is to prepare for his impending confrontation. The confrontation will not be with God but with some other adversary. This introductory section ends with God promising that when Job can prove himself victorious over this unnamed threat, God will pay him the homage due a conquering hero.

There are, in fact, two threats: Behemoth (40:15-24) and Leviathan (41:1-34), the exact identities of which are difficult to discern. Do they represent Mesopotamia and Egypt, Israel's formidable historical enemies? Are they mythic symbols of chaos from the religious literature of those cultures? Or are they merely the dreaded hippopotamus and crocodile, fearsome animals that mirror Job's own protest and struggle with suffering (Habel, 1985:557–58)? Whatever their actual identity, it is obvious from the text that they pose no threat to God. If they represent nations, they are in fact governed by God. If they symbolize chaos, it is clearly under divine control. If they are threatening monsters, they have clearly been tamed. To underscore further their dependence on God, they are both identified as creatures (40:15, 19; 41:33). The point of these descriptions and this questioning is evident: God has domesticated both Behemoth and Leviathan; what power can Job exercise over them? In other words, is Job on a par with God?

The speeches seem to provide another representation of God. Here, God speaks directly to Job in a way that calls for straightforward responses. God seems to be engaged with the rest of creation as well. When God refers to the structures and workings of the world and describes animal behaviors, there is a kind of pride and a sensitivity that bespeak both satisfaction in accomplishment and protective concern. Here God may not address the question of Job's moral integrity, but Job's ability to withstand an encounter with God, an encounter that will test his intellectual acumen and capacity to rule, is certainly an issue. In the heavenly council God may have conceded to the Satan, but here God yields to nothing and to no one. This is the creator, who alone understands and manages the entire sweep of creation, and who invites Job to contemplate its resplendence and complexity to the extent that he is able.

The question form that God employs in the speeches should not be overlooked. These are not requests for information but ironic questions that serve to correct Job's shortsighted perception of his ability to grasp some of the mysteries of life. They are rhetorical questions meant to lead Job to a depth greater than the information mere answers would provide. The marvel of this questioning approach is seen in its ability to bring Job to wisdom despite, or perhaps because of, its indirectness. God asks questions about nature and Job gains insight into human limitation.

Perhaps the most remarkable characteristic of this representation of God is the medium of the theophany. God is manifested through the natural world. The artistry of God can be seen in the splendor of the universe; God's wisdom in its delicate balance; God's imagination in its diversity; God's providence in its inherent fruitfulness. The natural world was not only born of the creativity of God, it also bears the features of this creativity. Every property of creation mirrors something of the creator. It is not enough to say that creation is the medium through which God is revealed; in a very real sense, the medium is itself the revelation. In his final response, Job testifies to having seen something of God, not merely the wonders of creation (42:5; Pellauer, 1981:79–80).

The final words of God (42:7-8) are spoken to Eliphaz the Temanite. They are fiery words of reproof, denouncing Eliphaz, Bildad, and Zophar for misrepresenting God. The second half of this reproach is even more puzzling than the first. God declares that Job is the only one who spoke accurately about God. How can this be when, in the first speech from the whirlwind, God claimed that Job "darkens council by words without knowledge," and in the second he is called "a faultfinder . . . who contends with the almighty"? Was there something in Job's replies to the speeches that has changed God's mind about Job's complaining words? Or might God be saying that, when all is said and done, Job was correct to disregard the counsel he received from others, correct to find fault with God and to argue?

It is important to note that here, as in the episodes in the midst of the heavenly council, every time God mentions Job's name it is prefaced by the laudatory phrase "my servant." This is a designation reserved for only the most prominent figures of the biblical tradition (Abraham [Gen 26:24]; Moses [Num 12:7]; David [2 Sam 7:5]; Isaiah [Isa 20:3]; the Suffering Servant [Isa 42:1; 49:3; 52:13]; Zerubbabel, the king in whom rested the messianic hopes of the nation [Hag 2:23]). In the opening scene, the phrase is followed by a formulaic description of Job's righteousness, "a blameless and upright man who fears God and turns away from evil" (1:8; 2:3). Although the description is not repeated here, it certainly comes to mind when we hear God call Job "my servant."

God directs Eliphaz to go to Job and there offer sacrifice to appease God's wrath. This is to be done while Job intercedes on behalf of the three men. God will only show favor to Job, will only spare them the consequences of their failure because of Job's prayer. Here, as in the prologue, God speaks about Job but never to him. In the prologue God uses the Satan as an agent of affliction; in the epilogue God uses Job as an agent of reconciliation. After Job intercedes for the very men who had denounced his claims of righteousness and refused him any consolation, God restores Job's prosperity twofold (42:10, 12). Since Job had been innocent from the start, this restoration should be seen as vindication of Job. It is also necessary as a kind of divine recovery; without this external manifestation of Job's vindication, God's behavior toward Job would be nothing less than abusive (Perdue, 1994:182). The text does not say that God explained to Job the reason for his reinstatement, but then, God never told him why his fortunes had been reversed in the first place. God seems never to have revealed why things happened to Job as they did.

The epilogue offers a third representation of God. Here God passionately supports what Job has alleged as opposed to what his visitors have claimed. This God is very demanding, setting high standards of truth and loyalty by which people will be judged. It is a God who makes the erring dependent on the devout and expects the righteous to speak on behalf of those who are at fault. God creates situations in the lives of people in ways unbeknownst to them. We may consider this unfair, but the fact remains that God leaves none of the major characters of this drama in distress. Job, who was put to the test, is vindicated; the visitors, who spoke falsely about God, are delivered.

The vocabulary used to identify God should also be noted. Although the speeches exhibit great variety of usage, the prologue and the epilogue are consistent. With three exceptions, only YHWH, the personal name of the God of Israel, is used here. (The exceptions are 1:22 and 40:2, where *'ĕlōah*, an ancient term for god, is in poetic parallelism with *šadday* [Almighty], and the figure of speech in 38:7). *'ĕlōhîm*, the plural form of the generic word for god, only appears as part of figures of speech (for example, fear of God [1:1, 8, 9; 2:3], curse god [1:5, 11; 2:5, 9], sons of god [1:6; 2:1; 38:7], fire of god [1:16], hand of god [2:10]). Since this word is always used with a singular verb, it is probably a plural of majesty rather than a true plural. In the speeches, the most frequently used terms are *'el* (in compounds and by itself), *'ĕlōah*, and *šadday*. *'ĕlōhîm* appears a few times and YHWH is used once (12:9). The characters avoid using the personal name of Israel's God but use various standard terms for god. This makes it impossible to know of which god they speak. It is clear from the prologue and epilogue, however, that the god of the narrator is the God of Israel.

At first glance, it appears that the three different sections of the book each furnish a different representation of God, and some of the features of one seem to conflict with features of another. These differences may be just that, however, differences but not contradictions. In this book God clearly is understood as both beyond the realm of the natural world and intimately involved in it; as acting through intermediaries and acting directly; as susceptible to the schemes of others as well as beyond another's influence (Alter, 1981:146–47; Miscall, 1983:17–23). Although God does indeed act irrespective of the constraints of retribution, the author does not fault God for this. Questions still remain: Has God changed in response to some of the words and actions of others? What is the final characterization of God with which the reader is left? These questions can only be answered after an examination of the other characters of the story.

The Foils

Two characters that appear in the prologue are the Satan and Job's unnamed wife. While they are never explicitly linked together, they have one significant feature in common: they both consider the possibility of Job's cursing God. Unlike Job's children and servants, whose importance lies less in their own individualities than in the roles they play in the description of Job, the Satan and Job's wife are actors in the drama.

The Satan appears in the heavenly council along with the rest of the divine court (1:6; 2:1). This is noteworthy, since a heavenly court is an assembly to which only the privileged have access. God and the Satan exchange words, further suggesting that this is an individual with stature. The conversation reveals that the Satan performs a rather significant role on earth, that of patrol. The text does not indicate whether this patrolling is for the sake of overseeing or of guarding or of spying. When God speaks with pride about Job, the Satan questions the quality of Job's integrity by claiming that Job's fear of the LORD, a disposition that normally implies humble reverence, is really a self-interested demeanor meant to ensure prosperity. The Satan suggests a way of showing that Job's virtue is hollow: take away his comfort and his prosperity and he will curse you. With God's permission, the Satan goes forth to execute the disturbing plan.

The word curse is really a euphemistic use of *bārak*, "to bless." (*Bārak* is used with the sense of cursing God only seven times in the entire Bible; four of these instances occur in the book of Job: 1:5, 11; 2:5, 9; 1 Kgs 21:10, 13; Ps 10:3.) The reason for the use of the opposite meaning is not clear. The thought of cursing God may have been too objectionable actually to use the maledictory language, or the author may be playing with the antithesis between bless and curse. They are both formulaic expressions that presume the legitimate use of divine power by one who is not divine. The language is performative, effecting what it describes. In a curse, the power is used to diminish or undermine something. It can be illegitimate or void in two ways: either the one pronouncing the curse does not have the authority to do so, or the content of the curse is beyond the competence of even this authorized person. The consequences of using divine power to curse cannot be underestimated. Whatever is being diminished most likely will do what it can to resist its diminishment, and the one cursing will be in direct line of this resistance.

To curse God is to assume divine power in order to diminish God. The effect of this can be nothing short of catastrophic. From God's point of view, it is blasphemy deserving of reprisal. From a human point of view, any possible diminishment of God might result in a diminishment of the very one who wields divine power. Thus, the one cursing could be trapped within the enactment of the curse itself. The gravity of the Satan's challenge can be seen in the use of *'im-lō*, a figure of speech used for emphasis and often translated "certainly" (1:11; 2:5). This exclamation, which introduces a promise or a threat confirmed by an oath, may have originally been a form of self-imprecation (for example, "The LORD do such-and-such to me if such-and-such does not happen").

On a second occasion, the Satan appears before God and accounts for his whereabouts. In this exchange, the Satan is rightly accused of having incited God against Job without cause (2:3). Undeterred, the Satan proposes a second, even more severe trial. Insisting that prosperity is one thing but personal physical integrity is quite another, the Satan dares God to "touch his bone and his flesh." For a second time, the imprecation *'im-lō*, reinforces the claim "he will curse you" (v. 5). Authorized by God, the Satan once again goes forth to afflict this innocent man. Having done this, the Satan disappears, not to be heard of again.

Just who is the Satan, and what role does this enigmatic character play in the story? If not a member of the divine council, the Satan is at least present with it. This is an audacious individual, who not only challenges God's estimation of Job but also entices God to submit Job to excruciating trials. This is not "the devil" of later tradition. The Satan afflicts Job but does not tempt him. If anyone is swayed by the Satan's proposal, it is God.

The fact that the Satan appears only in the prologue suggests that this is the only place where the Satan has a role to play. Actually, the role is twofold: to introduce the unthinkable proposal and, with authorization, to execute it. Without this proposition, Job would not be tested and there would be no story. Since the Satan does not have the authority independently to abuse Job but is responsible to God, this character apparently is nothing more than a foil of God used to create a situation wherein Job's righteousness might be demonstrated. The Satan serves a literary function by introducing the wager, the occasion for the drama, and a theological function, for as a foil, the Satan deflects responsibility for this tragedy from God.

Job's unnamed wife is both an important and an unimportant character (for a characterization of women, see Brenner, 1993:198–201). The fact that she is unnamed may reflect the male bias of the literary work. On the other hand, it might imply that, while the role she plays in the prologue is important, her personal identity is of little significance. Or perhaps both explanations should be assumed. At any rate, she confronts Job with a challenge: "Curse God, and die" (2:9). She seems to see no point in Job's unwavering virtue. Reasoning from the theory of retribution, if upstanding behavior yields good fortune, then, when good fortune is snatched away, virtue has little purpose. There is no point in Job's clinging to it. If Job curses God, Job will most likely die as a consequence. This kind of thinking is obviously at odds with that of Job, for he declares that she is speaking foolishness. He believes that there is merit in holding fast to virtue in the face of adversity.

Why does the author allow Job's wife to survive all of the disasters that befall him? Why does she not appear in the epilogue, where mention is made of the other children born to Job? Like the Satan, her significance is limited to the prologue. Unlike the Satan, she is not essential for the movement of the story. She too can been seen as a kind of foil, however, for her skepticism does indeed contrast with Job's constancy and serves to underscore the quality of his integrity. Another similarity between the Satan and Job's wife may be that they both seem to be trusted associates of their counterparts, associates who enjoy a degree of confidence. Perhaps they are even alter egos, who can make explicit (a curse) what the majestic God and the righteous Job would never even contemplate. However these two characters are understood, the wife offers, as a specific possibility, what the Satan insinuated: "Curse God and die!"

The plot is conceived. The stage is set. The drama unfolds.

In Defense of Justice

The three men who come to Job "to console and comfort him" (2:11), though possessing some distinctive individual characteristics, all embody the same worldview and promote the same message. They are all from lands renowned for wisdom. Eliphaz is the name of the firstborn of Esau also known as Edom, a land with a reputation for wisdom (Gen 36:4, 10, 15; Gen 25:30). Shuah is on one of the major trade routes through the Syrian desert, and Naamah is a Sabean city. Thus, the homelands of Job's counselors encircle the entire Arabian peninsula: Eliphaz from northwest Arabia, Bildad from the northeast, and Zophar from the south. Astonished by Job's appearance, the men rend their garments, sprinkle dust on their heads, and join him in his silent mourning. At the outset, they are portrayed as both wise and responsive friends to whom Job should be able to turn in his need.

Each man speaks in response to Job's outbursts and claims, yet there is little direct correlation between the specifics of one of Job's harangues and the immediate reaction to it. The arguments are repetitious and circular, beginning with counsel and growing into reproach. The recurrence of outcry, followed by response, followed by outcry, and so forth, creates a tension that heightens the frustration of all those involved. Job and his visitors are deadlocked in a standoff in which neither side agrees with the fundamental premise of the other. While the theory of retribution is a basic conviction held by all, they disagree about its universal relevance. The visitors presume that it is always applicable, concluding that Job's suffering is evidence of his offenses. Job demands that its principles be observed, insisting that he has been wrongly afflicted. No one thinks to challenge the theory's suitability as an explanation of the circumstances of life.

At the heart of the message of all three men is the axiom: the righteous will enjoy the fruits of their virtue, and the wicked will suffer the consequences of their sin. Should Job challenge this teaching, he would be placing himself above the wisdom of the elders (8:8-10; 15:9-10, 18), a wisdom confirmed by the order evident in nature itself (4:7-11; 8:11-12). On the other hand, if he admits his guilt and accepts God's chastisement, in due time he will be delivered from his adversity (5:17-27; 22:23). Should Job in fact be innocent, God will restore him (8:6). However, this last likelihood is slim, for his arrogant obstinacy itself puts him in the wrong (15:6). Job is admonished to trust God (4:6), for God is just (8:3) even though God's ways are at times unfathomable (5:9; 11:7-12).

These visitors actually touch on the truth of Job's situation without even realizing it. God's ways are unfathomable, and pondering the inexplicable workings of nature should confirm this fact. These men do acknowledge the incomprehensibility of God's ways, but at the same time they claim to understand them. Like God, they appeal to nature as an analogue for learning, but they do so in order to teach order and predictability while God reveals extravagance and mystery. Even if some of their counsel seems to be reliable, the worldview from which their thought proceeds is incompatible with that of Job, making a meeting of minds unlikely. In three different places (4:17-19; 15:14-16; 25:4-6) a carefully crafted rabbinic argumentation similar to argumentum a fortiori concludes that human beings, precisely because they are human, cannot be righteous before God. The argument claims that if beings that are far superior to mortals lack moral integrity, then inferior humans are surely corrupt. There is no way that Job can be innocent and God guilty. Job is either bearing the burden of his own particular failure or suffering the consequences of his sinful nature. Here human mortality is considered both the consequence of human iniquity (4:8-9) and the basis for it (4:19-21). In an attempt to legitimize this unsettling pronouncement, Eliphaz claims that it came to him in a night vision. This view of human nature would rather deny the fundamental goodness of creation (Gen 1:31) than reexamine the conventional view of God.

Their justification of God at the expense of Job might be considered testimony to the theocentric worldview of these men. This has really been a justification of traditional theology at the expense of truth, however, and their worldview is governed by static ideology and not by living faith. In their defense of divine management of the world, they renounce God's sovereign freedom to act as God would choose to act. Restricting themselves to the theory of retribution, they deny themselves the experience of mystery. Theirs may be a theocentric worldview, but it is narrow and restrictive and inadequate to deal with some of life's most pressing issues, to say nothing of the mystery of God.

The exchange between Job and his three visitors no sooner ends than a fourth voice is heard. Elihu is the only person with an Israelite name (1 Sam 1:1), and he shares ancestral ties with Job himself, being a descendant of Buz (32:2), the brother of Uz (1:1; Gen 22:21). This younger man, who claims that until now respect for his elders has restrained him, brazenly speaks out. He chides the three men for their inability to silence Job, and then he takes upon himself the task of convincing Job of his error. His protestations of originality notwithstanding, he too argues in defense of justice executed through divine retribution (36:5-12) and champions the sovereign rule of the creator (34:13-15). Elihu does not appear to be defending a theory so much as divine integrity, however. Nor does he appeal to human wisdom. According to him, God often speaks in dreams and night visions (33:14-16).

Elihu takes great pains to relate the incomprehensibility of God's ways to the wonders of creation, particularly the force displayed in the thunderstorm (36:26—37:13; Habel, 1985:502–14). Much of his teaching is based on empirical evidence, which gives his words more credibility than the hollow pronouncements of the others. Furthermore, he seems less concerned with human frailty and its consequences than with divine majesty and its manifestations. For these reasons, one might rightly say that Elihu espouses a theocentric worldview.

Elihu's last words to Job are ironic questions designed to force Job to acknowledge his own limitations before the wisdom and power of the creator. They are the same kind of questions that God will soon pose, questions meant to lead Job to the same conclusions. Earlier Job responded to the instruction and advice of his three visitors. He has no comparable opportunity to do so here. Elihu's interrogation about the splendor of creation is transformed into an announcement of a demonstration of that very splendor. All attention is fixed on the north, the traditional dwelling place of God. The Almighty is approaching.

Just as no explanation is given for his appearance, Elihu departs from the scene not to return. This man is not like the others who have addressed Job. Although he too offered Job counsel, he is not reproached by God. While the others rebuked Job's demand that God appear in court, Elihu sets the stage for the appearance of God in nature. He does not condemn Job of sin but of misunderstanding. This defender of divine majesty challenges both the rigid articulations of traditional teaching and the shortsighted claims of personal experience. He goes on to maintain that even a dynamic wisdom, one born of the dialogue between tradition and experience, cannot explain the mysteries of life. Elihu prepares Job, the visitors, and the reader alike for the theophany of God.

A Stand for Righteousness

The opening lines of the book identify Job as a man from Uz, a land linked with Edom, the famed center of wisdom. He is described as a righteous man par excellence, "blameless, upright, fearing God and avoiding evil." This is followed by a colorful delineation of his prosperity, life circumstances that were considered the consequence of his uprightness. He not only has great wealth, but his resources are in perfect balance, that is, they are counted in multiples of the mystical numbers of three, five, seven, and ten, numbers that symbolize fullness, entirety, perfection. He even has a balanced number of children, seven sons who will generate seven dowries and three daughters whose dowry disbursements will not result in financial hardship. This testimony of praise is rounded off with a second assertion of his preeminence. This man is "the greatest of the people of the east" (1:3), the region renowned for its wisdom. An example of Job's moral stature follows. His willingness to atone for any inadvertent transgression by his children illustrates the lengths to which this man will go in order to ensure not only his own but also his whole family's right relationship with God.

This portrait depicts a man without fault. Even God recognizes this and acclaims it to the Satan in the very words with which the description of Job's integrity begins (1:8; 2:3). The Satan does not really doubt Job's righteousness so much as the reasons for it. Is Job's piety disinterested or self-serving? Is it God he fears, or God's wrath? Does he turn from evil out of conviction, or because the circumstances of his life have protected him from invidious traps? If the securities of his life are taken away, securities with which God has blessed him, will he curse God?

The unfolding of the story shows that Job is unwavering in his commitment to God and actually accepting of his reversal of fortune. Having lost his possessions and his children, who were the guarantee of the continuation of his name, he dons the attire of the mourner, acknowledges the impoverishment of human existence, and actually praises God (1:21). He passes the second test, physical affliction, in the same fashion. He neither curses God nor questions the wisdom of his situation. In fact, he justifies it. Job's range of concern is defined by God's good pleasure, and his intention is commitment to God's designs. Job is definitely not an egocentric man. From a religious point of view, he is not anthropocentric either, although this is precisely what the Satan alleges. Even in his distress, Job espouses a theocentric attitude.

A close look at Job's two responses shows that they are not as similar as they might at first seem. They actually consist of three very different statements. Job first declares that we are devoid of possessions at birth and again at death. He then states that during life, God gives, and at death, God takes away. These two statements may be related, but they are not the same. Finally, Job asserts that God not only takes away our possessions but actually afflicts us with adversity. This seems to depict a progression of vulnerability: nakedness, dispossession, affliction. This is the fate of human creatures, and there is nothing to do but to accept it graciously. It should be noted that God decides this state of affairs, and there seems to be no causal correlation here with the moral character of human behavior.

The counsel that Job's wife offers may not be as illogical as sometimes alleged. From her point of view, this progression of vulnerability seems to be: nakedness, dispossession, death. If, in her eyes, dispossession is the companion of death, then death is the next logical step, and cursing God would certainly bring on Job's death. This kind of thinking arises from the traditional human theory of retribution, and yet Job rebuffs her counsel as foolish. He proposes a different wisdom. Defending the sovereign freedom of God, a freedom incomprehensible to women and men, he insists that they unquestioningly accept whatever God sends them, regardless of what it may be.

The Satan has been wrong. Job's words show that his piety is indeed disinterested; his virtue is genuine; and he has no intention of cursing God. The scene ends with Job sitting for seven days and seven nights, silently wrapped in his misery, accompanied by three friends who have come from afar to comfort him.

Job's period of mourning is complete, symbolized by the number seven. A flood of imprecations follows. Without cursing God directly, Job certainly does rail against God's creative designs on his behalf. He does not condemn the order of creation itself but, rather, the way it has impinged on his life. He seems to envision a kind of flexibility in creation, which would collapse the temporal order. This would enable it to reverse the course of time and return to the night of his conception and the day of his birth, in order to blot them out (3:3) or swallow them up (v. 8). What appears to be a fanciful notion of the natural world may be poetic hyperbole, but it does suggest belief in a kind of synergism in all of creation. In other words, what happens in one part or on one level (his life is in shambles) has repercussions elsewhere (cosmic upheaval). Job would have creation re-create itself in order to put an end to his adversity. This is anthropocentric self-interest in its most rudimentary form: anything for the sake of survival.

Job's words follow the formula of the curse. It can hardly be a legitimate one, however, because he has no authority to call for the reversal of creation. His words are condemnatory, not performative. The word used here for curse is qālal, meaning "to diminish," which is precisely what a curse is meant to do. The forcefulness of the imagery used shows that the intensity of Job's sufferings has brought him to regard his birth as a tragedy that never should have occurred. After censuring the cosmic order and the role that it played in his birth, Job bemoans the fact that he was not stillborn. Had this been the case, he would have departed immediately to the realm of the dead, where there is no social class, where the rich and the poor, the small and the great all endure the same fate. He denounces the granting of life to those destined to an existence of misery. He seems to suggest that for some, suffering is the very basis of reality rather than an intermittent occurrence. In this he is far from his previous understanding of suffering as merely one part of life, the other part being blessing (2:10). Here, God not only provokes distress but keeps the sufferer trapped within it (3:23). It is ironic that previously Job rebuked his wife for suggesting death, and here he pleads for it.

Do his curse and his lament imply that Job's virtue is wavering? Or has his view of human existence been subverted? Earlier Job might have presumed that life is fundamentally satisfying although it does include occasional setbacks. Now he seems to argue that it is an unbearable ordeal from start to finish, with little if any respite.

Job's condemnation of life is found in the dialogues as well. He perceives himself as defenseless, the victim of God's attacks, with no human support and no recourse. Life, as he sees it lived by others and now experiences it himself, is extraordinarily burdensome. It is a life of hard service, like that of a hireling or a slave, fraught with misery and trouble (7:1-5; 13:28—14:1, 6, 14), fleeting and devoid of hope (7:6-7, 16; 9:25-26; 10:20; 14:2-22). Job insists that he suffers all of this at the hand of God (19:6—21; 27:2), even though he is innocent of serious transgression (10:7; 16:17; 23:12). He admits that he has sinned, but he states that he did turn to God for forgiveness and cannot comprehend why God withholds it (7:21; 10:14; 14:16-17). When Job appealed to the people who knew him and who should have been willing to testify to his innocence, they not only refused him support in his misery, they turned against him (6:14-21; 19:13-19, 21-22). Job has little patience with the men who came to visit him to offer sympathy and advice. Their lives of comfort prevent them from understanding his distress (12:5; 16:4), and their defense of God is not only empty but false (13:4-5, 7-12).

Earlier, in his rejection of his wife's counsel, Job defended God's sovereign freedom and insisted that both good and evil come from the hand of God and should be accepted as such. Now his struggles show that he is not as committed to this opinion as at first it might have seemed. Instead, he looks for justice and agonizes over God's apparent disregard for its principles, not only in his own life but also in the lives of others. He is troubled that the disadvantaged are further oppressed (24:3-21) and the innocent suffer adversity (9:22-24). He observes that at times the wicked endure hardship (27:13-23), but at other times they prosper (12:6; 21:7-18, 30-33). He sees no pattern in God's manner of dealing with either the righteous or the wicked (10:3; 21:23-26). In desperation, Job resolves to summon God to appear before a court of justice (9:15-16; 10:1-2; 13:3, 18; 21:4; 23:2-7). The futility of this undertaking is obvious. God, who is the accused, is also the judge and the jury. There is no place to which Job can turn for justice.

Job does not see much hope in this life for wretched human beings. He makes this point by means of a poignant comparison with a tree. There is hope for a tree because, even if it is cut down, it can sprout again. A person who is cut down, however, does not have a second chance (14:7-14). Still, Job does not seem to prefer death. Although he certainly pleads for an end of his torment, he is more intent on knowing the reason for it. His vindication would be hollow in the realm of the dead (7:9; 10:21-22; 17:13-16), and so he does not entertain death as a possibility.

In the last analysis, Job blames God for his misfortunes (16:7-14; 19:6-12), and he will adhere to this allegation as long as there is breath in him (27:3-6). He admits that he is no match for God (9:2; 10:4; 23:8-9, 13), but he finds it incomprehensible that his creator has become his destroyer (10:8-11). Confident that God knows that he, Job, is righteous, he believes that he will emerge from this trial like refined gold (23:10). Although Job suspects that his adversity is a test, he sees it as a purification of imperfection, not as the test of loyalty that it is.

Job's predicament is less a struggle with suffering than a search for meaning. His unexplained adversity is the occasion of his search. His complaints are filled with frustration and despair of finding answers. He has been disappointed by experience, the great teacher of life, as well as by his religious tradition, the unassailable defender of God. In his final defense, he describes how human beings have been able to extract some of the riches of the earth and made progress along paths unknown even to adroit animals (28:1-11). They have not even found the dwelling place of wisdom, however, much less grasped its secrets (vv. 12, 20). Wisdom can be found neither in the land of the living nor in the realm of the dead (vv. 13-14, 21-22); nor can it be purchased with any of the treasures earned through human enterprise (vv. 15-19). Only God knows the way to wisdom, because only God "saw it and declared it; established it, and searched it out" (v. 27). The only course open to women and men is to fear the LORD and avoid evil (v. 28).

Job's declaration that wisdom is beyond his reach does not suggest that he has given up his struggle. On the contrary, he insists that he has in fact feared the LORD and avoided evil. In the past, this was recognized by all, and he delighted in the peace and satisfaction that came from this recognition (29:1-25). Now, for some reason he cannot apprehend, his world has been turned upside down. Respect has turned to disdain (30:1-11), and peace has given way to assault and anguish (vv. 12-19). Job has feared God, and God in turn has terrorized Job (vv. 20-31).

Job concludes his defense with a formal declaration of innocence (Habel, 1985:427–31). He lists the rules of conduct that have governed his behavior, and he insists that God either punish him if he is found guilty or vindicate him if he is innocent, as Job has claimed to be (31:1-34). If God would provide him with a comparable list of charges, Job would gladly carry it openly for all to see (vv. 35-37). He affixes his signature to his statement of innocence and awaits a reply from God. Job has forced God's hand. If his testimony has been false, God will surely punish him. If, on the other hand, he is not punished, it will be taken as vindication.

Not to be overlooked is the fact that Job's very last words acknowledge the relationship between social justice and ecoharmony. Job declares that any exploitation by him of either the land or its owners would earn him the same penalty: the land would produce thorns and weeds instead of wheat and barley. This declaration, which contains an acknowledgment of the affinity between human life and the rest of creation, corresponds to Job's first lament, wherein he curses the night of his conception and the day of his birth for their part in his wretched existence. Thus Job's speeches are framed by allusions to the synergy of the natural and human worlds. Although the different levels of creation individually follow their own laws, they can cooperate with each other in order to increase each other's effectiveness or, as here, accede to each other's requests (Stadelmann, 1970:7–8).

Job has appealed to nature on several different occasions and in several different ways. The easiest appeal to identify and to understand is the representation of God as the creator of the universe. God exercises authority over the heavens and the underworld, both establishing them and ruling them (9:5-10; 14:13; 26:6-14; 28:25-26). This sovereignty is further demonstrated by references to God's command of the powers of chaos depicted as mythical creatures: Leviathan, also referred to as Sea, Dragon, or Serpent (3:8; 7:12; 9:8; 26:12-13) and Rahab (9:13; 26:12). Poetic comparisons are drawn between aspects of human life and behavior and the features of other elements of creation (6:3, 15–17; 7:9; 14:18-19; 19:10). As God does in the speeches (38–42), so Job poses rhetorical questions about nature in order to illustrate something about human life (6:5).

A few passages may reflect something more than metaphorical flourish. In one passage Job bids his visitors inquire directly of the animals, the birds, the plants, and the fish. These creatures will declare that all things, Job's misfortune included, come from the hand of the LORD (12:7-9, the only place in the dialogues where the personal name of God appears). In another place Job directly addresses the earth (16:18), asking that nature not disregard his agony but allow his innocent blood to cry out (Gen 4:10). In these passages nature is not a silent disengaged stage on which human drama unfolds; it is active and dynamic, a possible ally for Job.

Quite clearly, neither the wisdom of traditional teaching as promoted by the visitors nor the insights that Job has recently gained through his own disturbing experience is sufficient to explain the mystery of innocent suffering. If Job's dilemma is to be resolved, he must look elsewhere for an explanation. At the end of his speech Job brings his doubts and questions, his frustrations and protests to the bar of God's justice and waits there to be heard (31:35). When God finally speaks, it is to question Job about creation, not to assuage his search for understanding (38:3; 40:7). Job's responses show that God's interrogation has accomplished its goal: Job has reached a new depth of comprehension. God began each series of questions by challenging Job to stand up like a man of valor (38:3; 40:7). In his responses at the end of each speech (40:3-5; 42:1-6), Job acknowledges how insignificant he is in the face of the magnificence of creation. Not only does he admit his inability to respond to God's questioning but he realizes how ineffectual his own questioning has been. These contrasts are ironic. On the one hand, the man called to be heroic is humbled; the one who posed questions cannot provide answers. On the other hand, Job's real heroism is found in his humble admission of human limitation; his questioning is satisfied by mystery.

Job does not disavow his integrity. But then, God did not speak about justice. This is a man who is in error, not in sin. He has been led to recognize the former and is not asked to concede the latter. What he does admit is that he spoke "without knowledge" (42:3). But knowledge about what? Or about whom? Has he been wrong about the religious tradition? He challenged its assertion that the righteous enjoy the fruits of their virtue and only the wicked must endure the burden of adversity. His own experience shows the fallacy of this contention, and so his criticism of this tenet is fitting. He has been wrong, however, to think that his religious tradition, as venerable and as sacred as it might be, can thoroughly resolve all of the critical issues that women and men must face in a lifetime. Job is wrong to expect this, and those who would uphold the tradition as absolute are wrong to presume it.

Has he been wrong about God? Throughout his complaints, he never denied God's power and majesty. On the contrary, he insisted from the start that God's advantage has been turned against him. In this he was correct (1:12; 2:6). He does presume, however, that God is bound to the same law and order assigned to human society and, being negligent in this regard, God is guilty of injustice. Although incorrect, this presumption is understandable. Job seems to have mistaken the synergy operative among the various dimensions of reality (the physical and the social) for univocity of operation. (In a synergy, individual agents follow their own respective laws even as they are cooperating. In a univocity, everything follows the same laws.) Job has labored under the assumption that human society, the physical world, and the mystery of God itself are all subject to the moral laws that Job knows (Fretheim, 1991:362). He expects God to enforce the causal relationship between human behavior and life circumstances that retribution, as he understands it, demands. In this he has been wrong.

Has he been wrong about himself? The reader knows that Job is not in any way responsible for his misfortunes. In fact, he was victimized precisely because he was so faithful. Therefore, he is correct to persist in his own defense. But he has an inflated notion of the reach of human comprehension. He may possess some limited understanding of human motivation and the consequences of human behavior, but he cannot fathom God's management of the world. Job has indeed spoken "without understanding," but he has not done so with malice.

With his last words, Job marvels at his encounter with God (42:5-6). This experience has opened his eyes and transformed his heart. He now recognizes God's sovereignty in the universe and, presumably, in the events of his own life. He no longer protests the circumstances of his existence but resigns himself to the modest yet remarkable condition of a mortal human being (v. 6). The narrowness of his former anthropocentrism has given way to a chastened theocentrism.

The epilogue shows that in many ways Job has been brought full circle. Once again he enjoys a special relationship with God (42:7; 1:8; 2:3), he acts on behalf of others as an intermediary (42:8; 1:5), and he is prosperous with a healthy posterity (42:12-13; 1:2-3). However similar the circumstances may appear, this is not the same man that we met in the prologue. Job has emerged from his ordeal transformed. There is no indication that he ever discovered the reason for his affliction, yet he seems satisfied. He had been treated insensitively by his visitors, yet here without a word he intercedes for them in their need. He had denounced faithless companions, and now he plays host to his fair-weather family and friends. Here is a man who has risen above egocentric inclinations.

A Victory of Faith

Certain questions remain to be answered: How had the visitors been wrong about God, but Job right? Their rigid interpretation of retribution convinced them that God would never afflict an innocent person as Job claimed had happened to him. Because they had not been present at the exchange between God and the Satan that took place in the heavenly court, they had no tangible way of knowing that their defense of God was false. Job, on the other hand, had no tangible way of proving that he had done nothing to warrant the kind of misfortune that had overwhelmed him. Nonetheless, he held fast to his innocence and drew the only conclusion that he could: God was in fact the cause of his adversity. In this, the visitors were wrong about God, and Job was right. Therefore, he was correct to disregard their counsel.

The fact that God spoke only about Job and never to him in the prologue and the epilogue is important in the final theological understanding of the book. It was in the prologue that the stage was set and the drama planned. It was very important that Job know nothing about this so that he could play out his part in faith and not with understanding. Job's misfortune was merely the occasion for his real trial: a struggle with the incomprehensible in life and with the incomprehensible God. This struggle was resolved at the conclusion of God's speeches, when Job admitted his inability to understand and his willingness to stand humbly and silently before the wondrous God. God's interrogation of Job had accomplished its goal, and so there was no need for God to speak to him again.

From beginning to end, Job knew nothing about the wager, and so he would not understand his suffering as a test or his concluding good fortune as a reward. Instead, his reinstatement as a respected member of the community was an external sign of his vindication (Janzen, 1985:267–69). Vindication and reward are not the same thing. Vindication is exoneration when guilt is erroneously presumed; reward is compensation for meritorious behavior. Job was indeed a righteous man who, nonetheless, endured misfortune. His vindication was evidence of his righteousness. Since Job knew all the time that he was innocent, his reinstatement was less a sign for him than it was for his family, friends, and acquaintances. There is no indication that Job ever understood why things happened in his life as they had. His encounter with God had provided him a glimpse of God's governance over all natural phenomena, but that was enough for Job to realize that God was indeed in charge. If God holds in balance the mysteries of creation with all their diversity and complexity, surely God would be attentive to the needs of human existence. Reassured by this conviction, Job sat calmly with his unanswered questions.

The final characterization of God that the reader retains is a composite of all the features revealed throughout the book. God presides over the heavenly council and oversees the events that unfold on earth. God is ultimately responsible for everything that happens in Job's life but is not bound to human standards of compensation in managing it. God created and sustains the universe and provides for the living creatures. Divine care for Job is shown in the magnanimous way in which God leads Job to new insight. It would be incorrect to maintain that God withheld knowledge from Job; rather, Job's human limitation prevented him from understanding mystery and, rather than allow this to crush him, God painstakingly brought him to realize this fact.

The prologue, the dialogues, and the epilogue all expose the limitations of the theory of retribution, which is really an example of religious yet human wisdom. From the outset, both God and the Satan acknowledged Job's virtue and yet they agreed on a plan to afflict him. This shows that the heavenly council was not bound by the expectations of the theory. Throughout the dialogues, Job clung tenaciously to his innocence. Although he challenged God, his own experience told him that there are times when the righteous do in fact endure inexplicable hardship. Thus the limitations of the theory were recognized as well by someone who suffered. In the epilogue Job is vindicated for the affront to his virtue. Those mentioned in the epilogue saw such reinstatement as an admission that an innocent man had been treated as one guilty of serious transgression. Thus in the end everyone, except for Job's wife who neither supported nor questioned his innocence, recognized the limitations of this theory.

To admit that something about the religious tradition is inadequate is not to dismiss it as irrelevant but merely to acknowledge its limitations as well as its strengths. Retribution may be the grounding for justice, a requirement for the stability of any social group, but the harmony within the physical universe depends on other laws. If this is true about the natural world, how much more is it true of supernatural reality? If God is omnipotent, as in this narrative, then no law can circumscribe God's activity. If the acts of God are inexplicable, then no theological testimony can capture God's reality. Theological assertions are testimonies to the experience of God, they are not exhaustive definitions of God's essence.

Perhaps the most significant insight that Job gained was anthropological. Contrary to his expectations, expectations supported by the dogmatism of retribution, Job could not understand his chaotic situation. Because he believed that ultimately God is responsible for everything, he pressed God for an explanation, not of the theory of retribution which he understood, but of God's designs beyond the scope of that theory. Job had an inflated notion of the capacity and quality of human comprehension. In order to understand the secrets of human life and to grasp its scope and the laws governing its function, he would have had to have been present at creation. Who was he to presume such privilege (15:7-8)? His encounter with the God of creation through God's creation brought him to a new anthropological appreciation. Human beings are part of the vast mystery of the universe, and only one who can grasp the totality of this mystery will be able to understand the secrets of life. Job admits his inability to measure up to such a challenge, and he willingly acquiesces to his human condition.

Rhetorical Function

The drama that unfolds within the book of Job was prompted by the Satan's challenge: Is Job's piety disinterested, or does he worship God for the sake of the blessings that will follow such devotion? Even the question presumes that some kind of good fortune is within reach of anyone who chooses righteous living. Such a presumption most likely originates from those who enjoy some degree of happiness and believe that they have a right to it. People for whom hardship and dispossession are constant conditions of life know from their own experience that virtue does not guarantee reward. While they may hope for advantage, they recognize it as a component of the lives of others.

The reader is appalled at the seeming injustice of Job's predicament. Here is a man who followed all of the standards of society and achieved what such fidelity promised, only to have it snatched from his grasp for no apparent reason. The conventional teaching of retribution does not satisfactorily address Job's situation. He is granted an extraordinary encounter with God, which brings with it a new understanding of the relationship between righteousness and success. Every one of the human characters in the book seems to presume the validity of the theory of retribution. Job's wife insinuates that righteousness in the face of suffering is worthless; the visitors maintain that justice is being served in Job's suffering; Elihu too defends the theory; and Job himself accuses God of violating its principles.

This is the perspective of the relatively comfortable. Disadvantaged people would not be appalled. They have probably both witnessed and experienced reversal of fortune despite having observed rules and regulations. They know that retribution is more a means to frighten them into compliance than a description of their reality, and they do not need a special revelation from God to recognize this. They are probably acquainted with many upstanding people who lack the comforts of life or who suffer great indignity. They may even count themselves among that group. Life itself has taught them that goodness is not always compensated.

People who are afflicted could view this book as a story with an ironic twist. They might be gratified watching one of the pillars of society fall from grace or seeing the defenders of orthodoxy reprimanded for their false teaching and then dependent upon the intercession of the one who not only suffered but who had to endure their ridicule in the face of it. They might read this account as an example of God using the weak things of the world to confound the strong. They would probably not identify with Job himself, because, while he may have endured much of the misery and disdain that they know so well, he experienced it as baffling loss and not as routine deprivation. Furthermore, he was eventually returned to a life of comfort and respect.

The book lends itself to two very different rhetorical interpretations. It can be directed to people who are prosperous or at least content. They will watch as their concept of justice is challenged and found wanting. From the outset, they will find themselves siding with the dissenter and, with him, will come to several new insights: success is ephemeral; it is not the sure sign of moral integrity; disaster can come to anyone at any time; and setbacks are not necessarily indications of moral frailty. At the end of the book, they will be brought with Job to the feet of God, there humbly to acknowledge their own limitations and their utter dependence on God.

The book can also be directed to those who live lives of desperation. Its dilemma will confirm their conviction that virtuous people can indeed be the victims of misfortune; that the frustration and anger of the poor can be justified; that the tradition often supports the status quo; that those who do not know tragedy can be quite self-righteous in their comfort. In the face of all of this, the book calls them to be steadfast in their own righteousness, persistent in their protest, and tenacious in their trust in God.

Regardless of the socioeconomic status of the readers, all will recognize the significance given to honest human experience. Job did indeed endure suffering that was in no way a consequence of his behavior. Although the visitors were ignorant of the wager in heaven, they knew of Job's reputation for wisdom and righteousness. Despite this, his claims did not conform to their framework of thought and so they refused to believe him. This obduracy on their part shows that empirical wisdom, which is actually a dynamic reflection of the genuine experience of life, can turn into rigid dogmatism, closed to whatever does not fit the theory. When this happens, the religious teaching, which both rests on and legitimates the sapiential tradition, ceases to be real wisdom. It did not appeal to Job's heart, and it will not appeal to the hearts of the readers.

Both Job and his visitors clung fast to what they believed was right, but Job was grounded in reality while they were caught in convention. Although true virtue will always be guided by sound convention, sometimes convention must give way to uncommon experience. God's defense of Job and rebuke of the others shows the preference for genuine experience over unyielding dogma, whether that dogma is found in a cultural or in a religious sapiential tradition. This divine preference probably made the standard-bearers of orthodoxy, whoever they might have been, feel very uneasy.

Job is portrayed as a model of personal integrity. He is an inspiration to those who, in the throes of distress with no support whatever, are tempted to compromise themselves. His response to his reversal of fortune, to God's silence, and to the denunciation by his visitors was not capitulation but fierce protest. Job would not tolerate meekly what he considered to be injustice on God's part and unsympathetic accusation on the part of others. From his point of view, he was a man of resolute virtue, his visitors were purveyors of empty platitudes, and God was an unreliable overlord. In his mouth, protest was nothing more than abused innocence demanding redress or human frailty crying out for release. Those in comparable situations will notice quickly that God does not fault Job for his outbursts. They will rightly conclude that, as harsh as they may have been, they were not inappropriate.

Unmasking the Powers

The first step in a liberationist reading, which is sensitive to issues of race or ethnic origin, class, and gender, is the disclosure of the centers of power. Both those who benefit from this power and those who do not are often either unconscious of its existence and influence in their lives, or they uncritically presume that the power structures are rooted in reality rather than in custom. This deceit must be unmasked and seen for what it is, discrimination of the worst kind.

Very little can be said about the ethnic origins of the characters of the book of Job, but what can be said is quite significant. All of the men, and presumably Job's wife, come from lands noted for wisdom. Although the author probably mentioned this so that the reader would appreciate the depth of their insights and the distinction with which each one spoke, it also points to the endorsement of such a tradition. The East was renowned for wisdom. But why? Perhaps it had been or continued to be a center of higher civilization and culture from which learning spread. Whatever the case, the reputation most likely arose out of factual circumstances which, over time, developed into a stereotype. Racial or ethnic stereotypes, even when they appear to be harmless characterizations, are seldom value-neutral. Like all stereotypes, they privilege some and hinder others. For example, those with wisdom do not have to listen; those without wisdom will not be heard. In the book of Job, the very stereotype that alerted the reader to the sagacious stature of each speaker prevented that speaker from being open to gain real insight.

Clearly Job belonged to the privileged class and presumed that his virtue entitled him to that prosperity. Although his encounter with God brought him new insight in this matter, at the conclusion of the story he is once again a prosperous man. What does the book really say about class privilege, and what are some of its unspoken suppositions?

The principles of retribution both reinforce and legitimate the stereotyping of class distinction. What may succeed as motivation for ethical living —goodness will be rewarded and wickedness punished—can be quite prejudicial when it becomes an explanation of life circumstance—prosperity is a sign of goodness and deprivation a sign of sin. These standards are manifest in the words of Job's visitors, who argue that neither the wicked nor their children will flourish (15:29; 20:10, 20–28). Job himself equivocates on this. In one place he complains that the wicked along with their children do prosper (21:7-16), and in another he maintains that, out of justice, God deprives the evildoers of their good fortune (27:16-19). The apparent incompatibility of this last passage with the rest of Job's protestations has led some interpreters to ascribe it to Zophar (Habel, 1985:383–87). This inconsistency notwithstanding, the attitude of the visitors about economic status is itself ambiguous. They believe that God intervenes on behalf of the poor (5:15-16) and punishes those who take advantage of them (20:19ff.). Job agrees (24:2-12, 18-24). But such a conviction contradicts the assumption that misfortune is the consequence of some kind of transgression. It also suggests that the righteous have a responsibility to relieve what is, in fact, divine punishment. In addition to this enigma, both Eliphaz (5:11) and Job (12:17-21) allege that God actually reverses the fortunes of some people for no apparent reason. The reader presumes that this is because they have sinned, but the text is not clear. For the humans, ambiguity on this matter reigns. For God, divine freedom is sovereign.

In his own defense, Job insists that he had not misused his position of privilege but had placed it at the service of those less fortunate than himself

(31:13-21). As far as abundance is concerned, he had put his confidence neither in his own wealth (31:24-26) nor in the wealth of others (6:22), and he recognized that no amount of gold or silver or precious gems can secure the wisdom for which everyone searches. Yet it is clear that Job believes that he had and continues to have a right to privilege. He is offended by the disdain of his former servants (19:15-16) and the loss of his prestige (29:7-10, 12, 25). He expects people to reverence his integrity, despite the loss of his prosperity. But without prosperity, his integrity is not recognized. The class stereotype that formerly endorsed him as honorable now convicts him.

Both Job and Elihu argue that God is no respecter of social position. Counselor, judge, king, priest, elder, and prince were all highly revered leadership posts. Yet those who occupied these seats of power could very well be deposed (12:17-21; 34:14-15, 24-28), and no class distinctions exist after life on earth (3:14-15, 18-19; 21:23-26).

The visitors and Job consistently defend retribution and the social categories that the theory ventures to define. They also recognize that God neither respects social hierarchy nor complies with the expectations of the theory. Since at the end of the story Job desists in his complaint against God in this regard (40:5; 42:3) and his visitors are reprimanded for their defense of God (42:7-8), it is apparent that the author intends the reader to be converted to God's point of view. This means that, while retribution may be an acceptable technique for motivation, it is an inadequate standard for evaluation. It also means that even good social hierarchy is tentative at best.

The third area of concern is the question of gender. It is clear from the outset that the story not only concerns a man and his male friends but is told from a male perspective. This in itself is not discriminatory. The bias becomes evident, however, when we recall that the misfortune that befalls Job and the struggle to understand its cause are not exclusively male issues. Women too endure such suffering, and they have a particular way of understanding it, which may or may not be the same as men's. To disregard this and to promote a point of view that represents only a male perspective is to relegate the experience of women to a position of insignificance.

A second indication of the gender preference is seen in the male characterization of God. Although the linguistic origin and subsequent meaning of the divine name YHWH are disputed, the Hebrew pronouns referring to YHWH are all masculine, signifying the intended gender of this representation of God. Yet any uncompromising insistence on God's masculine identity is challenged by the female imagery found in the first divine speech (38:28f.). When questioning Job about the origins of the cosmic marvels God uses different birth allusions, two of which are clearly female. One of the Hebrew verbs involved. (*yālad*) is used twice and can be translated either "to beget" or "to give birth." Since the verse (v. 28) contains internal parallel construction, and since the reference in the first line is to father, it seems fitting to translate the verb with the male connotation: "Has the rain a father? or who has begotten the drops of dew?" The second verse, (v. 29) however, contains clearly female allusions. "From whose womb did the ice come forth (*yāsā*)?" The use of parallel construction recommends that here *yālad* be translated "give birth": "From whose womb did the ice come forth, and who has given birth to the hoarfrost of the heaven?" Even though the verb forms in all cases are masculine, the imagery that alludes to God's activity is both male and female.

The only woman who plays a role in the story is Job's wife. This unnamed one-dimensional woman has only one line of dialogue, chiding Job for his steadfastness and counseling him to curse God. The author does not reveal her motivation for such a response to her husband's predicament. This lack of detail allows for a variety of conjectures about her disposition, all of which tells more about the interpreter than about the woman herself. Job's rejoinder creates the impression by which she has been remembered. Her words are foolish or shameless, a disgrace to the community. Job does not say that *she* is foolish or shameless, but that her words are. This kind of characterization has established the stereotype of the well-intentioned but senseless woman whose advice cannot be followed. An even more uncomplimentary interpretation identifies her with Eve. In this case both women are incorrectly perceived as gullible ploys of the devil, willing to take advantage of the marital relationship in order to ensnare their husbands. Thus the characterization of the woman as the temptress is reinforced.

Job's wife takes on a different profile if she is viewed more as a foil than as an individual, as I have proposed. This character is really a literary device serving to accentuate the quality of Job's moral disposition. The person in the story closest to Job, and the one the reader would expect to be most like him, is drawn in the sharpest contrast to him, thus highlighting his distinctiveness. This similarity/contrast is even more striking if Job's wife is viewed as his alter ego. The outer dialogue between the two then represents Job's personal inner struggle, and his marriage counterpart stands for his other self. In both cases, since this story concerns a man, it is understandable that his intimate would be a woman.

Job's wife does not stand in favorable light regardless of how her character is understood. But then, neither does anyone else who offers advice to him. He may have chided his wife, but he railed against his visitors, calling them liars and worthless physicians (13:4), miserable comforters with windy words (16:2-3) and closed minds (17:4). The point of the characterization of Job's wife is not the untrustworthiness of women but the inadequacy of any human counsel, even that which comes from one's most trusted ally, the companion of one's mind and heart. To read it as a denunciation of female integrity is to be guilty of a discrimination not found in the text itself.

A specific group of women is mentioned several times in the dialogues. In traditional patriarchal societies, widows were particularly defenseless. Once married, they no longer enjoyed the protection of their father's household. When widowed, they had no husband to provide for them. If they had no son to rely on, they were in dire straits. Humane communities assumed the responsibility for legally vulnerable groups such as widows and orphans. Concern for and care of them became the hallmark of the truly honorable person and, accordingly, a standard against which Job was judged. Eliphaz outrightly accuses him of disregard and abuse in this matter (22:9). While Job bemoans such wickedness in others (24:3, 21), he testifies to his own compassion and kindness (29:13) and confirms it with an oath (31:16). Job insists that he did not neglect those who were disadvantaged by the circumstances of life or the biased structures of society. Instead, he was their champion.

Job's own distorted view of women is shockingly evident in his oath of innocence, where he attempts to prove his sexual propriety. He disavows any adultery as well as the covetous lust that precedes it. He calls down upon himself, as penalty of any possible infraction in this regard, the defilement of his own wife. This declaration is abhorrent for at least two reasons. First, the punishment would be exacted in the flesh of the innocent wife, not the guilty husband or the other woman. Furthermore, it would be demanded by the offended husband. This seems to be an issue between the men and not between the women, although one of the women must pay for her husband's transgression. This clearly exemplifies how women were considered the property of the men and, as in any theft, stealing the pleasures of that property is a violation of the rights of the owner. This declaration by Job is also abhorrent in the crudity of the power Job presumes over his wife. Everything about the description of the defilement bespeaks vulnerability and subservience on the part of the woman and violence and domination on the part of the man, and this is intended to serve Job's claim of innocence. Perhaps according to the standards of his society Job is a righteous man, for this oath is precisely an asseveration of his innocence. Yet in no way are these particular standards of abuse and violence redeemable.

Finally, the reference to Job's daughters in the epilogue should be noted. Although disagreement exists over the number of children born to him after his ordeal (Habel, 1985:577), the description of them is of interest here. Unlike the daughters mentioned in the prologue, these women are named, so that they have a specific identity. Their names all signify beauty and delicacy, features highly praised in both the ancient and the contemporary worlds (42:14-15). More significant is the report about their inheritance. This is quite an unusual gesture on Job's part, since normally a woman only inherited in the absence of a male heir (Num 27:1-8). Even then the property would revert to the clan of her origin at her death, thus ensuring the integrity of its heritage.

Neither of these factors is reported for the sake of the daughters. They are both examples of Job's good fortune. The beauty of his daughters, a traditional chauvinist concern, redounds to his own reputation. The fact that they have an inheritance, even one that cannot be transferred to their husbands, makes them even more desirable. These are women who are not only beautiful but rich. They would certainly be welcome adornment in the households of their father and, later, of their husbands.

The portrayal of women in this book is consistent with a patriarchal androcentric worldview. Women are perceived and valued from a male perspective, and they serve to enhance the male ego and reputation. To say that despite this blatant bias Job is more sensitive to the women in his life than is customary is to beg the question. He is still a product of a worldview with a male preference. Something other than Job's own high ideals will have to intervene in order to redeem this story from its androcentric rule.

Into the Looking Glass

The advocacy stand that is sensitive to issues of race or ethnic origin, class, and gender not only critiques the Bible, as has been done above, but also sets the parameters for the challenge that the biblical material can offer. Light is now thrown on these specific issues in order to open to the transformative power of God's word the aspects of contemporary reality that they define. Thus the biblical message can function for the reader as a mirror and as a doorway to a new world.

Theology begins and ends with the activity of God. For that reason, the characterization of God sets the tone for understanding the dynamic of the book of Job. Everyone in the story addresses the nature and extent of God's involvement in human life. Even the Satan knows that God, although reigning from the far distant heavenly council, controls the lives and fortunes of people on earth. Job and his antagonists debate over God's compliance to the standards of retribution prescribed for human society. Is God in fact just? Is divine power used fairly, or are women and men victimized by it? With very few exceptions (11:7-12; 34:13-15; 36:26—37:13), the characterization of God espoused by these individuals is fundamentally anthropocentric, focused on God's relationship with human beings.

The divine speeches reveal an entirely different representation of God that is not simply one among many. This is a theophany, a divine self-revelation, through which God is revealed to Job as the source of mind-boggling creativity, not as an arbiter preoccupied only with human affairs. God shows that divine artistry and protection have been lavished on all creation, not merely on human beings. Furthermore, the value of this extravagant creation does not rest in its instrumental usefulness for humans. It is intrinsic to creation itself as having come from God. Furthermore, the imagery used to describe God's creative activity is female as well as male.

The wonders of creation that are paraded before Job were not unknown to him before this revelation. By and large, they constituted the world that he knew, but which he did not understand; the world within which he lived, but which he seems to have taken for granted. Job's breathtaking experience of creation has catapulted him out of his narrow confines of anthropocentrism into the vast expanses of mystery. His encounter with the ineffable Creator-God has led him to the new and transformative insight that human history unfolds within the broader context of the natural world and not vice versa; the natural world does not merely serve the ends of human history.

In his last response to God, Job admits that he has been converted to God's point of view. The God whom he previously knew and to whom he had been faithful was a God of righteousness who had recognized Job's integrity and had rewarded him for it. The God whom Job now knows is the mysterious power who brought forth the world, as a man begets or as a woman brings forth, and who is somehow revealed in and through that world. This God can provide for the entire resplendent universe without being distracted from the specific needs of fragile human beings, because God's designs are grander than, but do include, human history. God has taken suffering, the most pressing concern of human history, and has situated it within a broader context: that of material creation in its entirety. There, in the midst of measureless natural grandeur, the ambiguity of human life can be confronted with the honesty and humility that it requires, an honesty and humility that can admit to and accept the limited capacity of human comprehension. Creation itself has expanded Job's vision and called him to a deepening of faith that goes beyond understanding.

The implications of such an attitude are profound as well as wide-reaching. The shift from an anthropocentric to a cosmocentric worldview requires not only a new cosmology (Berry, 1988) but also a reexamination of many, if not most, of the tenets of the faith (Berry and Clark, 1991; Nash, 1991). Notions such as frugality and sufficiency, viability and sustainability play an indispensable role in theological discourse. The impertinence of human autonomous rule is replaced by a sense of responsible stewardship, and the bottom line of monetary calculation of resources gives way to aesthetic contemplation of natural beauty, a contemplation not unlike that of Job.

The book of Job also challenges ethnic stereotyping. The men who came to console and to counsel Job shared in and benefited from the reputations of their respective places of origin. In some of their exchanges with Job, they called upon their privileged status as endorsement of the legitimacy of their opinions and the error of his. Their own arguments exposed the fallacy of the stereotype, however; these men cannot be called wise, for they eschew the very criterion for wisdom, namely, deep and faithful reflection on life with all of its joys and sorrows. Job's experience of innocent suffering did not fit into their system, and so they dismissed it as fraudulent rather than afford it serious examination. While wisdom is faithful to traditional teaching, it is nonetheless attentive to new and different human experience. What the reader perceived through the unfolding of the story, Job knew by experience, namely, that these men taught unyielding doctrine rather than dynamic wisdom. God's rebuke of their unsympathetic counsel confirms this. The book of Job shatters the ethnic stereotype. The East does not have a monopoly on wisdom. What is true of this particular stereotype is true of all such ethnic or racial characterizations: they limit and confine, exclude and exploit.

Certain racial or ethnic groups do have distinctive characteristics that have developed as part of their adaptation to geographic, climatic, or social situations. But when the characterization that develops uncritically affords exclusive privilege and unjustified esteem to some but denies equitable opportunity and basic respect to others, it must be unmasked as the prejudice that it is. Neither wisdom, intelligence, wit, strength, agility, honor, nor any human value can be ascribed exclusively to one group. While human beings may be caught in the web of discrimination, the book of Job shows that God reads minds and hearts and is not confined by human stereotypes.

When one looks at the question of expectations from another angle, one can recognize the importance of human experience in the shaping of theology. Job's experience was judged theologically unsuitable because it was unconventional. This raises the question of power: Who determines what is conventional and what is not; what is theologically suitable and what is not? Whose experience shapes theology? The lines of power and credibility on this controversial question are well defined. Job's antagonists have both religious tradition and social convention on their side. They envision themselves and are perceived as being defenders of the faith and guardians of the sapiential legacy. There is no evidence that these men preach one thing and live another. They appear to be fundamentally good men who, according to Job's accusation, have been spared the ambiguities of life and mistake the tranquillity of their situations for virtue.

At first glance, Job is less credible. He is at odds with everything and everyone, bemoaning the fact of having been stripped of family, friends, and reputation for no apparent reason. He rejects his visitors' assessment of his condition and the pious instruction that they offer him, railing against them and against God. Certainly this kind of behavior does not produce authentic theology; at least that is what the dogmatist might think. That does not seem to be the way God sees it, however. Regardless of the vehemence of his outbursts, Job's rebellion is not considered a revolt against God. It is the cry of one whose life has been shattered and who is overwhelmed with confusion. He renounces traditional teaching because it denies the validity of his own assertion of innocence. Job's claims should have been heeded and his ordeal given serious consideration in the shaping, or in this case the reshaping, of theology. Although Job's visitors may not have held this opinion, it certainly is the view of the author, for throughout the book experience takes precedence over custom, the renegade over the establishment. In the end, this inverted point of view enjoys God's endorsement as well.

A theological insight that is experiential at base always has to prove its validity, since experience in itself can be quite unreliable. Genuine theology is never divorced from experience, however; it develops as a way of understanding it, of dealing with it, of shaping it. The more original the experience, the more distinctive the theology. The book of Job shows how the singular experience of one individual can challenge a theological tenet of a group. A comparable challenge arises when a communal experience of one segment of society contests the controlling theology of the dominant group. The breakthrough in perception realized by this segment follows the same path trod by Job. In the beginning they accept without question the interpretation of life supplied by the prevailing worldview. Anything that deviates from the standards is mistrusted, dismissed, or denied. But when such variation persists and cannot be made to conform, the way is open for the emergence of a new theological perspective.

Liberation theologies of all kinds have developed in this way. Convinced that their experience of life may be unique but is not fraudulent, people who have been minimized because of their gender, their race, their class, their age, their preference of any kind have developed various theological responses to the questions of life. Although their approach has much in common with theological contextualization (the development of theology with conscious and painstaking attention given to the distinctive details of the context), it does differ from indigenous theologizing. Liberation theologians seek first to free themselves of false identities and perceptions that have been forced on them by the prevailing worldview. They set out then to devise methods of understanding and approaches to life that are more compatible with their own experience. They have much in common with Job, who struggled with the prevailing view of retribution, refused to deny his own unconventional perspective, and in the end was praised by God for his integrity in this matter.

This leads to a third related issue, namely, the limitation of theology and the need to assess and revise it constantly. New experiences and new insight must not only be evaluated in the light of traditional teaching, they must also critique the claims of that teaching. Since truth is less an absolute that is discovered and applied to new situations than a judgment reached through assiduous investigation and astute evaluation, new data will always call for new interpretation. If this ongoing development is in any way thwarted, theology will become stagnant instead of dynamic, obsolete rather than relevant, illusory and not revelatory. Even the most conscientious theological articulations are limited, for they are finite expressions of infinite reality. When theological discourse crosses cultural boundaries, the variety in perception and expression is multiplied and complicated even more. This variety must be safeguarded and not stifled if theology is to be effective. Innovative racial, cultural, or gender theological studies must be encouraged and respected, for they enhance honest inquiry. Sometimes they provide a corrective, at other times they break new ground. They always reflect the diversity in human experience and its rich and resourceful response to divine promptings.

The ideological intransigence of Job's antagonists illustrates what can happen when people are unwilling or unable to admit the limitations of theology. They might not only misunderstand and alienate honest believers, they might sometimes even abuse them. Furthermore, they can misrepresent God with theology that is inconsequential at best, prejudicial at worst. Inflexible adherence to ideological preference should not be confused with fidelity to the religious tradition and the judicious caution that must be exercised in the matter of theological development. Theology is always somewhat conservative, for it has the responsibility of preserving the tradition as well as transforming it. Nor can the political dimension of theological development be denied. Just as liberation approaches promote the concerns of those who have been overlooked or otherwise disadvantaged, frequently the ones who refuse to acknowledge the limitations of theology are the very ones who benefit from its existing form, as happened with the visitors of Job. This book is unique in that God's approval is given to the one who claims that theology is limited and not to those who insist that it is adequate as it stands.

This last insight provides a way for those concerned with gender issues to discover the revelatory possibilities of this book. While the story contains an unmistakable gender bias, the message of the book itself can reflexively critique this bias. The story shows that, while people may be subject to the limitations of societal and theological perception and articulation, they must not cling to these limitations when corrective insights present themselves. The book of Job makes several claims that can be applicable here. From the point of view of the antagonists: First, deprivation is no indication of ethical indifference or inferiority. Second, conventional systems of understanding sometimes erroneously treat dissent and nonconformity as moral deviance. Third, when this happens, deprivation is then perceived as the consequence of dissent, and the circle of interpretation becomes tighter and even more vicious and incapacitating. Fourth, God condemns this kind of prejudicial thinking. From the point of view of the innocent sufferer, specifically those who are disadvantaged because of a gender bias: First, good and upright people do in fact fall victim to misfortune. Second, honesty and personal integrity demand that injustice be unmasked regardless of who the perpetrator seems to be. Third, solidarity with the oppressed is a religious as well as a humanitarian responsibility. Fourth, God stands on the side of human decency regardless of the distinction of an opposing theological theory.

Those committed to gender issues will also appreciate the characterization of the Creator-God, whose self-revelation springs more from the world of creation than from the world of social convention and is depicted by means of female as well as male imagery. Here God spurns conventional modes of judgment and praises the denigrated man for holding fast to his innocence and disregarding the false counsel given to him. In fact, this depiction of God can appeal to any group that has been maligned and marginalized. Those in the forefront of social or religious breakthroughs may suffer attacks on their integrity and even ostracism. This may be the price they have to pay for being faithful to themselves and to God's prompting in their lives. In the end, it can redound to the well-being of the very community that misjudged them.

In the Midst of Mystery

The book of Job demonstrates the profound human struggle between anthropology and cosmology (Perdue, 1991). It pits the search for understanding against the enormity of the universe in such a way that the human spirit is enraptured and not broken. The commonplace yet strangely unfamiliar natural world awakens amazement at its wonders and leaves the humbled gazer aghast. Having called on God to put things right in his life, Job was led by the magnitude of creation to see that he could not fathom the laws by which God governs. In the end, cosmology does not defeat anthropology; it opens its arms to welcome back its prodigal child.

This struggle, which is resolved in the cosmos, is played out on the stage of human exploration, where actors are fallible beings and the plot is the search for meaning. As the drama unfolds, the protagonist and antagonists alike adhere to the same rigid formula of retribution, an adherence that puts all of them in the wrong. The visitors uphold the formula and defend God and, consequently, falsely accuse Job. Job's support of it and defense of himself erroneously put God at fault. No one challenges the adequacy of the theory, one presumably based on experience.

God's concluding words to the guardians of the tradition charge them and us always to assess experience regardless of how distinctive or unconventional it may appear to be. Such assessment does not presume that experience is always adequately understood or always must generate theological reinterpretation. Job's ordeal of innocent suffering was authentic, but the theological conclusions that he drew from it were false. Presumptions and stereotypes must be assiduously scrutinized if the search for meaning is to be fruitful for all. Even then we may discover, as did Job, that the meaning for which we search is beyond our grasp, and the stand that we will take is in the midst of mystery.

Works Consulted

Alter, Robert. 1981. *The Art of Biblical Narrative.* New York: Basic Books.

Bergant, Dianne. 1982. *Job, Ecclesiastes* (Old Testament Message). Wilmington, Del.: Michael Glazier.

Berry, Thomas. 1988. *The Dream of the Earth.* San Francisco: Sierra Club Books.

Berry, Thomas, and Thomas Clarke. 1991. *Befriending the Earth: A Theology of Reconciliation between Humans and the Earth.* Mystic, Conn.: Twenty-Third Publications.

Booth, Wayne C. 1982. *The Rhetoric of Fiction* (2d ed.). Chicago: University of Chicago Press.

Brenner, Athalya. 1993. "Some Observations on the Figuration of Woman in Wisdom Literature." In *Of Prophets' Visions and the Wisdom of Sages: Essays in Honor of R. Norman Whybray on His Seventieth Birthday.* Edited by Heather A. McKay and David J. A. Clines. Journal for the Study of Old Testament Supplement Series 162. Sheffield: JSOT Press.

Childs, Brevard. 1979. *Introduction to the Old Testament as Scripture.* Philadelphia: Fortress Press.

Cooper, Alan. 1982. "Narrative Theory and the Book of Job." *Studies in Religion* 11:35–44.

Crenshaw, James L. 1984. *A Whirlpool of Torment: Israelite Traditions of God as an Oppressive Presence*. Overtures to Biblical Theology. Philadelphia: Fortress Press.

Dornisch, Loretta. 1981. "The Book of Job and Ricoeur's Hermeneutics." *Semeia* 19:3–21.

Fretheim, Terence E. 1991."The Reclamation of Creation: Redemption and Law in Exodus." *Interpretation* 45:354–65.

Gutiérrez, Gustavo. 1988. *On Job: God-talk and the Suffering of the Innocent*. Maryknoll, N.Y.: Orbis Books.

Habel, Norman C. 1983. "The Narrative Art of Job: Applying the Principles of Robert Alter." *Journal for the Study of the Old Testament* 27:110–11.

_____. 1985. *The Book of Job*. Old Testament Library. Philadelphia: Westminster Press.

_____. 1992. "In Defense of God the Sage." In *The Voice from the Whirlwind: Interpreting the Book of Job*. Edited by Leo G. Perdue and W. Clark Gilpin. Nashville: Abingdon Press.

Humphreys, W. Lee. 1985.*The Tragic Vision and the Hebrew Tradition*. Overtures to Biblical Theology. Philadelphia: Fortress Press.

Janzen, J. Gerald. 1985. *Job*. Interpretation. Atlanta: John Knox.

MacKenzie, R. A. F. 1979. "The Transformation of Job." *Biblical Theology Bulletin* 9:51–57.

Mettinger, Tryggve. 1992. "The God of Job: Avenger, Tyrant, or Victor?" In *The Voice from the Whirlwind: Interpreting the Book of Job*. Edited by Leo G. Perdue and W. Clark Gilpin. Nashville: Abingdon Press.

Miscall, Peter D. 1983. *The Workings of Old Testament Narrative*. Chico, Calif.: Scholars Press.

Murphy, Roland E. 1990. *The Tree of Life: An Exploration of Biblical Wisdom Literature*. The Anchor Bible Reference Library. New York: Doubleday.

Nash, James A. 1991. *Loving Nature: Ecological Integrity and Christian Responsibility*. Nashville: Abingdon Press.

Pellauer, David. 1981. "Reading Ricoeur Reading Job." *Semeia* 19:73–83.

Penchansky, David. 1990. *The Betrayal of God: Ideological Conflict in Job*. Louisville, Ky.: Westminster/John Knox Press.

Perdue, Leo G. 1991. *Wisdom in Revolt: Metaphorical Theology in the Book of Job*. Journal for the Study of Old Testament Supplement Series 112. Sheffield: JSOT Press.

_____. 1993. "Wisdom in the Book of Job." In *In Search of Wisdom: Essays in Memory of John G. Gammie*. Edited by Leo G. Perdue et al. Louisville, Ky.: Westminster/John Knox Press.

_____. 1994. *Wisdom and Creation: The Theology of Wisdom Literature.* Nashville: Abingdon Press.

Polzin, Robert M. 1977.*Biblical Structuralism: Method and Subjectivity in the Study of Ancient Texts.* Missoula, Mont.: Scholars Press.

Powell, Mark Allen. 1990. *What Is Narrative Criticism?* Philadelphia: Fortress Press.

Robertson, David. 1977. *The Old Testament and the Literary Critic.* Philadelphia: Fortress Press.

Seitz, Christopher R. 1989. "Job: Full-Structure, Movement, and Interpretation." *Interpretation* 43:5–17.

Sheppard, Gerald T. 1980. *Wisdom as a Hermeneutical Construct.* Beihefte zur Zeitschrift für die alttestamentliche Wissenschaft 151. Berlin/New York: Walter de Gruyter.

Stadelmann, Luis I. J. 1970. *The Hebrew Concept of the World.* Rome: Biblical Institute Press.

Terrien, Samuel. 1990. "Job as a Sage." In *The Sage in Israel and the Ancient Near East.* Edited by John G. Gammie and Leo G. Perdue. Winona Lake, Ind.: Eisenbrauns.

Tur-Sinai, N. H. (H. Torcyner). 1967. *The Book of Job: A New Commentary.* Jerusalem: Kiryat-Sefer, Ltd.

van Gennep, A. 1960. *Rites of Passage.* Chicago: University of Chicago Press.

Westermann, Claus. 1981. *The Structure of the Book of Job: A Form Critical Analysis.* Philadelphia: Fortress Press.

3

Psalms

Introduction

THE BOOK OF PSALMS, ALSO KNOWN AS THE PSALTER, is really a collection of five books: Psalms 1–41; 42–72; 73–89; 90–106; 107–150. Each "book" ends with a short doxology or hymn of praise: 41:14 (numeration in this study follows the Hebrew); 72:18f.; 89:53; 106:48; and 150, respectively. While some interpreters allege that this division grew out of the Jewish use of the psalms in a three-year lectionary cycle, a long-standing rabbinic tradition contends that the arrangement is patterned after the five books of the Torah (cf. Wilson, 1985:199–228; Seybold, 1990:14–23).

The Psalter itself contains evidence of the incorporation of even earlier collections. Several psalms are attributed to David, resulting in a popular but probably not historically accurate tradition that David himself wrote most of the psalms. Other psalms in the second and third books are ascribed to Korah and Asaph, the two great guilds of temple singers during the period of the Second Temple (cf. 1 Chr 6:33ff.; 25:1-2). These groupings may have been original collections around which other psalms were clustered. Finally, the fifth book is made up of a number of Songs of Ascent and psalms of praise known as Hallel or the Hallelujah collection.

These collections have another distinguishing characteristic, namely, variations in the preferred name for God. *YHWH*, translated LORD, is generally used in the first, the fourth, and the fifth collections. Hence, these are referred to by some scholars as the Yahwist Psalter. The name *'ĕlōhîm*, translated God, is preferred in the second and third books and thus they are sometimes called the Elohist Psalter (cf. Stuhlmueller, 1983:21f.). Many scholars believe that *'ĕlōhîm* is a substitution made by a postexilic editor who wished to show reverence for the divine name *YHWH* by avoiding its use.

Recently there has been a growing interest in considering the book of Psalms from a canonical point of view, that is, as a coherent literary composition (Childs, 1979:502–25; Wilson, 1985; Tucker, Petersen, and Wilson, 1988; Ceresko, 1990:227–30; Brueggemann, 1991; McCann, 1993b). The findings of this interpretive approach, which include identification of the introductory poem (Psalm 1) as a Torah psalm and the recognition of the editorial addition of superscriptions (for example, "of David," Psalms 19, 37; "of the sons of Korah," Psalm 49; "of Asaph," Psalms 73, 78; "of Solomon," Psalm 127, and so forth), have led a growing number of scholars to conclude that the final canonical purpose of the book of Psalms is meditation on the law rather than cultic use (Westermann, 1965:253; Wilson, 1985:207; Seybold, 1990:15; McCann, 1993b). These scholars contend that many or even most of the individual psalms may well have arisen out of and for the sake of liturgical practice, but that the Psalter itself is now independent of the cult and stands as a source of Torah piety (Mays, 1993:17; Wilson, 1993:72). They suggest that the psalms have in fact been scripturalized (Kugel, 1986:136).

Some contemporary scholars believe that certain literary features of the Psalter are clues to the theological intentionality of the editors. They contend that the psalms serve as "a guidebook along the path of blessing" (Childs, 1979:513f.), that the progression from the beginning of the Psalter to its end traces a movement from lament to praise (Westermann, 1981:257) or from obedience to praise (Brueggemann, 1991). Others claim that the royal psalms act as seams, bracketing books 1–3 and marking the division between books 2 and 3 (Wilson, 1992:133f.). According to this view, the strong Davidic flavor found in these collections characterizes the failure of the royal covenant, not its privilege. In support of this argument, its adherents point to the arrangement of various psalms in a definite pattern: lament/hope/lament/hope (cf. McCann 1987:97). They conclude that the psalms in books 4 and 5 underscore dependence on and trust in God alone, who was the refuge of the people long before the establishment of the monarchy (Wilson 1985:209–15, 227).

The instructional character of the Psalter can be examined in at least three ways. First, it has canonical significance as a book consisting of a wide variety of psalms, all of which, in this final form, serve as a means of meditation on life. Second, the specific wisdom psalms both explain and support the kind of behavior that is expected of the believer, whether ancient or contemporary. Third, the presence of wisdom motifs in psalms that do not fall under the wisdom category adds a didactic dimension to the entire collection (Ceresko, 1990:217–30). A thorough investigation to determine whether sapiential resignification of the entire Psalter occurred, a valuable project but one not yet undertaken, is beyond the scope of this study.

Any project that seems to isolate the language and motifs characterized as sapiential is already leaning toward an artificial dichotomizing of traditions (for example, wisdom versus prophetic, royal, legal, and so forth). The language and imagery of a culture may originate from within discrete segments of that culture, but as they become part of the common stock of expression they are normally appropriated and employed by all. When this happens, categorization according to origin loses its importance. An extensive examination of the wisdom influence in each psalm will not be undertaken here. This study is limited to an investigation of those psalms generally considered wisdom or Torah psalms.

Those poems identified as wisdom or Torah psalms are clearly different in both style and content from the prayers that probably originated in and were used during liturgical celebrations. They employ language and imagery characteristic of the wisdom tradition, that is, they are primarily concerned with the way of righteousness and the justice of God. Their manner of address suggests instruction rather than worship, calling people to listen and to learn, not to pray. Literary characteristics associated with the wisdom tradition can be detected in these psalms: "better . . . than" sayings (Pss 37:16; 119:72); numerical sayings (Ps 1:6); advice (Pss 37:2, 9, 17, 22); admonition to listen (Pss 49:1; 78:1); the macarism (Pss 1:1; 112:1; 119:1, 2; 127:5; 128:1, 2); rhetorical questions (49:6); the simile (Pss 1:3, 4; 37:2, 20; 49:12, 14, 20; 127:4; cf. Kuntz, 1974:191–99).

Scholars do not agree about which psalms belong to this category, but most interpreters include didactic poems (Psalms 1, 37, 49, 73, 78, 111, 112, 127, 128) and Torah psalms (Psalms 19, 119; for other classifications see Murphy, 1963:156–67; Perdue, 1977:261–343). Although wisdom psalms do not follow a uniform or distinct literary style, some of them do have recognizable characteristics that prove helpful for learning. One is the acrostic arrangement, a poetic form in which the sequence of letters in the Hebrew alphabet determines the initial letter of the first word of each successive line (Psalms 37, 111, 112, 119). Because they conform to this pattern, some commentators include here a few psalms listed under other categories (for example, the hymns, Psalms 34, 145; the lament, Psalm 25; the thanksgivings, Psalms 9/10; 34).

The Law Is the Way of Wisdom

Psalm 1

The didactic character of Psalm 1 is beyond dispute. This psalm contrasts two opposing ways of living, commending one and denouncing the other. It begins with the macarism (beatitude) "Happy is. . . ." This wisdom form, probably introduced into Israelite literature at a late period, is unlike the blessing, which invokes divine favor. It is more of a proclamation of the consequence of a specific course of action. Like many wisdom pedagogical techniques (for example, the proverb, the fable), the macarism describes how life works in certain situations and shows the desirability of a particular manner of behavior. It occurs extensively throughout the Psalter (cf. 2:12; 32:1, 2; 33:12; 34:9; 40:4; 41:2; 65:4; 84:4, 5, 12; 89:15; 94:12; 106:3; 112:1; 119:1, 2; 127:5; 128:1, 2; 137:8, 9; 144:15; 146:5), indicating the didactic quality of many psalms. Psalm 1 also contains parabolic sayings (vv. 3f.) and an antithetical proverb (v. 6) that summarizes the instruction of the entire psalm. The beatitudes that open Psalm 1 and close Psalm 2 form an *inclusio* that sets these two psalms apart as an introduction to the entire Psalter (Sheppard, 1980:136–44; Miller, 1993:83–92).

Psalm 1 is quite explicit: they are happy who follow the law of the LORD, who meditate on the law day and night (v.2). The psalmist is concerned here with more than an isolated occurrence. Meditation on the law and subsequent adherence to its teaching must be a full-time occupation if one wishes to be truly happy. This focus on the law has prompted some commentators to classify this, along with Psalms 19 and 119, as a Torah psalm (Mays, 1987). Although the word "law" invokes the idea of Israel's specific and extensive legal tradition, the Hebrew word *tôrâ* means "instruction," the tradition passed on by teachers. The first five books of the Bible are also called *tôrâ*, instruction. The parallel between the first books of the Bible and the books of the Psalter is no accident. In both cases, fidelity to the tradition found therein is the requisite for happiness.

In the wisdom tradition, "way" is understood in a figurative sense. It refers to the course of life that one chooses as well as the destiny that such a choice effects. A causal relationship, explained as divine retribution, was believed to exist between conduct and its aftermath. Righteousness is rewarded with prosperity; wickedness brings on punishment. This interpretation of retribution may describe some situations in life, but it also functions as an incentive for acceptable behavior. The path to happiness and success is the way of the law; the path to disappointment and failure is the way of dissolute living. This is a major theme of several other wisdom psalms (for example, 25, 37, 119).

Psalm 19

Even a cursory reading of Psalm 19 reveals its composite nature. The first part (vv. 1-6) is hymnic, praising God; the second part (vv. 7-14) extols the law. (Some interpreters distinguish vv. 11-14 as a humble prayer of supplication.) Form critical studies have added support to this division by uncovering the metrical differences between these parts. Despite the dissimilarities in meter and content, in its canonical form the psalm is a literary unit, and it is from this perspective that it will be examined here.

It is not the splendor of the heavens that is acclaimed in the opening verses, nor is it the psalmist who is praising God. Rather, creation itself glorifies the creator. Presumably it is by the very grandeur of its reality that it proclaims the wondrousness of God. Cosmic order is depicted in the regularity of day to day and night to night (v. 2) as well as in the universal governance by the sun (v. 6). As in the first part of the psalm, this section creates the context for understanding the second. The celebration of the law that follows should be read through the lens of these initial verses.

In six different ways, the law "of the LORD" is extolled and its effects are celebrated. It is perfect and trustworthy, right and clear, pure and true, all standard wisdom characteristics that exemplify proper order. The benefits that the law can grant, if heeded, are the blessings of a happy life. These are some of the delights that will be enjoyed by one who "meditates on the law day and night" (Ps 1:2). This instruction is not naive. In the final verses, the psalmist admits human frailty and prays for deliverance from serious sin.

Several theories have been advanced to explain how the distinct parts of the psalm interpret each other. The traditional position holds that this is merely a composite psalm made up of three very distinct units (Weiser, 1962:197). Since it begins with a psalm of praise and ends with a prayer of petition, it was normally classified as a hymn that had incorporated a bit of wisdom teaching. At first glance one might think that the order within the psalm permits a comparison between the grandeur of creation and the distinction of the law. Some interpreters believe that this arrangement suggests instead that the law is built into the very structure of the universe (McCann, 1993c:28). Still others contend that the cosmos may herald the divine majesty, but it does not reveal God's will. For that, the law is needed (Kraus, 1988:275).

The canonical approach to interpretation supports the belief that the law was built right into creation itself. This position is also in accord with the fundamental conviction of the integrity of all creation. Within the psalm, first the order made manifest through the heavens is praised and then the order brought about through adherence to the law. All three themes, that is, order, creation, and law, are prominent in the wisdom tradition. Psalm 19 may be difficult to classify according to form criticism's categories, but it is not a conundrum in the wisdom teaching. It carefully follows thematic development.

Psalm 37

In this acrostic poem each two-line saying begins with the successive letter of the alphabet, a popular technique that facilitates memorization (Mays,

1994:27–29). Actually, by structure and content each saying is a didactic proverb in its own right. Joined together as these sayings are here, they constitute a cohesive instruction. Characteristic of wisdom teaching, the psalm contrasts the fates of the righteous and of the wicked in a way that is not only descriptive but also persuasive. The way of righteousness is more desirable, despite what appearances might suggest. This opinion can be detected throughout the psalm, but it is explicitly stated in the wisdom form of comparison ". . . than" (v. 16, cf. 119:72; also Bryce, 1972:343–54). In yet another wisdom feature, the psalmist's own experience attests to the veracity of the teaching (vv. 25f.). This psalm addresses two very important wisdom issues: the ambiguity of human life and the limitation of the theory of retribution. It also gives evidence of the eschatological nature of the wisdom psalm.

Psalm 1 clearly and simply lays out the causal relationship between an action and its consequence. Certain behavior brings pleasure; other conduct produces distress. Apparently, individuals do have some control over the circumstances of their lives. Since they can choose their course of action, they are partly responsible for their situations. On the other hand, the admonitions found in Psalm 37 suggest that at times this causal relationship breaks down. Life is very complicated and seldom conforms perfectly to any scheme. What is true in one situation may not hold in another. Factors enter in that frustrate the flow of things, and the expected end is not realized. In other words, sometimes the wicked do succeed (v. 7) and the faithful suffer misfortune (v. 24).

The claim of causal relationship notwithstanding, the wisdom tradition does acknowledge and deal with life's inconsistencies. Proverbs, and wisdom instructions in general, are not inflexible canons. They are modest sketches of the ever-changing face of reality, capturing one aspect of life even as it unfolds into another. The wisdom tradition deals with ambiguity by adding new perspectives, not by correcting what has been preserved. It collects snatches of experience that together produce not a comprehensive picture but rather a collage.

To expect that life, with all of its ambiguity, will fit neatly into some theory, such as retribution, is to court disappointment. When circumstances do not follow the principles of causality, a dilemma often results that prompts many people to cry out in protest to God, or even to despair of life itself. Psalm 1 neatly articulates the theory, but Psalm 37 deals with its applications within the maze of experience. In fact, in the situation of the latter psalm the terms of the theory seem to be reversed: the wicked prosper and the righteous suffer. The psalm's admonition suggests, however, that such a situation is only temporary. In due time, the LORD will intervene with judgment, even death, for the wicked, but vindication for the blameless.

Psalm 37 urges the faithful to remain steadfast regardless of their present circumstances, to trust in God's protection in time of adversity, and to hope for eventual recompense. This promise of future blessing is a mark of the psalm's eschatological character. It holds out an assurance that the dilemmas encountered throughout life will eventually be resolved. This psalm acknowledges and deals with the ambiguity of life; nonetheless, its assurance of final vindication upholds the theory of retribution. It seems to say that recompense has not been denied; it has been delayed.

Psalm 49

This psalm begins with a long but important introduction (vv. 1-4). The summons to "Hear this" suggests that the instruction must be heeded. Typically, wisdom teaching is directed toward the young and naive or those suffering misfortune for no apparent reason. Significantly, the counsel given here is addressed to all people, regardless of social or economic class. Finally, the vocabulary, "wisdom, prudence, proverb, riddle," is reminiscent of the introduction of the book of Proverbs (1:2-7) and thus situates the instruction squarely within the wisdom tradition. Although wisdom and prudence are acquired through life experience, the lessons learned are not always obvious. Proverbs may appear to be self-evident, but riddles certainly are not. Since the instruction here is something of a riddle, the psalmist may have felt the need to gather all of his credentials as a sage—one who knows wisdom, has understanding, comprehends proverbs, and can solve riddles—in order to assure the instruction a hearing.

As in Psalm 37, the success of the wicked proves to be an enigma for the righteous. Unlike the earlier psalm that insisted on ultimate retribution, however, this psalm treats the issue from an entirely different point of view: it deals with the significance of wealth in the face of death. Psalm 37 states that the wicked will "perish and vanish like smoke" (v. 20), but it does not really confront the universal inevitability of death and the implications that this raises relative to the question of retribution. If we all die and must leave our possessions behind us, where is the value in amassing wealth?

Causal relationship between deed and effect explains why success and happiness were expected from a life lived in fidelity to the law. This also is the reason why wealth became a sign of one's fidelity and misfortune was considered an indication of wickedness. Death, which was always accepted as an inherent component of life, did not invalidate this view of retribution as long as it occurred after a full and satisfying length of days. It was the inopportune or untimely death, not the passing itself, that was perplexing.

The faithful Israelite expected a full life that would eventually end with death. Psalm 37 pondered the question of fidelity and the quality of life; Psalm 49 probes the quality of life in the face of death.

The heart of the teaching of this psalm is found in its short refrain (a riddle, according to Perdue, 1974:538): "One cannot dwell on the things one treasures" (translation by Brueggemann, 1984:109), for, like the animals, we all die (vv. 12, 20). This is a message that affluent and needy alike should hear. The prosperous have no advantage over the less fortunate. Their wealth is fleeting, for they will leave it behind when they die. They can neither keep their riches nor use their fortune to buy more time. Therefore, the wealthy should not put their trust in riches, and the needy have no reason to envy them.

The thought of death is accompanied by the mention of Sheol, the place of the dead (vv. 14f.). Just as death is no respecter of persons, so Sheol opens its door to both the wise and the foolish, the righteous and the sinners. Once again, retribution seems to play no role in the drama of death, but the psalmist does seem confident that, despite being destined for this fate as are all human beings, "God will redeem me from the power of Sheol" (v. 15). Is this a hope for resurrection after death? Or might it be a declaration in faith that although death has the last word in human life, God, not Sheol, has the very last word? Thus this psalm has moved from concern about reward and punishment to an attempt to offset the importance of wealth, to trust in God whose providence is beyond both retribution and death itself.

Psalm 73

The canonical shaping of the Psalter suggests that Psalm 73 marks a theological turning point in the book (Brueggemann, 1991:80–88). Psalm 1 set the design for observance of the law and the prosperity that is a corollary to this way of life. The royal psalms celebrated the monarchy as God's chosen agent leading the nation in a life of fidelity and bringing about its success. Psalm 72:20, clearly an editorial comment, announces the conclusion of the Davidic collections (Wilson, 1985:139, 208). Following this, Psalm 73 takes up the theme of Psalm 1 but immediately challenges its veracity. The monarchy was not able to actualize the vision sketched in Psalm 1, and now Psalm 73 questions the authenticity of the vision itself.

This psalm might be called "the journey of a soul." The psalmist admits having envied the prosperous wicked and having questioned the value of righteous living (vv. 2-12). Then, because of some insight received in the sanctuary (vv. 13-17), the psalmist realizes that God is neither unconcerned nor unable to mete out just recompense. As in the book of Job, no explanation of the troubling circumstances is given, but the insight gained appears to have been reassurance enough to restore the psalmist's confidence in God (vv. 18-28). What began as an admission of near apostasy ends on a note of commitment. Faith that is tested becomes faith that attests.

Like several psalms before it, Psalm 73 describes the scandal created by the success and affluence of the wicked. One might insist that such good fortune is fleeting and will not last (Ps 37), or that death, the great equalizer, abrogates wealth's importance (Ps 49; cf. Crenshaw, 1984:96). This teaching does not really explain, however, why God allows such situations to exist in the first place. This inequity is particularly troubling in face of the promises attached to observance of the law. The psalmist struggles with the problem of theodicy, that is, the justice of God in the face of evil. It is a universal and perennial problem that admits no rational solution.

The turning point in the psalmist's dilemma is reached in the sanctuary of God, when the final destiny of the wicked was considered. Was something revealed? We do not know, but something happened to the psalmist and, although there is a renewed acceptance of the traditional teaching, a transformed believer embraces this teaching. The final section of the psalm (vv. 18-28) leads us to conclude that the psalmist realized that the reward for observance of the law was not material prosperity but an intimate relationship with God (vv. 23-26, 28a). On the other hand, those who withdraw from God for the sake of the fortunes of this world are not to be envied. In a sense, they have already perished.

One might characterize Psalm 73 as a microcosm of the canonical form of the Psalter (McCann, 1993c:143). It begins on the positive note of Psalm 1, moves through the disorientation caused by human perfidy, comes to acknowledge the mystery of divine providence, and ends with a commitment full of trust in God. This is in fact a microcosm of the theology of Israel (McCann, 1987:247–57).

Psalm 78

This is a difficult psalm to classify. Although it is a narrative recounting selected events from the early days of Israel, it is introduced by wisdom language and themes. In its canonical form, it recounts the history in order to draw salutary lessons. For this reason, the psalm has often been considered part of the wisdom collection.

The very first verses of the introduction (1-2) are reminiscent of Psalm 49 (vv. 1-4; cf. Prov 1:8). The call to listen alerts us to the instructional character of the historical account that follows. The ancestors are mentioned three times, twice as those responsible for transmitting the tradition to the next generation and once as the unfaithful believers depicted within that very tradition. There is mention of tôrâ, proverb or parable and riddle, all of which give us direction for understanding the accounts that follow. History is more than a record of past events; it has lessons to teach, comparisons to make, and enigmas to solve.

The bulk of the psalm consists of two diverse accounts of the mighty acts of God, both of which follow the same theological pattern: a sketch of God's marvelous deeds; a report of Israel's infidelity; a description of divine punishment. Although this is a historical recital, the order within the psalm does not follow the chronology of history. Instead we find: the inconstancy of the northern kingdom, wilderness apostasy, the exodus event, and destruction of a northern shrine. The psalmist identifies the psalm as a proverb or parable. Perhaps this is because, as a negative example, it is intended to draw comparisons between the untrustworthy way the ancestors acted and the way present and future generations should behave.

The psalm also demonstrates that divine wrath is not capricious. God responded to Israel's infidelity, and the punishment corresponded to the crime. In each recital, the power of God initially acted as a blessing but was eventually turned against the people as divine punishment. In the first account, they longed for food; they were given food; they spoke against God and then died with the very food in their mouths (vv. 17-31). In the second, they were delivered from the gods of Egypt; they worshiped gods on high places in their own land; God allowed their enemies to destroy the sanctuary at Shiloh.

Originally the psalm may have been recited to bolster the cultic importance of Mount Zion (Clifford, 1981:137–41). Given the subsequent history of the Davidic monarchy, however, and the ruin of its shrine at Jerusalem, as well as the postexilic structuring of the Psalter, it now has a different rhetorical function. Neither the rebellion in the wilderness, nor the idolatry at Shiloh, nor the fall of Zion signals the end of God's mercy and providence. Each episode of history shows the fickleness of the people but the constancy of God. This history is enigmatic in two ways: How can a people so favored by God be so untrustworthy? And how can a God so defied continue to bless?

Psalm 111

Psalm 111 is a hymn praising the works of the LORD. The marvels alluded to are probably some of the blessings experienced by Israel because of its special election. This point is confirmed by the references to covenant (vv. 5,9) and to God's people (vv. 6,9). Many commentators consider it a wisdom psalm because of its acrostic style and the proverb with which it concludes. While the acrostic may be a fine mnemonic device, it does place restrictions on the content of the psalms. This is particularly true here, where the alphabetic sequence occurs at every half verse, preventing the full unfolding of any single thought. Despite this limitation, the hymnic quality of this short psalm is remarkable.

The most distinctive wisdom characteristic is the proverb in the last verse of the psalm: "The fear of the LORD is the beginning of wisdom." Regarded as the foremost wisdom statement (cf. Job 28:28; Prov 1:7; 9:10; 15:33; Sir 1:18), it encapsulates the essence of Israel's sapiential tradition. The fear referred to denotes awe and reverence as well as fear and trembling. It is a religious disposition as well, rooted in the acknowledgment of God's majesty and trustworthiness and in the human need to live faithful to God's will. Because human fallibility can thwart the search for wisdom, Israel was given the law to instruct it as to the will of God (cf. Kraus, 1989 [vol.2]:359). Clearly, fear of the LORD, which results in conformity to the law, is the beginning of wisdom.

Form critically, this proverb may appear to be out of place in a hymn that lists the marvelous works of God; yet it plays a very important role from a pedagogical point of view. When addressed to God, these statements signify praise; when directed toward human beings, they constitute instruction. Indirectly the proverb implies that anyone who stands in awe of and lives faithful to a God who can accomplish such marvels is truly a wise person.

Psalm 112

This is the companion to Psalm 111, sharing the same acrostic structure, common vocabulary, and even many of the same themes (cf. Mays, 1994:359). The psalms complement each other; the first praises the wonderful works of God, the second applauds the actions of the one who fears God. The complementarity suggests that this psalm should be interpreted in light of the previous one, particularly from the perspective of the fear of the LORD. Psalm 111 testifies to the preeminence of such fear and Psalm 112 lists some of its fruits.

The psalm opens with a beatitude (cf. Psalm 1) that reiterates the causal relationship between righteousness and well-being. Furthermore, it shows that righteousness is relational. The one who fears the LORD is generous, gracious, merciful, and just, all descriptive of social virtues. Just as God showed special favor to Israel, so the one described here excels in concern for others. The psalm ends with an interesting reversal of what is found in Psalms 37 and 73. There the just one was troubled by the prosperity of the evildoer; here the wicked are distressed over the good fortune of the righteous.

This psalm is a classic example of the retribution theory, but its verb forms suggest that the good fortune associated with virtuous living is in the future. This eschatological character augments the instructional value of the psalm. Anticipating the realization of well-being has proven to be a powerful motivation for people to live lives of integrity.

Psalm 119

This acrostic poem is the longest psalm in the Psalter. Each of its twenty-two stanzas is made up of eight lines, all of which begin with the same letter of the alphabet. It is a paean to the *tôrâ* (instruction), every line but one (v. 20) containing the word or one of seven synonyms for it (cf. Soll, 1991:35–56). Although the message of the psalm seems to enjoy a high degree of affinity with the theology of both Deuteronomy and Jeremiah, it lacks reference to specific laws. Rather, both its vocabulary and its general character suggest instruction of the sage rather than juridical or cultic regulation.

The orderly structure of the psalm reflects the harmony that a life of fidelity promises. The comprehensiveness with which it treats Torah suggests that the Torah itself covers every dimension of life. The poem includes features of several other types of psalms. It "praises the LORD, makes petitions, describes trouble, confesses need, makes vows, tells of salvation, asserts trust, describes the wicked—and so on" (Mays, 1987:7). Throughout the psalm, the ideal situation proposed by the introductory macarisms, namely, prosperity is guaranteed to the righteous, is challenged by examples from real situations that illustrate the unreliability of life. The psalmist is often vulnerable, even afflicted, and calls out in trust to God. This has led some to classify the psalm as a lament (Soll, 1991:59–86). In Psalm 119, however, all of the other psalmic features function pedagogically to encourage devotion to the instruction of the LORD (contra Soll, 1991:123–25).

The psalm opens with a pair of macarisms (cf. Psalms 1 and 112) that commend those who observe the decrees of the LORD. Although they fit into the acrostic pattern, the first three verses are descriptive, not direct address as is the case with the remainder of the psalm. The beatitude that they identify is held up as motivation for those who will hear or study the instruction on Torah piety that follows. Those who would aspire to happiness will have to follow the way of blamelessness (v. 1), the way of the LORD (v. 3). The parallel between Psalms 1 and 119 has led some to suggest that, at one point in the development of the Psalter, Psalm 119 concluded the collection (Westermann, 1965:252f.).

The psalmist frequently speaks of meditating on the law (vv. 15, 23, 27, 48, 78, 97, 99, 148). The Hebrew word *śiah* means "to talk" or "to babble," suggesting that this was not merely a silent interior activity. It might refer to the practice of reading or reciting in a kind of whisper or muttering fashion, a very common way of learning in many cultures. Personal reflection notwithstanding, the psalmist repeatedly prays for discernment or for some kind of divine illumination (cf. 1 Kgs 3:9; Job 32:7; Prov 2:6). Torah piety, like wisdom, is both acquired through one's own reflective living and bestowed by God. In fact, the psalmist recognizes three sources of *tôrâ*: the tradition that has been passed on through teachers (vv. 99-100); the natural law revealed in the order of the universe (vv. 89-91); and unmediated divine illumination (vv. 26-29; Levenson, 1987:570). In this, the psalmist has much in common with another great wisdom teacher, the author of Job (cf. Job 8:8-10; 12:7-10; 22:21-23).

Psalm 127

This psalm belongs to the collection known as "The Songs of Ascent" (Psalms 120–134). They may have been sung as pilgrims went up to Jerusalem to celebrate the major feasts, or as the men ascended the fifteen steps in the Temple from the Court of the Women to the Court of the Israelites. These psalms share several significant features that explain their assemblage: recurrent mention of the names Israel, Jerusalem, and Zion; frequent reference to "the house of the LORD"; routine use of liturgical expressions. The collection contains several literary types; however, only Psalm 122 referring to a pilgrimage and only Psalm 134 in any way processional. The content of the psalms reflects the interests and concerns of everyday life, but with a very particular focus: the indispensability of God's involvement in daily life. As they stand, the Songs of Ascent are instructional. This is particularly true of Psalms 127 and 128.

Psalm 127 consists of two short wisdom sayings (vv. 1-2; 3-5), both of which underscore how totally dependent human beings are on God. The Hebrew word *šāw'* (vanity or emptiness), considered part of technical wisdom vocabulary, is used three times in the first two verses, emphasizing this dependence. The expression "build a house" might be understood in any one of three ways: the literal meaning of building a dwelling; the cultic meaning of constructing the Temple; or the social meaning of establishing a family. The psalm's superscription "of Solomon" (v. 1) might relate to the Temple and thus reinforce the second meaning. Reference to children in the second saying could support the third. In whichever sense the saying is understood, the teaching is the same: While human labor is very good and necessary, nothing can be accomplished without the help of God.

The second saying extols sons, called "the inheritance of the LORD" (v. 3). They were both a gift from God and a promise of continued lineage. Posterity was viewed as one of the most important blessings from God (cf. Gen 15:5; 22:17). It assured the man of a defensive force when attacked, of assistance in old age, and of the perpetuation of his name and memory after death. The psalm ends with a macarism that celebrates a large household of sons. Like arrows in their father's quiver, they will be there, ready in his defense.

As part of a pilgrim liturgy, the psalm may have been intended to remind the Israelites of the need to trust God in all things, even in the mundane tasks of daily living and in the joys of family life. The Solomonic ascription invites us to read the psalm as a reminder to the monarchy that nothing will be accomplished without God's help (vv. 1-2). Furthermore, God promises both posterity and dynasty, and only through God's gift will these promises be realized (vv. 3-5). In its canonical form, the psalm critiques the aggrandizement of the monarchy.

Psalm 128

This psalm is a companion to Psalm 127, and possesses some of the same themes and vocabulary. It includes a macarism (v. 1f.), reference to the blessings of a large family (vv. 3, 6), and explicit mention of Jerusalem and Zion (v. 5). Both psalms consist of two sayings divided by the Hebrew *hinneh* (behold).

The psalm opens with a macarism, proclaimed twice (vv. 1-2), that celebrates the one who fears the LORD (cf. Psalm 112). Torah piety, described as walking in God's ways, will be rewarded. The psalm promises that the wife of the God-fearing man will provide him with a family of considerable size, the kind that will guarantee his own prosperity and security. Some commentators hold that the blessing statement that follows (v. 4) is a comment on this teaching. Since in that verse the Hebrew word for bless comes from *bārak*, the verb used in the saying that follows, others associate it with the second saying. The latter is the position held here.

The second Torah teaching redirects the focus from blessing on the extended family to that of the monarchic establishment. The reference to children's children holds both familial and civic importance. It bespeaks long life and the continuation of the family, but it also implies that the nation is prospering. Taken together, the teachings of Psalms 127 and 128 constitute a kind of chiasmic structure with attention to civic matters (127:1; 128:6) bracketing the blessings of family prosperity (127:3—128:3). At the center of this teaching are macarisms celebrating those who fear the LORD(128:1) and are blessed for this devotion (127:5). This is but another example of how the wisdom psalms foster trust in God alone and not in human accomplishment or institutions, not even the monarchy.

Rhetorical Function

This investigation of the Psalter maintains that the book's canonical purpose is instructional. The individual psalms may have grown out of Israel's various prayerful responses to events of life, both individual and communal, and they may continue to function as prayer today. As they stand in the finalized collection, however, they are independent of the cult and now serve as a guide for meditation on life, promoting a particular way of living. In other words, the psalms are prayer that has become teaching.

The canonical form itself makes a theological statement: we must place our trust in God and not in the monarchy. The experience of the exile challenged every aspect of the monarchy and threw into question the future of its authority and the possibility of its very existence. The people faced a serious crisis. If the monarchy, with the divine promise of abiding protection that it boasted (cf. 2 Sam 7:13-16), had not been a safeguard against the power of Babylon, could it be trusted to lead and to preserve the nation in the future? And if not in the monarchy, in what or in whom should Israel place its hope?

The Psalter, in its canonical form, was a response to this national dilemma. Its ordering leads the devout Israelite from an unquestioning reliance on the Davidic promises, through the collapse of royal privilege, to a contrite recommitment to Mosaic values and a renewed confidence in divine mercy and providence. This attitude toward the monarchy is not a rejection of it but a corrective of any exaggerated reliance on it. A careful look at Davidic covenantal theology clearly shows that its promises were always conditional and presumed fidelity to the more basic Mosaic covenant (cf. 2 Sam 7:14f.). As long as the king and the people were steadfast in their commitment, they could rely on God's protection. When they chose the path of defiance of or indifference toward the primary covenant, however, they forfeited this protection, making themselves vulnerable to "human chastisements."

The entire nation suffered the effects of the exile. All of the people, regardless of their political, social, or economic status, had to learn the lesson laid out by the Psalter. Those who had in any way enjoyed the fruits of the royal privilege probably endured the greatest reversal of fortune. They may have been forced to rely on God's mercy and providence in a manner previously unknown to them.

On the other hand, those who had never known political or social privilege probably reacted to the exile differently. Certainly there were many disadvantaged citizens who had hoped that they too might one day share in the benefits enjoyed by the privileged. The exile dashed these hopes, and they had to readjust their own expectations. There were probably others who, having been denied access to political or social advantage, always knew that they could not depend upon the monarchy. Not that they were necessarily more devoted to God, but they were less politically or socially optimistic. In fact, they may have been reassured by the Psalter's challenge of the trustworthiness of the monarchy. However, regardless of their political inclinations, all the nation would do well to heed an admonition to trust in God alone.

Even this theological counsel conceals a hidden bias. Accompanying the Torah piety advanced throughout the psalms is the promise of happiness, success, prosperity. This is a promise that may have been within the grasp of the privileged, but it was not always fulfilled in the lives of the dispossessed and the marginalized. While Torah piety is held up as the ideal for all, too often the standard used to judge the moral integrity of one's life was the degree to which the accompanying promises were realized. It was easy to believe that if the one who fears the LORD is happy (blessed), then those who enjoy blessing must do so because they fear the LORD. Conversely, those who suffer any kind of misfortune must be guilty of some kind of transgression.

The social bias in such a point of view is quite clear, but it is not unambiguously the position reflected in all of these psalms. The fleeting nature of abundance (Psalm 73) and wealth's inability to ward off death (Psalm 49) throw into question prosperity's claims of advantage and its subsequent identification with righteousness. While they may certainly hope for an improvement of the circumstances of their lives, the less fortunate within society could be heartened by this particular point of view. Its dissociation of virtue from wealth releases them from acceding to the contentions of any prejudicial stereotyping.

The theological intentionality of the Psalter remains the same today. Those who place their trust in human institutions, even institutions with divine legitimation, would do well to heed the instruction of the final editors. The same unwitting persons must remind themselves or be reminded that, remarkable as they may be, human institutions are limited. They are as effective as historical circumstances allow, and they are as trustworthy as the people who comprise them. The institutions themselves cannot save, and neither principle nor integrity should be sacrificed to save them.

The less privileged also have something to learn from the Psalter. Despite the promises that accompany the admonition to Torah piety, the collection of psalms taken in its entirety shows that a simplistic understanding of act–consequence does not always explain adequately the realities of life. Many of the laments issue from situations of anxiety or grief that are difficult to explain. They depict the righteous deprived of the joys of life, suffering at the hands of the wicked. They cry out to God for release or for comfort. Many of them express confidence that God will indeed hear and come to the aid of the sufferer. The hope set forth by these psalms is not a false hope but a trust in God's faithfulness in the face of life's ambiguity. This is the fundamental message of the Psalter: we must place out trust in God alone, not in human institutions or even in human explanations.

Unmasking the Powers

This study of the psalms has limited itself to the instructional purpose of the Psalter and to those poems that express Torah piety. Consequently, any liberationist reading sensitive to issues of race or ethnic origin, class, or gender will be incomplete. This imposed limitation does not, however, invalidate the insights that can be gleaned from even a partial investigation.

The Israelite origin and perspective of these psalms is obvious. For example, it was in Jacob-Israel that God established the law (78:5), and it is from Zion that God will send blessings upon Jerusalem (128:5). YHWH, the name of the God of Israel, appears in these psalms too often to list, and the standard Israelite wisdom phrase "fear of the LORD" plays an important role here (111:10; 112:1; 128:1, 4). Although the promulgation and enforcement of clearly defined statutes is a universal phenomenon, it becomes specifically Israelite when the reference is to the law of the LORD (1:2; 19:8-10; Ps 119). This ethnic or racial distinctiveness does not necessarily imply bias. On a most fundamental level, it is merely evidence of the particularity of all theology. One must read closely to discover whether this distinctiveness is a bias that in some way disadvantages others. Even the notion of election (God's people [78:10; 111:6, 9]; God's inheritance [78:62, 71]) denotes a kind of privilege that entails responsibility as well.

The accounts of Israel's history found here (78:9-64, 65–72) do indeed demonstrate divine preference for Israel over other peoples. They claim that God worked wonders on behalf of the Israelites at the expense of both the Egyptians (vv. 12, 43-53) and those living in the land that Israel sought to occupy (v.55; 111:6). As clear as this underlying ethnic preference may be, the real bias of this history is internal. The northern kingdom (Joseph-Ephraim [78:67]) is denounced in favor of the southern Davidic establishment (vv. 68-71). The recitals themselves recount the faithlessness and perversity of the people despite the extraordinary acts of God on their behalf. What was initially intended to be a blessing from God was turned against them and became, instead, a punishment for their sins.

The obvious internecine rift, which is eventually though tragically resolved, overshadows the more fundamental and lasting animosity that Israel felt toward the other nations. This latter enmity, which permeates the history from beginning to end, is never questioned, but is sanctioned by the theology of divine election.

A critique of these psalms from the perspective of class reveals a very complex perception. The traditional understanding of retribution, which was so often co-opted by the comfortable as justification of their social situation, does underlie much of the teaching. In it, peace and prosperity are perceived as the certain consequence of a life of Torah piety, and adversity is evidence of infidelity (Pss 1:3f.; 111:5f.; 112:3-10. But a very different lesson is proposed in passages that describe an apparent reversal of this perspective; the wicked are prosperous and the righteous are disadvantaged.

In some places the reversal is only temporary (cf. Psalm 37). The good fortune of evildoers will prove to be short-lived and the righteous will eventually delight in blessing. In other places (cf. Psalm 73), the prosperity of the wrongdoer is not denied (vv. 3-12), but its permanence is challenged (vv. 18-20). The virtue of the disadvantaged is ultimately acknowledged (vv. 23-28), even though the righteous do not experience reversal of fortune. All of this throws into question the ultimate value of wealth as well as the need for reversal of fortune for the innocent. In still other situations, where there is no reversal of fortune before death and no subsequent vindication of the righteous, wealth's value is nevertheless challenged by its powerlessness before the inevitability of death (Ps 49).

Challenge like this does not necessarily revoke the merit of the traditional view of retribution, but it does cast doubts on some of its component elements, chief among which is the character of the reward or punishment. This instruction questions whether they are really grounded in the realm of social, political, or economic reality. There is support for such questioning in the psalms themselves, where the psalmist delights as much in Torah piety as in riches (119:14, 162). In fact, the law is deemed of greater value than gold itself (119:72, 127; 19:11). The retributive principle may still be in effect, but it has been significantly resignified. It is no longer uncritically linked with economic prosperity.

It is the gender bias that is most pervasive and explicit in these psalms. In the first place, the language references and imagery describing God are all masculine. Such restricted literary usage suggests either that God is indeed male, or that only masculine references can adequately characterize a gender-neutral deity. The first view is a departure from one of the central tenets of the Judeo-Christian faith, namely, that God transcends all human categories. The second view can only be considered a patent gender bias. While it is true that feminine language and imagery are no more adequate in characterizing the reality of God than are masculine patterns, the exclusive use of one form over the other gives a very biased impression of the quality of the respective gender references. These psalms manifest an undeniably male preference.

Allusions to people are also exclusively masculine. The nation in general and both of the independent kingdoms are known by the name of a man, Jacob-Israel (78:5, 21, 71), Joseph-Ephraim (78:67), David (78:70). General references to individuals are all masculine, employing five different Hebrew words for man. When *'ādām* is used as a generic designation, it should be translated humankind. This inclusivity may have been the intent in several passages (cf. 49:12, 20; 78:60; 119:134), but in each instance the ensuing masculine pronouns employed betray the androcentric point of view. This is substantiated by the use of *'ādām* in parallel construction (73:5) with the word *ĕnôsh* (9:20), which conveys the notion of weakness and vulnerability and is unmistakably masculine.

A third word, *geber/gibbôr* (19:5; 37:23; 112:2; 127:4f.; 128:4) denotes a man at the height of his powers, a mighty man, a warrior. Even God is characterized as a *gibbôr* (78:65). The implications of this word are particularly distasteful when the prowess of the warrior is juxtaposed with that of the groom leaving the bridal chamber, both of them rejoicing in their respective conquests (19:5). The most frequently used word, *'îsh* (1:1; 37:7, 37; 49:8, 17; 78:25; 112:1, 5), designates an individual male. Because it emphasizes the male as distinct from the female, it is frequently translated "husband." Those passages that speak of the entire community use exclusively masculine language.

The final indication of gender bias can be seen in the content of the tradition itself. The lessons of history are about the goodness of God to the ancestral fathers despite their unfaithfulness (78:8f., 12, 57). Furthermore, this teaching was to be handed down from fathers to sons (78:3-6). Finally, the blessings of posterity are seen as fulfilled in sons, not daughters (127:3f.; 128:6).

Into the Looking Glass

It is not enough to critique the Psalms from the perspective of racial or ethnic origin, class, or gender. If they are to be revelatory for us today, we must be able to recognize our images in them as in a mirror and to step through them into a new world. Their multidimensional character includes not only their original cultic significance but also their final canonical function. Recontextualized psalms will yield meaning that is new and relevant yet faithful to a message that is long-lived and unfailing.

The theological concept of election by God is rich and multifaceted. The early biblical narratives that recount Israel's election (Gen 12:1-3; Exod 19:5f.) emphasize the gratuitous nature of this divine choice. Not only did Israel not deserve the initial selection, its subsequent behavior jeopardized its privileged status. The conviction of being God's chosen people should have grounded the Israelites in humble gratitude toward God. Instead, it was frequently used against other nations, justifying xenophobia and encouraging military aggression.

This divine election was not unconditional. Israel would enjoy the fruits of its privilege only as long as it held fast to the stipulations that accompanied the covenantal agreement. Disregard of these statutes and ordinances would be punished with political defeat and even expulsion from the land (cf. Deut 4:6-27). It could be said that Israel's election was as much a burden and a responsibility as it was a privilege. Or it might be better stated: privilege brought responsibility. Israel's history of infidelity demonstrates that it was no more committed to YHWH than were the nations that it disdained. In fact, the very distinction that it enjoyed as God's chosen people made its disloyalty to God even more heinous and its denunciation by God more severe. What may have begun as an ethnic privilege is portrayed here as a decided disadvantage.

Although the canonical message of the Psalter does disavow any inflated or uncritical veneration of a monarchy that proved to be ineffective, it does not leave the defeated and dispossessed people in despair. Instead, it recalls for them the true source of their distinctiveness as chosen and the original conditions of their blessing, and it does so in a way that inspires hope. The Psalter reminds the people that they must place their confidence in God and not in ethnic privilege, and that they must recommit themselves to the covenant with all of its attending responsibilities. As it stands, the Psalter possesses an eschatological character that opened Israel, and opens contemporary believers, to the promise of a special relationship with a generous and forgiving God who judges according to the heart and not in terms of ethnic origin.

Concerning class bias, we discover that these psalms do not offer a consistent view of the theory of retribution. The traditional teaching that goodness is rewarded in, and, therefore manifested by, material prosperity underlies the instruction found in many passages. This point of view is significantly altered, however, in psalms that depict the disadvantaged as righteous victims of the malice of sinners or that liken the merits of Torah piety to those of wealth. In the former psalms, the experience of the righteous demonstrates the inadequacy of the traditional understanding of the theory of retribution. In the latter, the fundamental concept of the theory is retained, but the character of reward is dramatically resignified.

When these psalms, with their teaching about retribution, are placed within the canonical context of the Psalter, they yield new and interesting meaning. The traditional position found in so many psalms not only provides an explanation of the collapse of the monarchy, the loss of the land, and the deportation into Babylon, but it also holds out a message of hope to all those, irrespective of class, who are willing to embrace the statutes and ordinances. To acknowledge that some people do indeed suffer through no fault of their own may neither alleviate the suffering itself nor abolish class differences; however, it does stand in opposition to the added onus of culpability in the face of the suffering and in opposition to any identification of prosperity with morality.

The most notable insight that this critique of class provides is the reevaluation and resignification of prosperity. When the charm of wealth is rivaled by the delights of Torah piety, it ceases to be a gauge of covenantal fidelity and it loses its ability to designate particular behavior as righteous. The instruction described above does not follow any consistent pattern. Accordingly, it challenges any rigid social, political, or economic understanding of the relationship of an act to its consequences and, thereby, nullifies any form of class bias based upon such an understanding.

It is in the area of gender that the contemporary revelatory possibilities of these psalms are most difficult to realize. This is because of the fundamental and pervasive androcentric bias of the tradition. Women are simply invisible unless they serve the objectives of men (78:63f.). Characteristics assigned to women are generally judged inferior and female imagery is usually derivative (19:5). Although specific biblical content may not be helpful in feminist resignification of the psalms, the canonical rhetorical intentionality may provide a window of opportunity.

The canonical structure of the Psalter is itself a theological instruction. It traces a movement from confidence in Davidic privilege, through an acknowledgment of disloyalty, to the realization of divine constancy and forgiveness, ending in commitment to and praise of God. The message it proclaims is: human beings and human institutions are finite and frequently ineffective; God and God alone is worthy of our trust and our unconditional devotion. The horizon that opens up in front of this pronouncement is unmapped, unprogrammed, unpredictable, and replete with eschatological possibilities.

Many feminists identify with the protests and supplications found in the individual laments (such as Pss 3–7). They perceive parallels to their own minimalization and subjugation in the oppression depicted there. Nevertheless, even a cursory look at the language of these prayers shows that the one praying is a man, and the God to whom the prayers are addressed is characterized as a male deity. Without minimizing its devotional value, such a practice frequently accepts uncritically the androcentric perspective of the psalms. Yet a canonical approach to the Psalter offers a method of interpreting constitutive parts of it that might critique this gender bias.

As stated above, the canonical message of the Psalter is: human beings and human institutions are finite and frequently ineffective; God and God alone is worthy of our trust and our unconditional devotion. This principle applies to all human cultural institutions, social and religious as well as political, a tradition of divine legitimation notwithstanding. Patterns of kinship, marriage practices, and gender relationships portrayed within the biblical traditions are all cultural constructions. The canonical principle articulated here suggests that they can all be critiqued and modified. In other words, the patriarchal structures and androcentric bias are finite and frequently ineffective; God and God alone is worthy of our trust and our unconditional devotion.

Finally, commitment to the concept of "the integrity of creation" leads us to an examination of the metaphorical use of nature imagery. Since this use is a characteristic of poetry generally, its presence in the poetry of the Bible is not exceptional. The fecundity of the natural world lends itself as a vehicle of meaning to the characterization of the righteous person, and the fleeting nature of life and the stark reality of decay and death to a comparable characterization of the sinner (for example, 1:3f.; 37:2, 35; 128:3). Although the psalms often descriptively ascribe to human beings distinctive traits of various animals (such as 49:15; 119:176), they do not blur the fundamental differences between species (49:12, 20; 73:22). Interestingly, they also use nature imagery in representations of the law (19:11; 119:72, 103).

In a more substantial discussion of natural creation, the psalms link nature imagery not only with the law (Psalm 19) but also with adherence to the covenant (Psalm 37) and with the mighty acts of God in the history of Israel (Psalm 78). As stated earlier, the canonical order of Psalm 19 suggests that the psalmist intended to depict the law as built right into natural creation itself. Such an assertion not only grants extraordinary legitimation to the law, it also provides some insight into the concept of causal relationship between reward/punishment and occurrences in nature. If the social and religious orders that the law intends to reflect and preserve are indeed a part of the very structure of creation, then the natural world will play a part in realizing the consequences of adherence to or disregard of that law (cf. 37:3, 9, 11, 20, 22, 29, 34). The interface of the orders of nature, society, and law suggests that the structures and functions of one order both support and influence the others.

Although the psalms presume that human beings are subject to these orders, they show that God is not so bound to them. In fact, the history as told is a history of divine intervention on Israel's behalf. There we see that God not only undermines the power and authority of other nations but also engages the forces of nature to do so (cf. 78:42-55). These forces serve other divine purposes both in providing for Israel's physical needs (cf. vv. 12-16, 20, 23-29) and in carrying out the sentence passed on it for its faithlessness (cf. vv. 21, 30f.). These miracles show that God alone controls the forces of nature and does so even in those lands that ascribe sovereign power to different deities.

These three psalms use nature imagery (19, 37, 78) to underscore the excellence of the law, the interrelatedness of the orders of law and nature, and the universal and exclusive sovereignty of YHWH. Nowhere do they reckon creation's significance from an anthropocentric point of view. It is perceived as *God's* handiwork, a *divine* blessing that flows from fidelity to the covenant, and it becomes the avenue through which *God's* miraculous power is manifested. God may use creation for the instruction and discipline of human beings, but as such it is at the disposal of God and not of the human beings that it serves. This fact is wonderfully demonstrated in the opening words of Psalm 19: "The heavens declare the glory of God, and the firmament proclaims God's handiwork."

Teach Me Your Law

The study of the Psalter as primarily a book of Torah instruction rather than temple prayer does not nullify the liturgical or devotional value of the psalms. Rather, it adds a further dimension to the surplus of meaning that they already enjoy. Taken out of their canonical context with its resistance to an uncritical reliance on the monarchy, they still attest to the religious aspirations that inspired them, aspirations that frequently mirror our own sentiments today. This is why the psalms can so easily become our own prayers, voicing our own praise, or complaint, or hope. Too often, however, we can discover no correspondence between the psalms we recite and the dispositions of our hearts. When this happens, the psalms lose their meaning for us and their continued use can become merely empty recitation.

The recontextualization of the psalms from a cultic setting to that of a carefully edited literary collection did not distort but rather added a dimension to their individual meanings. The praise, complaint, hope, and historical recital that they contain are now no longer merely occasional sentiments to be expressed according to our personal dispositions. Instead, they contain lessons to be learned again and again. Some of them explicitly trace a history that exposes the fallibility of human institutions and human leaders and then implicitly exhort us to trust in God alone. The cries of pain and despair that sprang from broken spirits are now gently cushioned by surrounding words of ardent hope for expected relief or humble gratitude for welcome deliverance. The psalms are constant reminders of life's inescapable misfortunes and of God's unfailing merciful love and salvific intervention. Torah piety does indeed promise blessings to those who embrace it, but it also teaches that such piety is often its own reward, more precious than gold itself.

The wisdom psalms, like all wisdom teaching, recommend a particular understanding of the meaning and purpose of life and advocate specific patterns of behavior that conform to that understanding. Since the details of this teaching are derived from a reading of empirical data, their claims are both authentic and authenticating: this is how things are, and this is how things should be. The solid empirical anthropological perspective notwithstanding, the Psalter is primarily a book of theology. It reminds us of what God has done in the past and what God is prepared to do in the future, if we but learn the lessons the Psalter has to teach and immerse ourselves in the Torah piety that it fosters.

Works Consulted

Brueggemann, Walter. 1984. *The Message of the Psalms: A Theological Commentary.* Augsburg Old Testament Studies. Minneapolis: Augsburg.

_____. 1991a. *Abiding Astonishment: Psalms, Modernity, and the Making of History.* Literary Currents in Biblical Interpretation. Louisville, Ky.: Westminster/John Knox Press.

_____. 1991b. "Bounded by Obedience and Praise: The Psalms as Canon." *Journal for the Study of the Old Testament* 50:63–92.

Bryce, Glendon E. 1972. "'Better'—Proverbs: An Historical and Structural Study." *Society of Biblical Literature Seminar Papers* 108:343–54.

Ceresko, Anthony R. 1990. "The Sage in the Psalms." In *The Sage in Israel and the Ancient Near East.* Edited by John G. Gammie and Leo G. Perdue. Winona Lake, Ind.: Eisenbrauns.

Childs, Brevard S. 1979. *Introduction to the Old Testament as Scripture.* Philadelphia: Fortress Press.

Clifford, Richard J. 1981. "In Zion and David a New Beginning: An Interpretation of Psalm 78." In *Traditions in Transformation.* Edited by Baruch Halpern and Jon D. Levenson. Winona Lake, Ind.: Eisenbrauns.

Crenshaw, James L. 1984. *A Whirlpool of Torment* (Overtures to Biblical Theology). Philadelphia: Fortress Press.

Kraus, Hans-Joachim. 1988. *Psalms 1–59.* Translated by Hilton C. Oswald. Minneapolis: Augsburg.

_____. 1989. *Psalms 60–150.* Translated by Hilton C. Oswald. Minneapolis: Augsburg.

Kugel, James L. 1986. "Topics in the History of the Spirituality of the Psalms." In *Jewish Spirituality from the Bible through the Middle Ages.* Edited by Arthur Green. New York: Crossroad.

Kuntz, J. Kenneth. 1974. "The Canonical Wisdom Psalms of Ancient Israel: Their Rhetorical, Thematic, and Formal Dimensions." In *Rhetorical Criticism: Essays in Honor of James Muilenburg.* Edited by Jared J. Jackson and

Martin Kessler. Pittsburgh: Pickwick Press.

Levenson, Jon D. 1987. "The Sources of Torah: Psalm 119 and the Modes of Revelation in Second Temple Judaism." In *Ancient Israelite Religion.* Edited by Patrick D. Miller, Jr., Paul D. Hanson, and S. Dean McBride. Philadelphia: Fortress Press.

McCann, J. Clinton. 1987. "Psalm 73: A Microcosm of Old Testament Theology." In *The Listening Heart: Essays in Wisdom and the Psalms in Honor of Roland E. Murphy, O.Carm.* Edited by Kenneth G. Hoglund, Elizabeth F. Huwiler, Jonathan T. Glass, and Roger W. Lee. Sheffield: JSOT Press.

—————. 1993a. "Books I–III and the Editorial Purpose of the Hebrew Psalter." In *The Shape and Shaping of the Psalter.* Edited by J. Clinton McCann. Sheffield: JSOT Press.

—————. 1993b. *The Shape and Shaping of the Psalter.* Sheffield: JSOT Press.

—————. 1993c. *A Theological Introduction to the Book of Psalms: The Psalms as Torah.* Nashville: Abingdon Press.

Mays, James L. 1987. "The Place of the Torah-Psalms in the Psalter." *Journal of Biblical Literature* 106:3–12.

—————. 1993. "The Question of Context in Psalm Interpretation." In *The Shape and Shaping of the Psalter.* Edited by J. Clinton McCann. Sheffield: JSOT Press.

—————. 1994. *The Lord Reigns: A Theological Handbook to the Psalms.* Louisville, Ky.: Westminster/John Knox Press.

Miller, Patrick D. 1993. "The Beginning of the Psalter." In *The Shape and Shaping of the Psalter.* Edited by J. Clinton McCann. Sheffield: JSOT Press.

Perdue, Leo G. 1974. "The Riddles of Psalm 49." *Journal of Biblical Literature* 93:533–42.

—————. 1977. *Wisdom and Cult.* Missoula, Mont.: Scholars Press.

Seybold, Klaus. 1990. *Introducing the Psalms.* Edinburgh: T & T Clark.

Sheppard, Gerald T. 1980. *Wisdom as a Hermeneutical Construct.* Beihefte zur Zeitschrift für die alttestamentliche Wissenschaft 151. Berlin/New York: Walter de Gruyter.

Soll, Will. 1991. *Psalm 119: Matrix, Form, and Setting.* Washington, D.C.: Catholic Biblical Association of America.

Stuhlmueller, Carroll. 1983. *Psalms 1* and *Psalms 2.* Old Testament Message. Wilmington, Del.: Michael Glazier.

Terrien, Samuel. 1993. "Wisdom in the Psalter." In *In Search of Wisdom: Essays in Memory of John G. Gammie.* Edited by Leo G. Perdue et al. Louisville, Ky.: Westminster/John Knox Press.

Tucker, Gene M., David L. Petersen, and Robert R. Wilson. 1988. *Canon,*

Theology, and Old Testament Theology. Philadelphia: Fortress Press.

Weiser, Artur. 1962. *The Psalms.* Translated by Herbert Hartwell. Old Testament Library. Philadelphia: Westminster Press.

Westermann, Claus. 1965. *Praise and Lament in the Psalms.* Translated by Keith Crim and Richard N. Soulen. Atlanta: John Knox Press.

Wilson, Gerald Henry. 1985. *The Editing of the Hebrew Psalter.* Chico, Calif.: Scholars Press.

_____. 1992. "The Shape of the Book of Psalms." *Interpretation* 46:129–42.

_____. 1993. "Shaping the Psalter: A Consideration of Editorial Linkage in the Book of Psalms." In *The Shape and Shaping of the Psalter.* Edited by J. Clinton McCann. Sheffield: JSOT Press.

4

Proverbs

Introduction

THE BOOK OF PROVERBS IS THE BASIC SOURCE of the study of biblical wisdom. Unlike Job, which has a certain literary cohesion, Proverbs is more a collection of collections. Several of these collections have distinct superscriptions, which usually introduce an assortment of proverbs boasting the same proverbial form: instructions (1:1-9:18; 22:17—24:22); sentences (10:1—22:16; 24:23—34; 25:1—29:27). The international character of the material is evidenced in the inclusion of collections ascribed to the non-Israelites Agur son of Jakeh (30:1) and King Lemuel (31:1). In addition to these collections, there are numerical proverbs (30:7-33), a poem (31:10-31), and an even further subdivision according to the specific form of proverb (10:1—15:33; 16:1—22:16). Despite the anthological character of the book, theories to explain some structural unity within its various components have been advanced (Whybray, 1994:157–65). The most interesting claims that the very composition of the book shows forth the design of the house that the author himself identifies as the house of Wisdom (9:1; cf. Skehan, 1971:27–45).

Although the individual sections probably originated at various times and out of diverse circumstances, there appears to be a definite structural framework that bespeaks editorial intentionality. Both chapters 1–9 and 31:10-31 declare the importance of fear of the LORD (1:7; 31:30), and each provides a description of what this means (1:2-6; 31:10-28). In both sections, the prominent figures are assertive women, not the docile women normally associated with patriarchal societies. The final poem is an acrostic, an alphabetic form that denotes completeness. Some interpreters believe that the final editor intended that this poem, both in form and content, echo the figure of Woman Wisdom found in chapters 1–9. The reason for the order of the other collections is not clear. The present examination of the book of Proverbs will follow the divisions determined by the superscriptions.

The book gets its name from the *mašhal* (proverb or saying). The word means both "to be similar to" and "to rule over." The proverb is a concise statement providing insight drawn from something that has been observed about life. Typical examples of the folk wisdom of many different peoples show a remarkable similarity in literary pattern and underlying meaning. These patterns point to several different things including identity, equivalence, or variable association of things; nonidentity, contrast, or paradox; similarity, analogy, or typing; disorder, futility, or absurdity; classification, or characterization of persons, behavior, or situations; value, priority, proportion, or degree; consequences of human character or behavior, and so forth (Scott, 1965:3–9). The import of the proverb lies not merely in its observational and descriptive character but also in its rhetorical function. It serves to persuade, describing how things work ("similar to") in order to give direction for living in accord with the order observed ("rule over").

Many proverbs have a narrative character, especially when they report the consequences of particular behavior or a specific course of action. Certainty regarding these consequences arises from dependence upon the theory of retribution or cause and effect, that is, righteousness will be rewarded and evil will be punished. Such predictability has earned proverbs the reputation of being conservative and supportive of the status quo. Because of their brevity of expression, the imagery in the proverbs is less elaborate than that found in the poetry of some of the psalms or prophetic announcements. Despite this, the regular use of metaphor provides a figurative quality that, while more implied than explicit, is, nonetheless, quite provocative. The descriptions themselves derive from what is commonplace in life. It is their clever artistic use that enables one to discern the exceptional in the familiar. In this way, the flexible quality of proverbs really does argue against rigid conformity to the structures of society.

The proverb itself is found in two basic forms: one-lined traditional sayings and two-lined artistic expressions. In the latter form, the second line somehow restates the thought of the first, either through agreement (synonymous parallelism) or through contrast (antithetic parallelism). It might also develop the thought in some way (synthetic parallelism). Parallelism is more than a repetition of thought. It is a technique wherein the interaction of the two lines creates new meaning. The unique literary style of the proverb is testimony to its artistic as well as its sagacious character. Penetrating reflections on life situations are expressed through finely honed pithy adages. This quality has gained wisdom the title "poetry of wit" (Alter,

1985:163–84). The poetic nature of the proverb enables one to teach to another the wisdom gleaned from the art of living, as one might teach any craft. Unfortunately, since Hebrew poetry follows rules of rhythm rather than those of rhyme, the vitality of the proverb is often lost in translation. The reworking in another language is seldom able to preserve the proverb's original accentual pattern and meaning. Still, the universality of life experience and the polysemic character of the proverbial metaphors ensure a rich variety of interpretive possibilities.

The Book

The Way of Wisdom

The first section of the book of Proverbs (1:1—9:18) is made up of a series of instructions addressed to "my son" (1:8, 10, 15; 2:1; 3:1, 11, 21; 4:10, 20; 5:1, 20; 6:1, 3, 20; 7:1) or "my sons" (4:1; 5:7; 7:24; 8:32). All these instructions have basically the same form: a call to take to heart the teaching given; mention of the motive for heeding the instruction; counsel to choose wisdom and avoid folly; and a prediction of the consequences that will follow one's choice (Scott, 1965:15–17). Besides the instructions, this section includes a few poetic speeches by personified Wisdom herself (1:20-33; 8:4-36).

The superscription that introduces this section identifies the collection as "the proverbs of Solomon" (1:1), thus according the highest sapiential authority to the instruction found therein (cf. 1 Kgs 3:5-28). This introduction is followed by an explanation of the purpose of the instruction given and the mention of several forms through which it is communicated (vv. 2-6). The introductory section ends with a proverb that establishes "the fear of the LORD" as the *rēšhît* (beginning, foundational or necessary condition) of knowledge. The position of this proverb at the beginning of the book (1:7) and its repetition at the end (31:30) creates a kind of *inclusio* that suggests that all of the learning and instruction contained within the book emanate from this religious attitude.

A second proverb expressing the importance of the "fear of the LORD" also appears at the end of the first section (9:10). Although reference to this religious disposition is found in several other places throughout the book, only in these two verses is the origin of "fear of the LORD" stated. (In one other verse it is associated with wisdom, though not with the beginnings of wisdom [15:33].) Elsewhere we read that the wicked disdain "the fear of the LORD" (1:29), while those who seek it will understand it (2:5). This attitude is the hallmark of the righteous (3:7; 8:13; cf. 14:2; 16:6) and their guarantee of blessing (cf. 10:27; 14:26, 27; 19:23; 22:4; 31:30). It is to be preferred above all else (cf. 15:16; 23:17; 24:21).

In two passages in this first section, wisdom is said to originate from somewhere other than with "the fear of the LORD." In one place, it begins with the very experiential process of becoming wise (4:7). In another, the cosmic Woman Wisdom claims to be the first fruit of primordial creation (8:22). The character of wisdom is noticeably different in these two references than it is in the earlier one, where wisdom refers to the sagacity handed down from the wise to the simple. From this we can conclude that wisdom can be perceived in various ways. The first and most accessible wisdom is that insight which is gained through reflection on experience itself (4:7). The second comes through the teaching, in this case the religious teaching, of the wise elders (1:7). The third is at the very heart of reality, intimately associated both with God and with the rest of creation, but beyond the grasp of human beings (8:22; cf. 3:19f.). This kind of wisdom is not gained empirically but is given by God (2:6).

The instructions themselves usually speak very generally about choosing the way of wisdom over that of folly. The first instruction (1:8-19) is typical of the teaching of the book. Here the use of parallelism (cf. Kugel, 1981) couples the advice of the father with the teaching of the mother and offers both as the course of action to be followed. The son or, as some suggest, the student is not only encouraged to live uprightly but is warned against the enticements of the wicked. In the midst of this instruction, the teacher, presumably the father, incorporates a proverb that metaphorically describes the way the innocent are lured unsuspectingly into a trap, just as birds are lured into nets (v. 17). This technique of illustration, called "proverb performance" (Fontaine, 1982), is also used to encourage enterprising planning (6:6-11) and to illustrate the suffering that results from an illicit sexual affair (6:27-28).

These are typical examples of how proverbs are used pedagogically. The proverb itself describes a situation in nature that is commonly seen and easily understood. It usually takes little insight to comprehend its message on this level; in fact, it is meant to be a very simple statement. Its artistry is in its precision of description accomplished through economy of words. The ingenuity of the proverb rests in its ability to help one to make connections between the situation described and some unspecified facet of human life. When a proverb stands alone, the intended connections may not be obvious, but the referents are much clearer within the context of an instruction, such as is found here.

The counsel found within these instructions suggests that the choice set forth is unambiguous: one selects either the way of wisdom or that of folly (1:15; 2:7-9, 12-15, 20; 3:6, 17, 23, 31; 4:11-19, 26; 5:8, 21; 6:23; 7:25). The most commonly used word for "way" is *derek*, which is derived from the

Hebrew for "to tread" or "to trample." It suggests a path worn by constant use (Habel, 1972). This is an apt metaphor, because both wisdom and folly describe patterns of behavior rather than isolated individual acts. Despite the concrete features of the metaphor, the purpose of this "way" is the formation of an interior disposition (2:1f, 10; 3:1, 3, 5; 4:4, 21, 23; 6:21; 7:3).

Most of the counsel found in the instruction in this section is somewhat general, but in some instances specific advice is given. For example, the son is admonished to be independent of others (6:1-5), to be industrious (6:6-11), but most of all, to beware of women who might lure him into adulterous liaisons (2:16-19; 5:3-6; 6:24-29; 7:5-27).

The oral character of the teaching is unmistakable. The son is exhorted to listen (1:8; 4:1, 10; 5:1, 7; 7:24) to the words of his father (2:1; 4:5, 20; 7:1) as well as to those of Wisdom herself (1:20-23; 8:6-36). There is something very dynamic about learning through word of mouth, since the speech-act is immediate and, presumably, nuanced by the tone and inflection of voice. Much of this is lost in the act of transcription and, as a consequence, it falls to the reader to revitalize the sayings by recontextualizing them in real-life situations (Ricoeur, 1976:25–44; Camp, 1985:167–73). The fact that proverbs are often considered static and lifeless can be traced to failure on the part of the readers and commentators to do this recontextualizing.

Incorporated within the instructions are three poems that stand out as unique creations, independent of their literary contexts. These take the form of speeches by a mysterious figure, personified Woman Wisdom (1:20-33; 8:1-36; 9:1-18; see Brenner, 1993:193–98; Whybray, 1994:35–43). In the first poem, Wisdom cries out from the busiest corner at the gates of the city. Since this is where most people will likely be found coming in and going out of the city, conducting public business or gathering for social occasions, Wisdom stations herself there, calling out to all, offering herself to whoever would be her disciple. As a woman who is alone and aggressively soliciting companionship, she is not unlike the wanton woman who frequents the streets in order to entice the unwary (Camp, 1985:129–32). Wisdom invites them to fear the LORD, not to forsake their integrity. But the naive are not always astute enough to discern the difference, and so they often accept the wrong invitation.

Many of the traits that characterize Woman Wisdom are found throughout the book of Proverbs, describing either the wise teacher or the wisdom teaching itself (Perdue, 1994:77–122). This wise woman offers both counsel and reproof, which unfortunately are often ignored (1:24, 25, 30). She warns that, in the end, the consequences of rejecting her ministrations will be distress and anguish (v. 27).

The attitude suggested by the poem differs significantly from that found in the instructions themselves. The latter urge the youth to seek wisdom, and to do so diligently and with perseverance. Here it is Wisdom who does the pursuing. She takes the initiative, goes in search of the youth, and persists in her attempts at wooing the simple ones. It is almost as if the search for wisdom is perceived differently by the one searching than by the personified object of the search. To the searcher, wisdom is elusive. To Wisdom, the search appears to be halfhearted at best. This is an important distinction, for it determines how one understands responsibility for the lack of wisdom. One cannot be held accountable for one's folly, if wisdom itself is relatively inaccessible. On the other hand, if the search for wisdom is done unenthusiastically, no one else can be blamed for one's lack of insight.

The second poem (8:1-36) finds Wisdom again at the crossroads, at the gate of the city. From this vantage point she cries out to all who would hear her, assuring them that her words are righteous and her instruction is as valuable as silver or gold or precious jewels (vv. 1-21; in 3:14f and 8:10f. they are more valuable). She offers herself to the simple (v. 5) just as she has offered herself to kings, rulers, and nobles (vv. 15-16). This initial characterization of Wisdom is the same as that found in the first poem. As the poem continues, this unusual woman becomes even more unique. After praising her own merits, Wisdom recounts her beginnings. From the pathways of human society, she transports her hearers to the primordial arena of creation (vv. 22-31).

The exact relationship between this mysterious figure and the creator is not clear. Wisdom admits that she herself was created (v. 22). She also claims to have had some part in other acts of creation (v. 30). Is this mysterious figure a personification of some divine attribute, in other words, merely a stylistic feature employed by the author? Such an explanation does not take into account the fact that Wisdom is identified as an entity separate from the creator (v. 22). It is apparent that once Wisdom is created, she has a life of her own. Clearly, too, she is a creature with cosmic dimensions. She existed before the rest of creation, and she appears to have been active beyond the confines of space and time. All of this suggests a mythological origin (Lang, 1986).

The poem ends where it began, with a summons to listen to Wisdom's instruction, which alone will guarantee a happy life. There is a slight but important nuance here. Where previously Wisdom stood at the gates (1:21; 8:3), now, those who listen to her stand at her gates (v. 34). The image here is altogether different. The gates of the city, where Wisdom sought disciples, included the broad open areas on both sides of the gate itself, not unlike an open public marketplace. Wisdom's gate is more like a swinging door, the device for opening and closing an entryway. It is used only in connection with a constructed house. This is the entryway to a private dwelling. It seems that Wisdom goes out into the marketplace in order to invite the simple into her home.

Just as "proverb performance" can be adequately understood only when considered in context (cf. 1:17), so this description of the cosmic dimensions of Wisdom should be interpreted within its literary context. The placement of this unusual characterization in the midst of an account of Wisdom's involvement with human beings is rather interesting. In the earlier poem, Wisdom reports that her counsel was rejected and her invitations ignored (1:24f.). In this poem she affirms her importance by claiming that the influential leaders of the community owe their success to her (8:15f.). Is this mere boasting on her part, or is it a means of prodding those who earlier had shown themselves reluctant to listen to her? If the latter is the case, as proposed here, she reinforces her distinction by revealing her mythological character and origins. If the youth cannot independently recognize the value of her advice, then he (or they) should accede to it on the basis of her cosmic stature.

This poem makes another notable point. If the figure of Wisdom is the same on earth as in the primeval realm, then a connection exists between the insights garnered in the marketplace and the very structures of creation. This leads one to conclude that the various kinds of wisdom delineated above are not so much separate realities as they are different aspects of the same reality.

The third wisdom poem (9:1-18) consists of invitations to two different banquets and an assortment of miscellaneous proverbs. The first banquet is held in the house of Woman Wisdom (Skehan, 1971:27–46), the second in that of the foolish woman. These two figures vie with each other for the attention of the simple. This passage reveals the same unambiguous distinction between the way of wisdom and the way of folly mentioned above, but here the female characters assume the aggressive role (Camp, 1985:125-33).

The unit appears to end on a negative note. It states that the fate of those who are seduced by folly is death or the depths of Sheol. Since all of these instructions really function as exhortations, the descriptions of reward or punishment function more as motivation for future behavior than as mere reports of previous situations. Thus, the section is really open-ended. The youth is left with a decision; either choose wisdom and the happiness that it can provide, or embrace a life that squanders potential and carries with it a penalty. Ending with an image of suffering may be an effective pedagogical technique.

The last question to be examined is the role that creation plays in this instruction. As already mentioned, the metaphorical use of nature imagery, a literary technique found in most folk literature, is used here to encourage a variety of values, including marital fidelity (5:15-19), speed and agility (6:5), and diligence (6:6,8), as well as to warn against taking steps that will eventually lead to being trapped (7:22f.). The most significant discussion of nature occurs in the references to wisdom's role in creation. Although there is no personification in the first reference (3:19f.), wisdom's instrumental role is explicitly acknowledged. In the more lengthy description of the primordial events (8:22-31), personified Wisdom maintains her place of distinction as the first fruit of God's creative venture. First came Wisdom and then followed the material universe.

In order to understand exactly her role in creation, one would have to determine the meaning of 'amôn (v.30). Is she a participant in the events as a "craftsman" (NAB and NJB), "master worker" (NRSV)? Or is she merely a spectator, a "darling" (NEB)? The Hebrew is not clear (for a summary of positions see McKane, 1970:356–58).

As noted above, the placement of this description of the creation of the universe provides cosmic legitimation for experiential wisdom. In other words, from the point of view of literary content, the description of cosmic events is bracketed between two references to the marketplace. The meaning intended by this literary arrangement calls for an interesting reversal, however. In reality, the wisdom of the marketplace is authenticated by its presentation here within the context of the unquestionable wisdom displayed in the marvels of the cosmos.

The Proverbs of Solomon

The second section of the book of Proverbs (10:1—22:16) is an assortment of discrete two-lined sayings. There appears to be neither internal structure nor thematic organization here. This does not mean, however, that the proverbs have been collected haphazardly. Careful scrutiny shows that occasionally proverbs are grouped according to some catchword. This may have been a mnemonic device meant to facilitate rapid recall. The universal applicability of the type of counsel contained here is readily attested to by the fact that many of these maxims have been invoked by countless generations. For example: "Spare the rod and spoil the child" (cf. 13:24); or "Pride goes before the fall" (cf. 16:18).

The collection itself can be further divided into two smaller collections of approximately equal length (chs. 10–15 and chs. 16–22). Most of the sayings in the first half are in antithetic parallelism, while those in the second half contain synonymous and synthetic parallelism as well. These two quite different collections appear to be linked together by a group of proverbs containing characteristics of each of the two dissimilar collections (14:26—16:15). It seems that an editor brought these collections together in order to bring the total number of proverbs in this section to 375. This number corresponds to the numerical value of the Hebrew for Solomon, the great wisdom figure to whom the superscription (10:1) attributes authorship. This is a very creative way of according the section the highest sapiential authority (Skehan, 1971:17–20). All of this bespeaks careful literary design.

The use of antithetic parallelism produces some unambiguous comparisons. Chief among them are contrasts between the righteous and the wicked, the wise and the foolish, the rich and the poor, the diligent and the lazy. These individuals and their good or bad fortunes are distinguished in order to encourage appropriate behavior in the students, presumably the "sons," addressed in chapters 1–9. While most of the proverbs are descriptive, their instruction is by inference. The proverbs describe for the students the value in lives of honesty (11:12; 14:5), diligence (12:11; 13:4), obedience (10:8), and docility (10:17); of discipline (14:30), restraint (10:19), and civic responsibility (11:10f.), to name but a few prized attributes. These descriptions are intended to persuade the students to live accordingly in order to be happy and successful. The most frequent exhortation is to a life of righteousness (10:16; 11:18-21; 12:2-7; 13:2; 14:9; 15:8-10), which is the path chosen by the wise (11:9; 12:23; 13:14-16; 14:6-8; 15:20f.). The rewards of such a way of life include success (10:3f.; 11:16-18; 13:3f.), security (10:30; 11:3-9; 14:26f.), relative peace (10:10-13; 12:21; 15:1), and a reputation for integrity (10:7; 11:2; 14:20).

The collection of proverbs in the second half of this section (16:1—22:16) differs considerably from the first. Besides proverbs in synonymous and synthetic parallelism, this section contains more "better . . . than" sayings (Bryce, 1972:343–54) than the rest of the book, and the name YHWH appears more frequently here. (It appears eleven times in 14:26—15:33, the group of proverbs that seems to link the two collections, but only nine times in the other 141 proverbs found in chapters 10–15.) Explicit attention is also given to the importance of the king, of good family relations and order, and of trustworthy and socially appropriate speech.

The "better . . . than" saying (12:9; 15:16f.; 16:8, 16, 19, 32; 17:1; 19:1, 22; 21:9, 19; 22:1; also 25:7, 24; 27:5, 10; 28:6) is a clever device that provides insight into the priorities of the society. Unlike synonymous parallelism, which sets up a correspondence between two objects or antithetic parallelism, which contrasts them, this figure of speech provides a form of prioritization. One thing is judged to be better than the other. Three of these sayings assert something about a wife. Five others exalt a virtue. All of the rest allege that some social value is better than good fortune. It is more likely that this attitude would be advanced by the comfortable rather than by the needy.

As already stated, empirical wisdom is garnered from serious reflection on the experiences of life. That reflection is always done from the perspective or worldview fashioned by previous reflection on experience or by the worldview into which one has been socialized. If that worldview is religious, then one's judgments and insights will have a religious dimension to them. Many of the proverbs in this second collection show Israel's belief in YHWH's involvement in human life. YHWH, who is the maker of all (20:12; 22:2), originates and manages the events of life (16:2, 4, 9, 11, 33; 19:14, 21, 23; 20:24; 21:1), meting out reward for wise or righteous living (16:3, 7, 20; 18:10, 22; 19:17; 21:3; 22:4) and punishment for folly or wickedness (16:5-7; 17:5, 15; 20:10, 23; 22:12, 14). YHWH is powerful (21:30f.), testing and weighing hearts (17:3; 21:3).

It is easy to see that, when one discovers a way to live a well-ordered life within the regularity observed in both nature and social exchange, that person could be led to believe that there are certain beneficial patterns inherent in the structures of creation. From such a point of view, the search for wisdom would be perceived as a search for these patterns for the purpose of living in accord with them. When one believes in a God who creates and maintains all of creation, this search can become a search for God's plan or will. Such a faith is implicit in these references to YHWH's involvement in human events.

With the exception of two references in the linking passage (14:28, 35), the king is not mentioned in the first collection. There are several references in the second collection, however. The king holds a special place in society because it was believed that the throne had been established by YHWH (16:12). Not only does the king expect righteousness from others (16:13), he is obliged to act out of righteousness himself (16:10; 17:7; 20:28). He exercises exceptional power over his people (16:14f.; 19:12; 20:2), exacting judgment on them (20:8, 26). All of this privilege notwithstanding, the king is himself governed by YHWH (21:1). If YHWH has established the throne and continues to govern the king, one can easily conclude that the king acts as a mediator of God's will to the people. This view would give the king tremendous power over the people.

Family cohesiveness is seen in the joy and pride that members take in one another (17:6) as well as in the suffering and shame that one member can bring upon the rest (17:21, 25; 19:13, 26). There are injunctions to discipline children (19:18; 22:6, 15) and warnings of the punishment they will face if they dishonor their parents (20:20). The one family member who is singled out is the wife. If she is a good wife, she is considered a gift from YHWH (18:22; 19:14). But if she is contentious, the husband might just as well retreat into isolation (21:9, 19).

The importance of appropriate and pleasing speech in the transmission of tradition cannot be overemphasized. If speech is not trustworthy, the very foundations of a society are threatened (16:27f.; 17:4; 18:21; 19:28; 21:6). The king, who is responsible for the vitality of the community, expects honesty from his subjects (16:13; 17:7; 22:11). While foolish speech carries bitter consequences (18:6f, 13; 20:19), the speech of the prudent yields satisfying fruit (17:27f; 18:4; 20:15; 21:23). The tradition of wisdom is one of prudent choice. In order that the appropriate advice be followed, one should be not only forthright in one's words but also persuasive (16:21, 23f.).

Words of the Wise

The next two sections have the identical superscription. (They are short and therefore will be treated together.) Strictly speaking, the first section (22:17—24:22) has no superscription. The superscription of the second (24:23), however, claims to belong to another assortment of "words of the wise," leading one to conclude that the preceding is itself a discrete collection. The descriptive style of the preceding instructions gives way here to imperatives. The section itself seems to be instruction to one person ("my son" [23:15, 19, 26; 24:13, 21]). There is a definite design to this unit. It is almost all in synonymous parallelism, and its length too appears to be specific, "thirty sayings" (22:20; for discussion about possible historical influence see Bryce, 1972:15–87). On the other hand, the second section (24:23-34) is a very short assortment of miscellaneous proverbial forms.

Reference is made to written tradition (22:20), even though the oral character of the instructions can be seen in the summons to "hear" (22:17; 23:19, 22). The proverbs address the typical wisdom themes found in earlier collections: learn the wisdom of the society (22:17) from your fathers and your mothers (23:22, 25f.); stay away from harlots and dangerous women (23:27f.); be prudent in the presence of the king (22:29—23:3; 24:21f.). The most important lesson is: be faithful to YHWH (22:19, 23; 23:17; 24:18, 21). The young man is admonished to be industrious (24:27, 30f., 33f.), prudent (22:26; 23:4) and honest (22:22, 28; 23:10) in his dealings. He is warned about the dangers of intoxication (23:30-35) and encouraged to develop a class consciousness that will advance his own social standing (22:29). This young man is not himself a child, for he is given counsel about how to discipline his own son (23:13f.).

The Men of Hezekiah

The second collection of proverbs attributed to Solomon (25:1—29:27) is said to have been compiled by the men of King Hezekiah (cf. 2 Kgs 18–20). Just as the first collection claiming Solomonic authority (10:1—22:16) was skillfully crafted in order to comply to a certain pattern, so the hand of an editor has fixed the number of sayings here as well. There are approximately 140 proverbs in this collection, the numerical value of the name Hezekiah (Skehan, 1971:44). This identification, along with the concern for court etiquette found within many of these proverbs, suggests that the monarchy played a prominent role in gathering and arranging, though not necessarily originating, this wisdom teaching.

This collection is like the first in another way. The proverbs lack thematic development but often seem to be gathered together by means of some catchword ("fool" appears eleven times in 26:1-12) or onomatopoeic devices. Differences in form and content enable this section to be divided into two subdivisions (chs. 25–27 and chs. 28–29). A good deal of the material in the first half is in the form of prohibition, while the second half contains antithetic parallelism. Almost all of the comparisons with the natural world are located in the first half and all but one reference to the LORD in the second, thus again indicating that distinct units have been brought together. These differences notwithstanding, together the two halves comprise an assortment of teachings, some of which echo earlier counsel and some which is distinctive in itself.

The entire unit begins with a tribute to the king (25:2-5) and follows with directives for behavior at court (vv. 6-7, 15). This theme occurs again in the second part, where the privileged position of the king is asserted (28:2). Despite his prominence, the king is still required to act with wisdom and justice (28:3, 15f.; 29:4, 12, 14). The law (28:4, 9; 29:18) and the law courts (25:8-10) play important roles in the lives of the people. Since the courts were an acknowledged institution within the monarchy, and since the king had the serious responsibility of assuring justice for all of his subjects, understandably a close relationship existed between the monarchy and the court. Despite the king's role in executing justice, the sages believed that righteousness itself came from the LORD (29:26). These proverbs clearly state that the LORD is the arbiter in the realms of justice (25:22; 28:5, 25; 29:25f.) and that God's justice is enjoyed by all (29:13).

Some particularly interesting features appear in this section. The first is repetition. A proverb in this collection (25:24) is also found in an earlier section (cf. 21:9). Another technique is contradiction. A proverb recommending the manner of dealing with a fool is followed by a second proverb that gives exactly the opposite counsel (26:4f.). This juxtaposition of contrary advice highlights the essence of wisdom teaching. A proverb is not a formula to be followed but an example of how one aspect of life unfolds under a particular set of circumstances. This dimension of life may not transpire in the same way under different conditions. The difference between mere observation of life and wise judgment about it is the ability to decide, from among many possibilities, which course of action is appropriate for which set of circumstances. A wise person will take note of all of the particulars of the situation, consider possible avenues to follow, and make a decision. Thus, the answer to the question: How should one deal with a fool? is: It depends upon the circumstances.

Many proverbs teach through comparison. Frequently something known from the natural world is said to be "like" something in human experience (25:11, 13; 26:1f., 8, 11, 18, 23; 27:8; 28:15). In other words, the values of the group are compared with silver, gold, or precious jewels (25:11f.), human behavior with elements of nature (25:13f., 25f.; 26:1f.; 27:19), with habits of animals (26:11; 27:8; 28:15), and with examples of violence (25:18; 28; 26:6, 8-10; 26:18f.).

The admonitions in this section presume that the one for whom the advice is intended already possesses material assets that will increase if managed prudently (27:23-27; 28:19). Prudent use includes providing for the needy (29:7), even if they have been considered enemies (25:21f.). Wealth may be desirable and it may be seen as evidence of honorable living, but being overzealous in amassing it can work to one's detriment (28:8, 20, 22). Respect and tranquillity within the home (25:24; 27:11, 15f.; 28:7, 24; 29:3, 15, 17) and commitment to friends (27:10) are also values necessary for a stable society.

The Poetry of Wit

The last two chapters of the book of Proverbs are rather difficult to classify. Although they contain two superscriptions (30:1; 31:1) and, therefore, are comprised of at least two discrete collections, they also include a prayer, a selection of numerical sayings, an instruction for a specific individual, and an acrostic poem. Each of these sections displays a high degree of literary composition, testimony to the careful refinement which the proverbs had undergone. The artistry that they exhibit confirms their poetic character; the ingenuity of their performance demonstrates wit that they communicate.

The meaning of the Hebrew of the first verse of chapter 30 is uncertain. Both the forms and the message of the ensuing teaching are clear, however, though unusual in three ways. First, unlike the other collections of the book that describe order or counsel a pattern of behavior, this section begins with a very pessimistic disclaimer. The sapiential tradition consistently maintains that wisdom is attainable through reflective living, through the process of socialization, and through the religious tradition. Agur disputes these claims. He declares that he has neither empirical wisdom, nor traditional wisdom, nor knowledge of God. The questions that he then poses (v. 4), questions similar to YHWH's initial inquiry in the book of Job (ch. 38), suggest that only one who has traversed the cosmos and has held sway over it can possibly attain wisdom. Where does this leave the human searcher? The teaching that follows may provide an answer.

The three proverbial statements of Agur (the expression of cynicism [vv. 2f.], the questions [v. 4], and the saying [vv. 5f.]) originally may have been independent of each other. Juxtaposed as they are here, however, they create a kind of progression of thought. People lack understanding because what they want to know is really beyond their limited human capacity. Real knowledge comes from God. In the end, we must accept the "sayings of *'elōah*" and not augment them, for they are the words of God.

The second unusual feature of this section is the inclusion of a prayer (vv. 7-9). Wisdom teaching normally appears in descriptive maxims or imperative exhortations. Although hymnic prayers do appear elsewhere (for example, 8:22-31; Job 28), they are usually part of another proverbial form. Prayers of petition are rare (Whybray, 1990:78–81). Following the progression of thought found here, it appears that what began in skepticism (vv. 2f.) ends in piety.

The third unusual feature is the numerical proverb (vv. 15b- 16, 18f., 21-23, 24-28, 29-31; cf. 6:16-19). By means of its unique structure (x, x+1), this poetic composition gathers phenomena that, at first glance, are notably different in order to compare one common feature (Roth, 1965). This is a singularly creative way of ordering or categorizing information. Like the riddle, it is occupied with paradoxes, phenomena that are so very different and yet so much alike. While the riddle teases one into discovering the commonality, the numerical proverb begins with a clear identification of that common element. This is an ingenious mnemonic method of collecting and teaching information. Like all wisdom teaching, these proverbs are intended to throw light on human conduct. Like many other expressions, they call on the observed habits of animals to provide this. Comparing the behavior of human beings and animals in this way suggests that somehow all are governed by the same kind of laws.

Chapter 31 is comprised of two literary pieces: an instruction of a queen to her son Lemuel (31:1-9), and a hymn of praise in honor of an industrious wife (vv. 10-33). The women that we glimpse in these two passages differ significantly from the inconsequential or disreputable women referred to throughout the book. These two women are strong and influential in their own right. Their positions as wives and mothers have not restricted them but, on the contrary, have given them an arena within which they can exert power. The power that they employ is neither oppressive nor exploitative nor manipulative. It is used for the benefit of others. The picture of womanhood sketched here is highly complimentary.

Many narratives recount the influence that mothers exerted in the lives of their children (such as Rebekah [Gen. 27:5-17] and Hannah [1 Sam 1:21-

28]). There are also signs that on occasion women in the royal family wielded extraordinary power over the nation (such as Bathsheba [1 Kgs 1:11-23] and Athalia [2 Kgs 11:1-3]). This is the only place in the Scripture, however, where a mother is presented as the primary source of vocational education of her son (for historical precedents, see McKane, 1970:407f.). The content of her instruction is identical to what is found earlier in the book. She warns him against women (v.3), but not against quarrelsome women (19:13), or contentious women (21:9, 19), or debauched women (6:24). One can only presume that the reference is to threatening women, but the text is not specific. The warning here is general; it is against women.

She also cautions him about the dangers of strong drink (vv. 4-7). If the king is to be a reliable ruler of the nation and defender of the rights of all, he must not allow inebriation to impair his performance in any way. Intoxicating drink may be put to good use as a medicinal palliative to alleviate suffering, but it is detrimental to good administration. Drink seems to be a major concern, for it is the major portion of her exhortation.

The queen's final counsel addresses the matter of advocacy. An honorable king will not only judge impartially but will defend the rights of the defenseless. It is very important to be equitable in one's governance. But when the structures of society privilege some and disadvantage others, as many structures do, it might become necessary to act on behalf of the disadvantaged. This royal mother urges her son to assume such responsibility should it arise.

The criteria for an ideal king are followed by a poem celebrating the ideal wife (Camp, 1985:90–93). This poem is acrostic in form, the verses beginning with consecutive letters of the alphabet. Acrostic structure provides a clever mnemonic device, but it limits the possibilities of the features that can be included in the description and it prevents the poem from having any kind of consistent development of thought.

After characterizing the wife in a manner earlier ascribed to wisdom (v. 10b; cf. 3:15), the poem sketches the advantage that she brings to her husband (vv. 11f.). This is a woman of high social and economic standing (vv. 21f.), whose husband occupies a position of importance within the community (v. 23). She appears to make business decisions independently (vv. 16, 18), providing for her own household (vv. 15, 21, 27) as well as for the needs of others (v.20). She is not only successful but also virtuous (vv. 25f.). This is a very successful and prosperous woman. She has much to be happy about (v. 28; cf. 23:25).

This poem not only stands on its own as a literary composition but also employs some of the same female imagery found in the very first section of the book (chs. 1–9). Both sections allude to the teaching of the mother (1:8;

31:1). Both Woman Wisdom and the industrious wife are more precious than jewels (3:15; 31:10), and whoever finds them will not lack material gain (3:13-14; 31:11). Just as Woman Wisdom can be found at the city gates (1:21), so this woman is praised at the city gates (31:31; see Camp, 1985:188f.). Finally, the book of Proverbs begins and ends with "the fear of the LORD" (1:7; 31:30). These correspondences create a kind of *inclusio*, suggesting deliberate literary composition.

Rhetorical Function

The objective of these instructions is quite clear. The unspecified character of some of the counsel given suggests that it is a general motivation urging compliance to the accepted mores and customs of society (Nel, 1982). The explicit advice of the directives reveals the specific customs and mores that are being advanced. The young student is admonished to listen to his elders and to pattern his life after theirs. Success and prosperity are placed before him as incentives to conform; the threat of failure and deprivation is meant to deter him from unacceptable behavior. Because such socialization seldom questions the appropriateness of the social mores and customs, it tends to reinforce the authority of the status quo. While it produces a sense of belonging, it also restricts exploration and creative expression. A form of social homogenization takes place that defines who belongs and who does not, who is acceptable and who is not, who will succeed and who will not. Those who resist socialization often become marginal to the group or are considered social deviants who seldom enjoy the rewards the society bestows on those who conform. The presuppositions of such socialization underlie the teaching found in the rest of the book as well.

The teaching also presumes that socialization is the same for all. It uncritically supposes that all sectors of society face life in the same way and gain the identical insights into their experience. Its conclusions further claim that the rewards for compliance to social patterns are available to all. Those with the power to decide that their insights are superior to the insights of others and should be deemed universally valid thus install their values as norms for all to follow. Relating wisdom as defined by them with the wisdom at the heart of the structures of reality (ch. 8) gives cosmic legitimation to their particular teaching. The instruction of Proverbs is a powerful political tool in the hands of the established institutions, whether these institutions are based on kinship, such as the family, clan, or tribe, or on political organization, such as court or scribal schools (McKane, 1965:23–47; Scott, 1965:xxv–xl; Whybray, 1990:69–72).

Despite the limitations of the group's mores and customs, the importance of the marketplace as the site of the encounter with wisdom cannot be minimized. The accessibility of this place democratizes the acquisition of wisdom and places at least one dimension of it at the disposal of the general public. The social status of those who congregate in the marketplace may vary, but all classes of people are found there, and Wisdom cries out to all of them (8:4; the Hebrew "sons of Adam" is meant to be inclusive). Since one's social location influences one's perspective, the diverse members of the crowd in the marketplace are bound to yield an array of discerning points of view. The dispossessed will hear certain characteristics of Wisdom's voice and the social elite will hear others. The question is: Whose point of view will be considered reliable and offered as universally normative?

Since the one who chooses wisdom will enjoy the good things of life, while the fool has embarked on a path that leads to death, the metaphors of banquet and eating lend themselves to understanding the life-giving qualities of wisdom. Although both Wisdom and the foolish woman prepare food for the simple youth, the dissimilarities of the meals are striking. Wisdom's fare of meat, bread, and wine (9:2, 5) is offered honestly and, presumably, eaten openly. On the other hand, the foolish woman's bread and wine are taken in secret and those who partake of them do so without realizing that they have been tricked (9:17). Wisdom's nourishment leads to life (v. 6). In fact, she is called a "tree of life" (3:18). On the other hand, the provisions of the foolish woman bring her guests to death, to Sheol (9:18). The menu offered by Wisdom would be common fare of those who eat well and the preferred food of those who eat poorly. But the destitute would probably eat whatever was offered to them from whoever thought to offer it. Thus, the banquet metaphor with its bill of fare, as effective as it may be in highlighting some of wisdom's vivifying attributes, has certain presuppositions about class.

Gnomic sentences typical of all wisdom literature are simple descriptions of insights culled from life. Each proverb records a conclusion drawn from experience. Usually its authority rests on the accuracy of its description, and it is only validated by another experience. Since each proverb is but one frame in the assemblage of pictures, views from different vantage points are collected in order to create a kind of collage of life experiences meant to communicate the social values of the group. Most likely, only the proverbs whose insights expressed the views of those in power were handed down as normative for the entire group. In this way the dominant worldview was furthered.

Two proverbial forms in particular, antithetic parallelism and "better . . . than" sayings, are inclined to estrange different groups within society. The first establishes unambiguously which behaviors and situations in life are acceptable and which are not. Such differentiation can not only reinforce the mores and customs preferred by those in power but also alienate those who do not measure up to the established standards. In a similar way, the "better . . . than" saying can diminish the value of something that is good but not better. Evaluations such as these probably exerted pressure on members of society to conform lest they be judged inadequate. Those who were unwilling or unable to comply to these pressures may have found themselves estranged from the mainstream of society.

Another literary device, comparison, betrays the bias of the proverbial material. These comparisons will only be meaningful if the circumstances to which they allude are within the scope of the experience of the people. If the element of observation is taken from the natural world, it is more probable that people of every class or subgroup will be able to appreciate the comparison. If it is derived from an aspect of the culture or a specific set of values, however, only those with access to the culture or who share the values will think much of the comparison. The elements of the comparison betray the biases of those using them. This is another method of socialization.

In the first collection, the wisdom of the marketplace was combined with wisdom in the cosmos, thereby granting divine legitimation to social mores and customs. The second achieves the same end by relating the worldview and conventions of society to the designs of YHWH. Divine authority is also bestowed on the political structures by the claim that YHWH established the monarchy. The strength and extent of this controlling power cannot be minimized. If the origins of the monarchy are rooted in God's designs, resistance to royal rule can be construed as opposition to the divine will. Since devout people would probably not challenge what they regarded as God's plan, the monarchy could, and probably did, wield tremendous political, social, and religious power.

Obedience to the law is essential if a society is to be healthy and secure. This means that instruction in its statutes and ordinances must be part of the socialization into the group. Where there is law, there will be a means of enforcing it and of deciding how and when it has been violated. Some form of court procedure is a part of every legal system. But those in power usually unduly influence the character of the law, the manner of enforcing it, and the means of judging its violation. The lower classes of a society frequently lack power in this regard. The teaching here seems to presume that the laws are equitable, that all members of society have recourse to the courts, and that the vulnerable will receive the same justice as will the privileged. The disadvantaged know from experience that this is seldom the case. The optimistic view of the legal system seems to be class-conditioned.

Socialization begins within the family. It is there that the values of the broader society are first learned. It is logical to presume that the social patterns learned in the family will be transferred to interaction within the social groups of the broader society. The proverbs that address family matters not only counsel behavior but also suggest responsibilities within the family. Parents are to instruct; children are to respect and obey; wives are to be amicable. No directives are given explicitly to husbands regarding their attitudes or behavior toward their wives. If this implies that husbands had no obligations in this regard, it is an indisputable sign of gender discrimination.

Finally, the significance of speech, especially in an oral culture, should not be overlooked. Words not only describe reality, in a very real sense they fashion it. Words are not merely vehicles of communication but also expressions of the very personality of the speaker. Words transmit truth. A society will not survive if it is based on deceptive words. Therefore, it was incumbent on all members of the group to speak honestly and wisely.

It is apparent that all of this counsel is intended to prepare a young man for responsible adulthood within society.

Unmasking the Powers

The focus of this liberationist reading of the book of Proverbs turns now to the issues of race or ethnic origin, class, and gender to discover some of the presuppositions of the teaching. Proverbs are defined as pithy depictions of some facet of life. Although this is true, they are really value-laden descriptions. They interpret a facet of life from the prevailing worldview of the society. As already noted, the rhetorical function of proverbial teaching is the socialization of members into the mores and customs of the group. Whatever does not conform to these norms is suspect at best or in extreme cases becomes the object of discrimination. Accordingly, what is strange or foreign is often distrusted and treated with suspicion.

If there is resistance to unconventional behavior within the society itself, there was even more xenophobia when what was strange was foreign to that society. Thus, to warn that strangers or foreigners will savor the fruits of one's labor (5:10) does not merely mean that someone who did not endure the struggle required in accomplishing the task might reap the benefits; it also suggests that the rewards of hard work may go to outsiders or non-members and, if this happens, the entire community will be deprived of its due. The Hebrew word used here is not *ger* (sojourner or resident alien) but *zerim,* from the verb meaning "to turn aside, to depart." It has the connotation of loathsome or unlawful and usually refers to a dangerous or hostile stranger, an enemy.

Several proverbs go further in this regard and actually advise against sharing with these strangers (5:17) or intervening economically on their behalf (6:1; 11:15; 20:16; 27:13). Along with the vulnerability that attends being an outsider, these people are not only deprived of the privileges of membership but members are advised not to assist them in their need. To recommend caution in the face of the uncertainty posed by the unknown is one thing, but to disdain the legitimate needs of strangers violates the principles of hospitality and, in fact, disregards the admonition to alleviate the needs of enemies (25:21f.; cf. 24:17f.). To advocate such behavior in a society whose legislation seems already prejudiced against the outsider only compounds any discrimination the stranger might already experience. The dangers of ethnocentricity are apparent.

The real disapproval of outsiders is directed against the seductive strange or foreign woman (2:16; 7:5; 27:13; see Camp, 1985:265–71). This temptress is also described as evil (6:24) and noisy (9:13). It is difficult to decide if the reference is to any woman who is "loose" (a translation of *zarah*, the Hebrew for "to be stranger to") and who seeks a sexual partner outside of her family or marital commitment, or if the instruction intends to malign the foreign woman by characterizing her in such a negative way. In one reference (23:27f.), the parallel construction suggests that she is in fact a prostitute. The bias here is more ethnocentric than directed toward women in general, since the foolish woman has a wise female counterpart who is praised (contra Camp, 1985:115–20).

Gender bias does exist, however. In the first place, the only references to the deity identify God with the divine name YHWH and the male pronouns that attend it. Second, there is a definite androcentric character to the advice given. Without exception, the students are referred to as sons and the socialization takes place between father and son. The teaching reinforces the values and customs of a society that is patriarchal in structure and androcentric in perspective (Newsom, 1989:142–60). Although in some passages the mother's teaching parallels the instruction of the father (1:8; 4:3; 6:20; 10:1; 15:20; 19:26; 20:20; 23:22, 25), with only one exception (31:1) it does not appear as the sole source of guidance as the instruction of the father does. It may be that mention of the mother's teaching is really a poetic fiction used to produce parallel construction, rather than a reference to social reality.

The male perspective of the instruction is also seen in the recurrent warning about the temptress, found in the first section (5:3-6; also 29:3). She is depicted as worldly-wise, taking advantage of the naivete of the young and innocent. The truth is that women are no more captivating or provocative than are men, who can be just as attractive and irresistible. The fact that only a woman is portrayed as alluring says less about the seductive character of women than about the gender bias of the writer. Furthermore, the tantalizing woman is not only a temptress but an adulteress as well (2:16-19;

6:24-29, 32-35; 7:5-27). This fact compounds her guilt, for she both leads the unsuspecting youth into the ways of folly and profanes her own commitment in the process.

The most obvious gender question is seen in the characterization of three female figures: personified Wisdom; the queen mother of Lemuel; and the industrious wife. Why are these three women described as independent and influential in a society that is certainly patriarchal? What is their importance in teaching that is definitely androcentric?

Several explanations for the female personification of wisdom have been advanced. Some believe that this is a remnant of ancient Near Eastern worship of a goddess of wisdom (Lang, 1986; for a summary of theories see Camp, 1985:23–36). They contend that its survival within an indisputable patriarchal religion indicates either a deeply rooted popular devotion to a female deity or respect for the characteristics of YHWH that correspond to what was considered female. Others understand the characterization as hypostatization, taking what is normally a personal trait and transforming it into a person with its own existence (Whybray, 1965:92–104). Still others see it as merely a development from the feminine form of the Hebrew ḥokmah (wisdom).

Whatever the origin of this representation, at issue here is its rhetorical function. The most widely accepted explanation for the female characterization can be found in the nature of the society itself. In this tradition, wisdom was regarded as the most desirable possession. In a patriarchal male-preferred society such as the one portrayed in the text, it is understandable that what is desired would be personified as a woman. The same is true for folly. Women are no more inherently wise or seductive than are men; however, they better represent what heterosexual men find enticing. Both demure Wisdom and the seductive woman are interested in securing the allegiance of young men. They prepare meals that are meant to entice them, a role that traditionally has been assigned to the woman (Camp, 1985:133–37). This characterization, which at first glance appears as enhancement of the female character, is actually a device used to further male objectives.

The second woman characterized is the queen mother of Lemuel. The instructional role that she plays is not as significant as is the content of her instruction. She is concerned that her son rule as king according to the way the monarchy was understood in their society. She does not train him in a different model. She actively takes part in the formation of the next patriarch. Furthermore, her caution against women is not only blatantly androcentric but stereotypically discriminatory as well. Of the three different admonitions she gives, two are warnings: one about women and the other about strong drink, two evils that undermine the effectiveness of kings. What at first glance looks like unusual privilege is in reality collusion in the perpetuation of a system and attendant attitudes that prejudice the gender group of the counselor.

The third characterization is of the industrious wife. As with the previous sketches, this depiction can also be deceiving. She may be a model wife, mother, and provider, but it is the prevailing model fostered by the patriarchal society. While her husband is seated with the elders at the gates of the city, presumably conducting the public business of the society, she is busy providing for the private needs of the household. Although several of her transactions are carried on outside the family, they are, nonetheless, for the sake of the family. The patriarchal character of this society is laid bare when the woman is referred to as daughter (*bat*, 31:29). Who is calling this woman "daughter"? Hardly her father, for he is not even mentioned in the poem. Certainly not her children. If it is her husband, then he would clearly be her patriarch.

Finally, the last verse of the poem is expressed in the imperative. To whom is this direction given? Not the woman, because she is the intended recipient of the favor proposed. Whoever is being addressed is advised that the woman be given a share of the fruit of her hands and that she be praised at the city gates. This is an unnecessary directive if the woman does indeed have control of the material assets described in the poem. It is good that she should be praised at the city gates, but that this has to be proposed suggests that such commendation is not customary. While it is true that this is an acrostic poem which places extraordinary restrictions on composition, still the character of the traits chosen for this description betray its androcentric bias.

The word *'iššâ* is translated both as "woman" and as "wife." The context within which it appears influences which rendering is preferred. In very few passage are the statements about women merely descriptive. Most of them are either pejorative or they depict women in subordinate positions. The subordination is reinforced by the use of the Hebrew *bā'al*, a word that is translated as "husband" but also as "owner," lord" or "master" (12:4). Wives are described as quarrelsome (19:13), contentious, and fretful (21:9, 19; 25:24; 27:15). A beautiful but senseless woman is compared to a gold ring in a pig's snout (11:22), not a very complimentary image. The good wife is valued as an adornment of her husband (12:4), something that he has found (18:22), or a gift to him from God (19:14). The woman's value is ordinarily judged according to her usefulness to the man.

One female reference stands out as unusual. In a warning against the strange woman, the youth is told to treat wisdom as a sister, an intimate kinswoman (7:4). Within patriarchal societies, sisters, and brides who are often called "sister," are considered dependents. Such is not the case here. Nowhere in the book is wisdom envisioned in a subordinate position. The intimate relationship proposed is more like that in the Song of Songs (4:9f., 12; 5:1f.; 8:8), where the relationship between the woman and the man is one of mutuality.

The final aspect of the advocacy critique concerns class. Actually, the principal group categorization is the distinction between the wise and the simple, not between different social or economic classes. Nonetheless, the doctrine of retribution displays an obvious class bias favoring good fortune, as can be detected in the correspondence of prosperity and want with specific social groups (3:13-15; 6:9-11). Furthermore, part of the allurement of both Woman Wisdom and the foolish woman is the experience of luxury offered to the simple youth (8:18-21 and 7:16f.).

The youth being addressed is assumed already to possess certain material assets and the means to increase them (3:9f.; 25:21f.; 27:23-27). Either this prosperity is inherited capital or the young man is singularly and shrewdly industrious, acquiring assets at an early age. Because in the latter case he would already be wise and in need of no one's direction, it is more likely that he has inherited his assets. Clearly the admonition deals not with the acquisition of material resources but with their wise use and investment. Good management and investment are clearly concerns, if not of the upper class, at least of those with moderate means (Whybray, 1990).

A kind of ambiguity toward wealth does appear in several places. For example, despite the high regard accorded good fortune, there is a warning about the peril that awaits those who covet riches (1:13-19; 28:20, 22, 25). Since the craving for wealth occurs in all segments of society, there is no way of knowing the social station of the intended recipient of this counsel. In another passage, theft motivated by need is considered a lesser offense. This would probably be a point of view held by the impoverished. Nonetheless, dire circumstances do not mitigate the punishment facing the perpetrator if caught, a policy most likely supported by those who are financially comfortable (6:30f.). Poverty is not always regarded as evidence of estrangement from God. In fact, YHWH is described as the defender of the poor (22:23; 23:10f.). Hence, those who oppress these vulnerable people will face the opposition of God.

Being wealthy has its own pressures. It may enable one to acquire a certain amount of protection (10:15), but it can also make one vulnerable to the wickedness of others (13:8). Although wealth seems to attract admirers (14:20), it cannot always be trusted (11:4, 28). In addition, the prosperous have the obligation of using their wealth responsibly (13:11, 22; 14:21; 20:13;

22:9, 16; 28:27). Although such pressures are real and cannot be ignored, they are still the pressures of the privileged. There is a definite class bias behind much of this teaching.

Prosperity is not the only avenue to attaining privilege. The kind of social stratification that normally accompanies the institution of the monarchy also benefits some within the society more than others. Even though rulers have the responsibility of administering justice to rich and poor alike (29:4, 13f.), access to the corridors of power (25:6-8) is usually limited to certain classes. These proverbs presume that the young man has such access, thus hinting at his social status.

The expectation of definite consequences following certain actions underlies much of the instruction given. Several proverbs presume that hard work will always be rewarded (10:4; 12:11, 14, 27; 13:4; 14:23; 27:18; 28:19-22), and good fortune is generally the fruit of righteous living (10:3, 22; 11:24f.; 13:18, 21; 15:6, 25, 27). As is usually the case with the theory of retribution, this is the point of view of those who have known success and expect to experience it again and again. The dispossessed or disadvantaged within the society know from their own experience that righteous living cannot insure good fortune. Furthermore, only those who do not suffer want would claim that, under certain circumstances, a meager existence along with virtue is better than an abundance without it (15:16f.; 28:6). It is acknowledged that at times the wicked do succeed (10:16; 13:22), and their prosperity may have been acquired through devious means (10:2; 11:1). Still, the presumption is that their good fortune is short-lived and they will ultimately be deprived of their success (10:2; 13:22). Thus the theory of reward and punishment stands.

The perspective from which these proverbs originate is clearly anthropocentric, indeed, it is androcentric. Although the immensity of the universe is acknowledged (25:3), references to the broader natural world are usually metaphorical formulations that serve anthropocentric objectives. For example, the tree of life is reward for righteousness (11:30), animals satisfy human needs (14:4) or are figurative allusions to human situations (11:22; 17:12; 19:12; 20:2; 22:13; 23:5, 32). The righteous may know what their animals require (12:10), but it is not clear whether they meet these needs for the sake of the animals or out of their own economic interest. Since this wisdom teaching is preoccupied with the successful orientation of the young to the customs and mores of society, its anthropocentric focus is understandable. The point to remember is the cosmological legitimation of Woman Wisdom.

Into the Looking Glass

Now that the advocacy stand sensitive to issues of race or ethnic origin, class, and gender has critiqued the counsel found in the book of Proverbs, the revelatory power of the sapiential tradition can be directed toward these issues. The biblical message can again function as a mirror into which the reader looks, as well as a doorway to a new world into which the reader steps. Reading the book of Proverbs from an advocacy stance is not difficult, but examining the advocacy issues of race or ethic origin and class from the perspective of the biblical material is far from easy. Proverbs is a collection of insights, the underlying values of which are tied to a particular worldview, and the worldview is quite restrictive. There is no narrative development here, as there is in the book of Job, nor is there dynamic conversion. The challenge here is to find something within the teaching of Proverbs that lends itself to the advocacy stand and that can be used as a lens to look at the contemporary world. The theme chosen to do this is: wisdom as the way to life.

This study contends that the primary function of the teaching found in the book of Proverbs is the socialization of members into or within the society. By means of several different literary devices, it captures moments of life, snippets of action, and flashes of insight. This book is a treasury of wisdom, not because reality is fixed forever in its poetic forms but because it supplies us with limited yet accurate glimpses of the same phenomena from several different angles. This variety of perceptions is evidence of the ambiguity within life and acknowledges the need continuously to weigh circumstances and to make discerning judgments. Each judgment, and the course of action that it engenders, is an expression of the values of the group, values into which the young are initiated.

Relying on past insights, wisdom sets a direction for successful living in both the present and the future. Wisdom itself is dynamic, not static. Whoever clings rigidly to the insights of the past may be knowledgeable but is not necessarily wise. However, the wise person will be imbued with wisdom in order to be influenced by it, for one does not so much apply wisdom as act out of it. In the midst of ambiguity, wisdom takes stock of the situation, scrutinizing each circumstance and weighing every possibility. Within the process of socialization, conformity does not call for wisdom, discretion does. In order for one to exercise discretion, one must think flexibly and be able to adapt to various situations.

In the book of Proverbs, and especially in the first section (chs. 1–9), the image that characterizes the direction set by wisdom is "the way" (see Habel, 1972). Wisdom sets the direction. In a certain sense, wisdom *is* the direction. Wisdom is the way. But the way to what? Wisdom is the way to life. This is very clearly stated by Woman Wisdom herself: "Whoever finds me, finds life" (8:35; cf. 4:13; it is also the "tree of life" [3:18] and the "fountain of life" [16:22]).

Life is more than mere physical vitality, although length of days is a treasure to be desired (3:16; 9:11; 10:27). Real life is the ability to exercise all of one's vital power to the fullest. It includes health and security, prosperity and respect. Life is meant to be enjoyed in the midst of family and friends. This relationship is symbolized in the figure of Wisdom, who stands majestically, like the Egyptian goddess *Ma'at*, with life in one hand and riches and honor in the other (3:16; see McKane, 1970:295f.). Physical existence deprived of this fullness, this *šalom* (3:17), is not really life but a form of death. All of our days we are torn between life and death, between the fullest enjoyment of our powers and total deprivation.

If wisdom is the way to life, what is to be said about those who are deprived of the means of life? What of the stranger who, already in a vulnerable situation, is refused assistance and thus put into even greater jeopardy? And what is it that makes the stranger a potential enemy? We would be naive to close our eyes to the causes of any long-standing deep-seated ethnic animosity, for if ignored it might only fester and spread. But does there not come a time when, with eyes open, we consign enmity to the past and move forward together, committed to equitable and peaceful alliance? Xenophobia has no place in a "global village." In this we can look to Proverbs, which in advocating such conciliation speaks against its own ethnocentricity. It not only denounces delighting in the misfortunes of strangers (24:17f.), it also recommends providing for them in their need (25:21f.). The world in which we live provides us with ample opportunity to respond to this admonition.

Racial or ethnic prejudice is not the only obstacle to the means of life. Poverty can dehumanize and grind people into the dust. Although it is not uncommon that racial or ethnic discrimination and abject poverty are found together, most social groups have their own economic stratifications. Despite the claim of the act/consequence principle of retribution, that prosperity will be found where there is goodness and misfortune will accompany infidelity, Proverbs does not condemn the poor. In fact, it instructs the youth to be generous toward them (14:21; 21:13; 22:9; 22:22; 28:27). Even the king is told to provide for them (29:14; 31:9). Such concern may in fact be condescending and not at all disinterested, because reward is often promised for following this advice. Nonetheless, part of this instruction directs the youth to treat the needy with respect, because all, rich and poor alike, have been made by the same God (14:31; 17:5; 22:2; 29:13). Acknowledgment of the common origin of all is the basis of human rights and human solidarity.

While the description of human women is very disparaging, the depiction of Woman Wisdom is just the opposite. She is strong and independent, discerning and self-sacrificing. Her integrity is beyond question and her dignity unshakable. The features of her portrait may have been engendered by a patriarchal perspective, but she does not conform to the patriarchal stereotype of woman. Although she figures only in chapters 1–9, she becomes the characterization of wisdom as found throughout the book (Camp, 1987). More to our point, her metaphorical characterization can reflexively delineate the profile of the human woman (Camp, 1985:71–77), who might also be strong and independent, discerning and self-sacrificing, with integrity beyond question and dignity that is unshakable. The women pictured in this book may have been circumscribed by the stereotypes of the culture of the writer, but the metaphor of Woman Wisdom allows contemporary women to move beyond such restriction (McFague, 1982).

The final issue to be considered is the cosmological character of wisdom. The substance of much of the gnomic teaching presumes a knowledge of the working of the natural world. In fact, much of the comparison found in the proverbs actually requires such knowledge. Since the intention of this knowledge is practical (success in human endeavor), might we conclude that the similarities described in the comparisons are more than figurative? The ants, the badgers, the locusts, and the lizard all display a certain kind of wisdom (30:24-28), a wisdom that would benefit humans as well. Amidst the incalculable diversity of natural phenomena, might their common origin from God through the agency of wisdom (3:19f.) and their similarity of behavior suggest that on some level there lies a type of commonality or affinity? Some have referred to this affinity as "the order of reality" (Perdue, 1994:46–48).

We have seen that Woman Wisdom who calls out in the marketplace is none other than the Wisdom present with God at the creation of the universe (8:1-34). She made this known in order to confirm the authority of the wisdom she offers to the youth. In other words, the wisdom of the marketplace is authenticated by its presentation here within the context of the unquestionable wisdom displayed in the marvels of the cosmos. All of this leads to the following conclusion. The counsel found in Proverbs may be manifestly anthropocentric, but the wisdom which is the real goal of the sapiential teaching is broader than any limited human focus.

The Teaching of the Wise

"The teaching of the wise is a fountain of life" (13:14). The search for meaning and for a satisfying life is a universal quest, the dream of all people and the goal of every society. Those who are new to the task look to the ones who are practiced in it; those with questions turn to the ones with answers. The lore that is handed down continues to refresh, like an ever-springing fountain. The success of yesterday becomes the possibility of today; the failures of the past are warnings to the present. And so life unfolds as before.

The book of Proverbs is just such a life-giving fountain. It describes and it instructs; it teases and it forewarns. It has passed the test of time, and its counsel is as pertinent today as it was at its first articulation. The pictures sketched by its idioms have retained their energetic quality, capturing the habits of a world that never ceases to fascinate. The truths enshrined therein need only opportunity to be tested, for it will only be authentic wisdom when it is actually directing the lives of a new generation of searchers. They are the ones who will appraise the effectiveness of Proverbs. It is their recontextualization that will determine its value.

Regardless of how wise this teaching is or how faithfully it is transmitted to others, it bears the mark of human limitation. Its focus and its imagery spring from experience that is always circumscribed. In itself, this does not discredit the trustworthiness of the counsel. But when the insights of some are disregarded while those of others are extolled as normative, the teaching can become distorted. Presuppositions, which are always subjective, can become very biased and discriminatory. People outside the dominant group are often forced either to disregard their own insights and conform to the status quo or retain their points of view and be relegated to the margins of the society. If this happens, the life-giving quality of the teaching dries up for all. Those who are disadvantaged by the bias of the tradition are not able to be refreshed by it or to refresh others with the rejuvenating riches of their own wisdom. In like manner, those whose wisdom has become normative for all are deprived of the richness of perceptions which they would not come to on their own. In this case, all are impoverished.

The ethnic, class, and gender biases of the book of Proverbs are quite obvious. But so is the all-encompassing call of Wisdom and the very general, polysemic character of her message. For this message to be authentic wisdom, it must be recontextualized again and again. The waters of the fountain can both refresh and cleanse, and in this way bring forth treasures of wisdom, both old and new.

Works Consulted

Alter, Robert. 1985. *The Art of Biblical Poetry*. New York: Basic Books.
Brenner, Athalya. 1993. "Some Observations on the Figuration of Woman in Wisdom Literature." In *Of Prophets' Visions and the Wisdom of Sages: Essays in Honor of R. Norman Whybray on His Seventieth Birthday*. Edited

by Heather A. McKay and David J. A. Clines. Journal for the Study of Old Testament Supplement Series 162. Sheffield: JSOT Press.

Bryce, Glendon E. 1972. "'Better'—Proverbs: An Historical and Structural Study." *Society of Biblical Literature Seminar Papers*: 108:343–54.

Camp, Claudia V. 1985. *Wisdom and the Feminine in the Book of Proverbs.* Sheffield: Almond Press.

_____. 1987. "Woman Wisdom as Root Metaphor: A Theological Consideration." In *The Listening Heart.* Edited by Kenneth G. Hoglund, Elizabeth F. Huwiler, Jonathan T. Glass, and Roger W. Lee. Journal for the Study of the Old Testament Supplement Series 58. Sheffield: Sheffield Press.

Fontaine, Carole R. 1982. *Traditional Sayings in the Old Testament.* Sheffield: Almond Press.

_____. 1993. "Wisdom in Proverbs." In *In Search of Wisdom: Essays in Memory of John G. Gammie.* Edited by Leo G. Perdue et al. Louisville, Ky.: Westminster/John Knox Press.

Habel, Norman C. 1972. "The Symbolism of Wisdom in Proverbs 1–9." *Interpretation* 26:131–57.

Harris, R. Laird. 1980. *Theological Wordbook of the Old Testament,* Volume 1. Chicago: Moody Press.

Kugel, James L. 1981. *The Idea of Biblical Poetry: Parallelism and Its History.* New Haven: Yale University Press.

Lang, Bernhard. 1986. *Wisdom and the Book of Proverbs: An Israelite Goddess Redefined.* New York: Pilgrim Press.

McFague, Sallie. 1982. *Metaphorical Theology.* Philadelphia: Fortress Press.

McKane, William. 1965. *Prophets and Wise Men.* Studies in Biblical Theology 44. London: SCM Press.

_____. 1970. *Proverbs.* Old Testament Library. Philadelphia: Westminster Press.

Murphy, Roland E. 1990. *The Tree of Life: An Exploration of Biblical Wisdom Literature.* The Anchor Bible Reference Library. New York: Doubleday.

Nel, Philip Johannes. 1982. *The Structure and Ethos of the Wisdom Admonitions in Proverbs.* Beihefte zur Zeitschrift für die alttestamentliche Wissenschaft 138. Berlin: Walter de Gruyter.

Newsom, Carol A. 1989. "Woman and the Discourse of Patriarchal Wisdom: A Study of Proverbs 1–9." In *Gender and Difference.* Edited by Peggy L. Day. Philadelphia: Fortress Press.

Perdue, Leo G. 1994. *Wisdom and Creation: The Theology of Wisdom Literature.* Nashville: Abingdon Press.

Ricoeur, Paul. 1976. *Interpretation Theory: Discourse and the Surplus of Meaning.* Fort Worth: Texas Christian University Press.

Roth, W. M. W. 1965. *Numerical Sayings in the Old Testament: A Form Critical Study.* Vetus Testament Supplement 13. Leiden: E. J. Brill.

Scott, R. B. Y. 1965. *Proverbs, Ecclesiastes.* Anchor Bible 18. Garden City, N.Y.: Doubleday.

Skehan, Patrick W. 1971. *Studies in Israelite Poetry and Wisdom.* Catholic Biblical Quarterly Monograph Series 1. Washington, D.C.: The Catholic Biblical Association of America.

Whybray, Roger N. 1965. *Wisdom in Proverbs.* London: SCM Press.

_____. 1990. *Wealth and Poverty in the Book of Proverbs.* Journal for the Study of the Old Testament Supplement Series 99. Sheffield: JSOT Press.

_____. 1994. *The Composition of the Book of Proverbs.* Journal for the Study of the Old Testament Supplement Series 168. Sheffield: JSOT Press.

5

Ecclesiastes

Introduction

ECCLESIASTES (OR QOHELETH) DOES NOT ENJOY THE popularity of the book of Job. A superficial reading has left many people with the impression that the man described here is a skeptic, a cynic, even a hedonist. His view of life seems too pessimistic for some and, unfortunately, he is then dismissed without a hearing.

The first two chapters of the book have the literary characteristics of a Royal Testament, a common form of the ancient Near East wherein a king imparts advice to his successor. Other typical pedagogical genres used by the author include proverbial quotations, contrasting proverbs, and rhetorical questions (cf. Loader, 1979:1–28; Murphy, 1981:129–49). As with many books in the First Testament there are unresolved questions about this book's authorship, dating and provenance, structure and composition.

The book recounts the author's struggle with the limitations of the theory of retribution, the inevitability and universality of death, and the sense of futility that this often accords life. Death is not the only reality that challenges the purposefulness of life. Since the direction taken by life is often completely out of human hands and the search for wisdom is endless, the acquisition of goods can be experienced as pointless. Qoheleth looks at human striving in general and asks an encompassing and profound question: "What is the meaning of life?"

Many attempts have been put forward to identify the literary structure of this book (cf. Crenshaw, 1987:34–49; for polar thought patterns see Loader, 1979). Most obviously, there is a superscription (1:1), a kind of introduction (1:2-11), and an epilogue (12:9-14). A closer look has revealed a number of definite literary forms and patterns of expression, especially numerical patterns and the repetition of interpretive phrases (Wright, 1968, 1980; contra Fox, 1989:155–62). Since the major portion of the book is a first-person account, the third-person form of the superscription and the epilogue suggests editing by another hand. The phrase "Vanity of vanities; all things are vanity!" 1:2; 12:8) forms an *inclusio*, which rings the body of the book, a further example of its literary unity.

In addition to the lack of obvious literary structure, the book is fraught with internal contradictions. In an attempt to reconcile these contradictions, various interpretive approaches have been suggested (cf. Fox, 1989:19–28). Harmonization, the traditional approach, maintains that statements conflict because the same words are used in different ways or treat different matters. When this method fails to answer all questions, the inconsistencies are explained as additions to the text. Another theory suggests that Qoheleth first states an adage from traditional wisdom and then refutes it with another proverb (Gordis, 1968:95–108). No method of explanation is totally successful, and none has been universally adopted.

The Book
The Preacher

The very first verses of the first chapter (vv. 1, 12) describe but do not identify the speaker of the book. As mentioned earlier, the Hebrew title of the book and the name of the protagonist is *Qoheleth*, the one who presides over the *qahal* or assembly. The Greek rendition of the word is *Ekklēsiastēs,* an official of the *ekklēsía* or assembly. The speaker is further identified as the son of David, king of Israel. No doubt the reference is to Solomon, the one esteemed in popular devotion as the wise man par excellence. There is a tradition that Solomon was not only versed in human wisdom (1 Kgs 3:16-28) but had encyclopedic knowledge as well (1 Kgs 4:29-34). Actually, most ancient Near Eastern societies held that the monarch possessed extraordinary and even superhuman wisdom bestowed by the gods. Such royal pretensions were ascribed to Solomon, and he was thus credited with exceptional human insight and divinely allotted wisdom.

The biblical tradition states that this extraordinary wisdom was a reward for Solomon's devotion to God. Since the theory of retribution claims that wealth and prosperity are bestowed in proportion to one's righteousness, the affluence identified with royalty was frequently regarded as the fruit of unflinching fidelity. Thus the king was not only wealthy and wise but considered upstanding as well. When Qoheleth assumed this royal identity and ascribed to himself all of its advantages, he was establishing himself as one whose insights into life had undisputed credibility regardless of how unconventional they might be at times.

The Hebrew word *Qoheleth* is itself a feminine participial form of the verb. This has led some interpreters to wonder further about the identity of this teacher. Given this feminine form, the indication that this is clearly not the historical Solomon, as well as the literary evidence that elsewhere (Prov 8) the figure of Woman Wisdom both enjoys access to public life and gathers the simple into her house to impart her teaching (Prov 9), feminist interest in the identity of the preacher is understandable. However, the fact that the principal characterization is male cannot be denied (for characterization of women, see Brenner, 1993:201–3).

Qoheleth represents himself as a wise king who surpassed those who preceded him in Jerusalem (1:16). Still, he was not satisfied with what life had provided him, and so he set out to discover the depths and the breadth of all human endeavors. Possessing the necessary wisdom, wealth, power, and freedom, he was better equipped than most to embark on this quest. Using the insight he had already gained, he resolved to know wisdom by experiencing its opposite, folly. He tested the extent to which pleasure or success could give ultimate satisfaction. In all of this searching, he was disappointed (2:1-2; 11).

He then turned his attention to the search for wisdom itself. Despite the advantage that wisdom and the wise may claim to have over folly and the foolish, this advantage is only temporary and even questionable. In fact, he discovered that the fool who disregards the conventions of life may have an edge over the person who conforms at the cost of enjoyment. At this point in his observations, the specter of death appears for the first time. Since everyone faces the same destiny, the wise appear to have no advantage in this regard. This realization unsettled the seemingly impersonal Qoheleth and he cried out against life itself (2:17).

The Vanity of Life

The book of Ecclesiastes may be unfamiliar to many people, but one of its most frequently used phrases, "Vanity of vanities; all is vanity!" is well known throughout the world. Qoheleth's teaching begins (1:2) and ends (12:8) on this note. The basic meaning of the Hebrew word *hebel* (vanity) is "wind" or "breath," and it denotes something that is ephemeral, fleeting, quickly fading. The wind is, by its nature, ephemeral or fleeting, but when the word is used to describe something that should be enduring, constant, or firm, it signifies disparity between what is expected and what really is. The word then takes on the connotation of futility (Hubbard, 1976) or absurdity (Fox, 1989:29–51). It seems that in his probing of "all that is done

under heaven" (1:13), what Qoheleth presumed would be enduring, constant, or firm turned out to be ephemeral, fleeting, quickly fading. His
expectations proved to be absurd, like "a chasing after wind" (1:14).

"What profit can be gained from all the toil done under the sun?"
(1:3).This disconcerting question is really a challenge to the experiences of
life, indeed, to life itself. The very first reported words of Qoheleth have
already declared that "all things are vanity." Therefore, the answer to this
question should be obvious: "What profit can be gained?" None! Lest this be
understood as a specious claim of a petulant cynic, Qoheleth gives evidence
to support the assertion. First, he claims to "have seen all things that are
done under the sun, and behold, all is vanity and a chase after the wind,"
and then, in more detail, he recounts his observations.

Represented as king (1:1, 12), Qoheleth would have had the means and
the time to launch the kind of investigation that he described. In his pursuit
of pleasure, he denied himself nothing, quenching his thirst for aesthetic
beauty and skill, for sexual and other physical delight, for possessions and
power (2:1-9). He found pleasure in his toil (v. 10) but no profit, and he saw
this as "vanity and chasing after wind" (v. 11).

The pursuit of wisdom did not provide him with any greater sense of success. While wisdom is certainly more desirable than folly, the wise are subject
to death and oblivion just as the fools are (2:12-16). To expect otherwise is
"vanity and a chasing after wind" (vv. 14, 17). Not only must one die, but that
for which one toiled is left to another, and there is no guarantee that this other
will appreciate the fruits, much less the toil (vv. 18-21). This too is vanity (vv.
19, 21). Qoheleth maintains that all the energy put into toil is to no avail. It is
all vanity (v.23). All one can do is enjoy the simple pleasures that life has to
offer as they come along (vv. 24-26). These observations end with the sobering assessment: "This also is vanity and a chasing after wind" (v. 26).

Qoheleth declares that there is a definite order in nature (1:4-7) as well as
in the events of human life (3:1-15). This order, which appears to be fixed
(1:14; 3:15), is the object of the human search for fulfillment yet beyond
human comprehension (3:11). Qoheleth concludes that this disparity
should bring human beings to see that, in this, they are no better than animals, which are also subject to unfathomable natural laws, particularly the
laws of life and of death (3:18-21). To think otherwise is vanity (v. 19).

Social conventions were not spared his critique (4:4-12). The solitary life
and life in community each has its drawbacks. On the one hand, to toil
relentlessly and have no one with whom to share the fruits of such toil is
vanity (v. 8). On the other hand, sometimes our feverish labor springs from
envy of and competition with others. This too is vanity (v. 4). Finally, there
is no permanence in leadership either. The most unlikely frequently take the

reins for a time and then lose the esteem of the governed. "Surely this also is vanity" (v. 16).

Covetousness and greed are not only forms of vanity in themselves (5:10, 12); but they also eat away at the fabric of society. They frequently breed injustice or are the basis of personal financial ruin and the subsequent impoverishment of one's descendants (vv. 11-17). For any number of reasons, wealth itself does not ensure happiness (6:1-6). Some of the rich cannot delight in bequeathing their prosperity to their own offspring. Instead, a stranger acquires it (vv. 1-2). Certainly this is vanity (v. 2). Even those of the rich who have children do not always enjoy life. Finally, human desire itself is insatiable. This acknowledgment brings Qoheleth to his characteristic conclusion: "This also is vanity and a chasing after the wind" (v. 9).

Qoheleth was troubled over many things in life. One was the advantage that the wicked who prosper seem to have over the righteous who do not (4:1; 7:15; 8:10-14). Society does not seem to operate according to laws of equity, and this he saw as vanity (vv. 10, 14). He was also concerned that all enjoy to the full the life that they do have, for death will come to everyone and will put an end to all enjoyment. Neither pleasure nor youth nor the energy normally associated with youth is lasting. Everything is vanity (11:8, 10).

Advice for Wise Living

Besides assessing what his observations had uncovered about the value in or futility of life, Qoheleth also offers advice for living. Identified with and having identified himself with the Solomonic tradition of wisdom (1:1, 12), his advice enjoys the authority of that tradition even where, or perhaps especially where, it may appear to be unconventional.

Qoheleth declares that all of life unfolds "under the sun." The phrase, which is found nowhere else in the Bible, appears thirty-five times in this short book (a variant, "under heaven," is found in 1:13; 2:3; 3:1). This phrase is generally taken to mean "everywhere on earth," emphasizing the universal sweep of what is being discussed. It also has a cosmological dimension, attesting that this universal sweep is not determined by the earth but by the sun.

Qoheleth's consciousness of the natural world can be seen throughout the book. He uses examples from nature to make his points, a familiar technique of the wisdom teacher (2:13; 10:8-11, 20; 11:3f.). Nature imagery figures in his description of old age (12:2-6) and his references to death (3:19-21; 12:7). The metaphor "chasing the wind" (1:14, 17: 2:11,17,26; 4:4, 6, 16; 6:9) is not only remarkably creative in its characterization of futile pursuit but it reveals a keen observation of the elusiveness of this natural phenomenon.

The ordinariness in and the regularity of the natural world, used in early wisdom books to encourage social harmony (cf. Prov 30:15-33), are characterized here as monotonous and devoid of any kind of progress (cf. Crenshaw, 1984:80–84). The earth follows the same seasons, the sun the same cycles, the wind the same currents, and the rivers and streams empty into an insatiable sea. Like nature, human striving after gain is nothing but wearisome labor that must be repeated and repeated with neither promise of conclusion nor assurance of satisfaction (1:1-8).

Qoheleth was well aware of the expansiveness of and patterns within nature, but he did not see any advancement realized from its activity nor profit accrued to human beings.

In one of the rare instances in the wisdom literature where attention is given to religious observance, Qoheleth discusses the custom of making vows (5:1-6; cf. Deut 23:21-23). He does not really promote practices of piety as much as faithfulness to one's word. He warns against the tendency of multiplying words at prayer. Many people believe that "more is better," a principle that Qoheleth regularly refutes. The messenger referred to (v. 6) may be a temple official who has come to collect the promised monetary or material payment. To fail to meet this payment is to risk divine punishment. Qoheleth insists: do what you have said you are going to do; carry out your responsibilities. He ends his counsel with the classic exhortation of the wisdom tradition: "Fear God!" (cf. 12:13).

In one place, Qoheleth seems to foster a compromise of principles (7:16-18). Can one be too righteous? Perhaps these curious admonitions flow from a realization that happiness cannot be assured by any particular form of behavior. Qoheleth is probably suggesting that it is far better to live a balanced life than to pursue anything to excess, even virtue.

Qoheleth may question the meaningfulness of much of life, but he is not an iconoclast. He does not promote the overthrow of social or political structures. If anything, he is troubled when they do not seem to function as he expects they should. In line with this, he advocates adherence to social practice and respect toward and obedience to legitimate rulers (8:2-5; 10:4-9). He further counsels perspicacity and diligence in work (11:6), the enjoyment of youth as long as it lasts (11:9), but with mindfulness of the creator (12:1; contra Crenshaw, 1987:184f.).

Like all wisdom teachers, Qoheleth instructs indirectly through the use of proverbs. In some instances he uses them to illustrate a point that he is making. Examples of this include: human beings are unable to change what God has established (1:15, 18); wisdom is to light what folly is to darkness (2:14); toil accomplishes nothing permanent (4:5f.); speech should be discreet (5:2, 6; for a treatment on "proverb performance" see Fontaine, 1982).

More frequently the proverbs are together in collections: examples of the relative worth of things (7:1-14); distinctions between wisdom and folly (9:17—10:4; 10:8—11:5).

In six different places throughout the book, Qoheleth exhorts his hearers (or readers) to savor the simple pleasures of eating and drinking and to take whatever enjoyment they can in their toil (2:24-26; 3:12f., 22; 5:17; 8:15; 9:7-9). This is not encouragement to launch into a hedonistic life but sage teaching that maintains that people should find satisfaction in living life itself and not merely in the profit that one might derive from certain life activities (Collins, 1980:73f.). The pleasure that accompanies human activity is part of the natural order and comes from the hand of God, and so it should be relished (Collins, 1980:90).

The Lot of All

Perhaps the issue that troubled Qoheleth the most was the apparent indifference of death in the face of good or evil. Death cancels all personal accomplishments, thereby obliterating anything that might distinguish the fruits of virtue from the wages of wickedness. Not only are the righteous thereby deprived of the rewards of their labor but their righteousness appears to be to no avail. Human beings are all powerless in the face of death (6:6, 12; 8:8; 9:2f.).

In his search for wisdom, Qoheleth concedes that eventually he will face the same fate as does the fool, and so he wonders: "Why then have I been so wise?" (2:15). His commitment to upright living might have value if his integrity will be remembered after his death. But he probes further and has to confess that this will not be the case. The wise and the fools all die, and they are also all forgotten. This certainly is "vanity and a chasing after wind" (vv. 16f.).

Qoheleth believes that there is a time and place for everything (3:1-8). Human beings cannot adequately grasp this order, however. Qoheleth wonders why God has planted the desire to know in the human heart, yet has kept the realization of this desire out of human reach (v.11). This is true of divine retribution as well. Although he asserts that God will in fact pass judgment (v.17.), he does not believe that human beings will always witness it. This he decides, is God's way of testing them in order to show that they are little more than animals. Having claimed that death strips humans of all that might set the righteous apart from the wicked, he implies that they have no advantage over animals, because all die and there is no evidence that after death one is privileged over the other (vv. 19-21).

Qoheleth does not suggest that *death* is vain. Rather, its universal and indiscriminate nature casts doubt on the meaningfulness of *life*. In light of this, he declares that the dead who no longer have to contend with life's inequities have an advantage over the living who do. Better off than both are the unborn, who know nothing of life's struggle (4:2f.; also stillborn, 6:3). At times, he seems to prefer death over life (7:1-4). At other times, however, he quite clearly prefers life under any conditions. He insists that the living, even though they know that they will someday die, still have hope, while the dead have nothing (9:4-6, 10). Qoheleth may have been quite harsh in his assessment of the meaningfulness of life, but he did not totally reject it. In fact, as has been seen, he encouraged its enjoyment (2:24f.; 3:12f., 22; 5:18; 8:15).

The Editor

The last six verses of the book (12:9-14) suggest an addition from another teacher, one intent on having the instructions of Qoheleth accepted as genuine wisdom (cf. Sheppard, 1980:121–29). There is ample literary evidence to support this opinion. Most obvious is the form of the pronouns used. Qoheleth speaks in the first person, while the writer here, and also in the first verses of the book, uses the third person. A disciple of Qoheleth or an adherent of his teaching may have collected some of his insights, adding this epilogue, which is neither a supplement to nor a correction of the basic teaching of the book. Rather, it testifies to Qoheleth's legitimacy as a purveyor of wisdom, thus indirectly validating the teaching itself.

The epilogue designates Qoheleth as a wise man. Not content with learning wisdom himself, he taught it, critiqued it, and organized it. He is further recognized for his literary skills and his trustworthiness. This appraisal gives approbation to the teaching found in the book, even though it frequently challenged the customary wisdom point of view. Perhaps the editor felt it necessary to include such accolades, lest Qoheleth's insights and conclusions be disavowed. Still, if "the sayings of the wise are like goads," then Qoheleth qualifies as a sage. He not only offered guidance for behavior but he urged his hearers (or readers) to confront life as it really is and to come face to face with its mysteries.

Some commentators believe that verses 12-14 constitute a second epilogue, because of their rather critical opinion of books such as Qoheleth's and because of what appears to be the traditional expression of retribution with which the book ends. If this is indeed a second addition, it may demonstrate how yet another editor felt obliged to temper Qoheleth's teaching in order to preserve it. Addressing the reader in the classical wisdom manner, "my son" (cf. Prov 1:8, 10, 15; 2:1; 3:1, 11, 21; 4:10, 20; 5:1; 6:1, 3, 20; 7:1; 19:27: 23:15, 19, 26; 24:13, 21; 27:11), the editor warns against adding to the speculative kind of teaching found in this particular book.

A close look at the concluding verse will show that the final statement need not be read as a reiteration of the theory of retribution (contra Crenshaw, 1987:192). While it does maintain that "God will bring everything into judgment, including all that is secret, what is good and what is evil," it does not assure the reader that the judgment will follow the principles of retribution. Most commentators presume that this is implied. Qoheleth would not, however. At the heart of his critique is the realization that ultimate justice is indeed in the hands of God, but human beings cannot be sure that or how it will be enacted, because it is beyond human comprehension. The final statement counsels: fear God and keep the commandments; everything else is out of your hands and in God's.

Rhetorical Function

The musings, opinions, and advice of Qoheleth issue from a worldview firmly grounded in the theory of divine retribution, that is, God will reward righteousness and punish wickedness. This theory is based on two fundamental assumptions: (1) that the world and its functions are grounded in and directed by moral not merely physical laws; (2) that these laws are contingent on human behavior. Though considered *divine* retribution, this is essentially an anthropocentric perspective, since the character of human behavior governs the character of God's involvement in human affairs.

Although Qoheleth does subscribe to this theory, his experience of life prompts him to question its applicability. He clearly maintains that, just as God fashioned an orderly universe, directing its movements according to established rhythms and patterns (1:5-7), so God designed human life, appointing a time for everything under heaven (3:1-8). His observations of the way life actually unfolds suggest, however, that human beings are bound by an order that they cannot fathom and over which they have no control (3:11). The disparity between the theory of retribution and the realities of life is the source of his frustration and resulting skepticism.

It may be true that people generally want to know, to understand, even to control the world. But only people with a certain degree of self-direction or personal authority presume that they in fact can. Those who lack autonomy have no illusions about their ability or opportunity to determine the course of events. They might hope for a world of order founded on integrity, but they know that too often something or someone beyond their control is in charge. The assumptive world of the book of Qoheleth seems to correspond to people who normally exercise some kind of control over the circumstances of life.

Qoheleth's experiences and observations challenge the accuracy of this assumptive world. For this reason, the counsel that he gives frequently sounds unsettling, even bleak. He insists that his hearers (or readers) must face the facts about life. There are no guarantees for either the wise or the fool; all must face life's ambiguity and, ultimately, all must die. Furthermore, even when life does unfold as expected, it does not yield fruits that endure. No group within society has an advantage over another. Qoheleth clearly deplores this fact of life, thus laying bare his own bias. Still, his censure can alter nothing. He realizes that he must live with what he cannot change, and he sets out to teach this lesson to others as well (cf. Scott, 1965:204–7).

The ones in need of learning this lesson are either those who share Qoheleth's worldview and presume a definite correlation between behavior and the circumstances of life, or those whose experience corresponds to his and who have the opportunity to exercise some control over their situations. Like Qoheleth, they must be brought to acknowledge the limitations of human comprehension and the extent of human dependence on structures and systems beyond their control.

The book can also speak to those who are impoverished or deprived of self-determination. If they share the assumptive worldview of Qoheleth, they might judge their deprivation either as the consequence of sinful or foolish living or as testimony to God's unreliability. They too can benefit from Qoheleth's skepticism, though to a different end. The difficult circumstances of their lives have already taught them to accept the fact of life's ambiguity and to live with what cannot be changed. Now they must be brought to see that this lesson, which they have already learned, does in fact contain true wisdom. They too must relinquish any insistence on rigid application of the theory of retribution.

Finally, Qoheleth may have lost hope in the possibility of securing some kind of advantage from his undertakings, but he does not despair of life itself. His admonition to enjoy life's simple pleasures as they come rather than neglect them in the hope of gaining some kind of profit from toil is advice that can be heeded by all, regardless of class or social standing.

Unmasking the Powers

A liberationist reading of Qoheleth, attentive to questions of race or ethnic origin, class, and gender, reveals some of the presuppositions underlying the message of the book. Very little if anything betrays a racial or ethnic bias. Although both Qoheleth (1:12, 16; 2:7, 9) and the editor (1:1) make references to Jerusalem, they allude to the Davidic house that ruled in that city and not to any predilection in favor of the racial or ethnic identity of the city itself. Still, these references are not completely devoid of bias. As the city of the son of David (presumably Solomon), it is the center of royal wealth and wisdom. It is included in the pseudoidentification of Qoheleth in order to confer legitimacy on his teaching. The bias here is one of class. Jerusalem is privileged because it is the city of the ruling circle.

Class bias can be seen in other places in the book as well. Qoheleth describes himself as surpassing everyone in wealth (2:4-10). He even possessed slaves (v. 7). His observations and evaluations are from the particular perspective of wealth and power. His class consciousness cannot be easily masked. Being a man of integrity, he disapproves of crediting royal might with saving a city when the feat was really accomplished through the wisdom of a poor man (9:14-16). Yet, he is upset when members of the lower class assume the standing of the privileged (10:7, 16). He counsels compliance with royal bidding, not merely because the king exercises authority and obedience is his due (8:2-4) but as a safeguard against royal requital (10:20) or capriciousness (10:4). Still, he does not question the legitimacy of royal rule. Although he does value wisdom more highly than he values money, the distinction between them is not always sharp (7:11f.).

An adherent to the theory of retribution, Qoheleth believes that the prosperous should be allowed to enjoy the wealth that they can amass (2:18; 6:2). Despite his obvious class bias, he is still concerned that the less fortunate be able to enjoy life and not be victimized (4:1; 5:8; 6:8). This concern leads him to question not the social structures but the faithfulness of people within these structures. He observes that life does not always follow the path envisioned by retribution, but he certainly would have preferred that it did.

Another pervasive bias pertains to the question of gender. The search for meaning in life is done from an exclusively androcentric point of view. Not only is the protagonist a man (a king, 1:1, 12), but the one to whom the instruction is given is addressed as "my son" (12:12). Qoheleth considers dimensions of life that are customarily associated with men in a patriarchal society. In such a society the major events of men's lives take place in the public rather than the private domain, in the workplace, in the marketplace, at court. He discusses the struggles, joys, and sorrows of men (*'ādām* [1:3; 2:12, 24; 3:22; 6:1, 7, 10, 11, 12; 7:2, 20, 29; 8:1, 6, 8, 9, 15, 17; 9:1, 12; 10:14; 11:8; 12:5, 13]; *'iš* [1:8; 2:12; 6:2, 3; 7:5; 9:15]; *'ĕnôš* [9:14; 12:3]), of the sons of men (1:13; 2:3; 3:10, 18, 19, 21; 8:11; 9:3, 12), and of young men (*baḥûr* [11:9]; *yeled* [4:13, 15]), but not those of women or girls. Royal allusions are to kings and princes (2:8, 12; 4:13; 8:2-4; 9:14; 10:4f.) but not to queens; the solitary (4:8) is one who has no son or brother. Women are equally paired with men only in the reference to slaves (2:7f.), and the wife is mentioned in the exhortation, directed to the man, to enjoy the simple pleasures that are at hand (9:9). There are two passages wherein female imagery appears in a positive fashion. One uses the mystery of gestation to illustrate the mysterious workings of creation (11:5). In the other, daughter appears as a metaphor for the songbird (12:4).

Even more distorted than the general disregard for the presence of women, their participation in society, and their concerns in life is the way Qoheleth characterizes them when he does refer to them. He states that the woman who is like a trap, whose heart is snares and nets, and whose hands seem to shackle a man is more bitter than death (7:26). Although this harsh statement does not appear to be a judgment on all women, what follows shows that he does not have high regard for any women (vv. 27f.). From beginning to end, Qoheleth's perspective is quite biased and judgmental.

Into the Looking Glass

Once the liberationist critique of the book is complete, attention can be given to its new revelatory possibilities. The message that it furnishes can act as a mirror into which the reader can gaze, as well as a doorway through which a new world can be entered. Interestingly, the very skepticism that has caused some to question the religious merit of this book may in fact be the best key for opening it to contemporary interpretations.

First and fundamentally, Qoheleth questions the legitimacy and value of an anthropocentric understanding of the theory of retribution. While some may presume that human beings can and should be able to discern the patterns within the mysterious workings of the world, he has come to realize that this is impossible and that it is "vanity" to expect otherwise. He never really doubts the existence of order. On the contrary, he perceives order in the patterns and regularity of nature (1:5-7) and maintains that there is also a proper time for everything pertaining to the events that constitute human life (3:1-8). He does not believe that human beings will ever be able to comprehend, much less exploit, this order. He argues that the meaning and control of all things are found in God and in God alone (v. 11). This is the basic new insight from which flow all of Qoheleth's exhortations.

Appropriating this pivotal insight would oblige us to reevaluate how we perceive the relationships between the cosmic order, the social order, and the moral order. It should deter us from forcing the meaning of our lives into inadequate systems of interpretation and from employing these systems to pass precipitous judgment on the circumstances of the lives of others. We cannot be certain about the appointed times for ourselves, and we are certainly less equipped to assess someone else's life.

Skepticism about the presence of a reliable and discernible order can affect our analysis of societal structures. Like others who interpret prosperity and power as the consequence of wise or righteous living, Qoheleth exhibits very little sympathy for the disadvantaged and even less interest in changing the social structures that may have disadvantaged them. In fact, he is disturbed by what he regarded as irregularity in social propriety: the poor were in places that were normally allotted to the rich, and the rich were in situations usually relegated to the poor (10:6, 16). Had he been able to free himself of his class biases, Qoheleth might not have been so quick to place blame for misfortune in the way that he did. Instead, he might have thought that while we have the desire to grasp the meaning of life's twists and turns, comprehension is beyond us and, therefore, so is judgment. Questioning the applicability of retribution casts a shadow of doubt on the reliability of its implications. Qoheleth may not have been able to revise his thinking in this way, but contemporary readers certainly can.

The revelatory possibilities of this book are not quite as easy to discover in the area of gender. As it stands, there is nothing here about women or what is associated with women that can be interpreted in a way that enhances their dignity or intrinsic worth. Qoheleth's basic insight, that the order established by God does not conform to human standards, can, however, be directed toward his gender bias, both challenging it and moving beyond it. In other words, his gender bias can be seen as one of those human standards that falls short of the order established by God.

A second theme that lends itself to feminist reinterpretation is the notion of the universal breadth intended by the oft-repeated phrase "under the sun." It embraces everything and everyone. Although Qoheleth uses the phrase in criticism of shortsighted human aspirations, the phrase itself bespeaks comprehensiveness. It includes women and the concerns of women. These two concepts, the finite character of human standards and the all-encompassing scope suggested by the phrase "under the sun," yield a vision of inclusivity that can shatter all prejudicial social customs and structures, whether they are related to race or ethnic origin, class, or gender. Qoheleth may have been a chauvinist, but the message of this book need not add support to chauvinistic proclivities.

The Gift of God

It is fitting that Qoheleth be associated with the phrase that begins and ends his teaching: "Vanity of vanities! All is vanity!" (1:2; 12:8). However, the significance of his message will only be grasped satisfactorily if we understand exactly what it is that he considers vain. He does not maintain that it is vanity to toil, for he exhorts his hearers (readers) to take pleasure in their toil. He does argue that it is vain to toil for the sake of some kind of profit, for there is nothing to be gained beyond the toil itself except the immediate pleasure that it engenders (1:3; 2:11; 3:9; 5:15).

In several places throughout his instructions, Qoheleth declares that there is nothing better to do than eat, drink, and enjoy what is within one's reach (2:24; 3:13; 5:18; 8:15; 9:9). He is not promoting forbidden pleasure for, in each instance, he declares that this enjoyment comes from God. Such admonition should not be confused with the hedonistic saying that bids us to "eat, drink and be merry, for tomorrow you die." Despite the great similarity in the two statements, they signify very different directives. Within the context of hedonism, a doctrine built on the premise that pleasure is the highest good and should be the ultimate end of all our actions, the statement promotes the immediate pursuit of pleasure. There is an urgency to this pursuit, for death is imminent and will put an end to all enjoyment. Therefore, self-indulgence is encouraged.

Qoheleth proposes a notably different perspective and subsequent manner of behavior. He addresses his teaching to those who appear to judge the value of an undertaking according to the tangible even measurable effect that it can produce. He too realizes the inevitability of death, but he focuses on the fact that it disregards social and economic distinctions, stripping everyone of what they held so dear in life. Qoheleth would have us gratefully savor pleasure, not feverishly pursue it.

Qoheleth does not disparage human ingenuity and the myriad of enterprises that spring from it. He directs his disdain toward judging the worth of human endeavor in terms of the amount of output rather than the quality of input. He is able to discern the very thin line that exists between training all of one's energies toward the accomplishment of a worthy goal and sacrificing everything for the sake of success. He brings this insight to his critique of the accumulation of wealth, the ascent up the ladder of prominence and power, the pursuit of acceptability in prestigious social circles, the search for wisdom and the reputation that it affords.

Qoheleth is not insensitive to the disappointments and tragedies of life, but he does realize that many things are beyond human power to control and they must be accepted as part of life. While it is true that this kind of thinking has been used to hinder social change, within its own context it is a message of profound religious significance. Life and the things of life are in God's hands, and we must learn to accept and enjoy whatever is within our reach.

At the heart of Qoheleth's message is a profound appreciation of the fact that life is primarily for living and every human endeavor, regardless of its own intrinsic value, holds a secondary place. All toil, all progress, all organization have merit to the extent that they promote and enhance living. This is a religious message for Qoheleth, who maintains that the creator has implanted the capacity for happiness in each and every human heart, has made living an exciting venture, and wills that every person be afforded the opportunity to find pleasure in living (Bergant, 1982:291–94). Anything else would be "a chase after the wind"!

Works Consulted

Bergant, Dianne. 1982. *Job, Ecclesiastes.* Old Testament Message. Wilmington, Del.: Michael Glazier.

Brenner, Athalya. 1993. "Some Observations on the Figuration of Woman in Wisdom Literature." In *Of Prophets' Visions and the Wisdom of Sages: Essays in Honor of R. Norman Whybray on His Seventieth Birthday.* Edited by Heather A. McKay and David J. A. Clines. Journal for the Study of the Old Testament Supplement Series 162. Sheffield: JSOT Press.

Collins, John J. 1980. *Proverbs, Ecclesiastes.* Knox Preaching Guides. Atlanta: John Knox Press.

Crenshaw, James L. 1984. *A Whirlpool of Torment.* Overtures to Biblical Theology. Philadelphia: Fortress Press.

——————. 1987. *Ecclesiastes: A Commentary.* The Old Testament Library. Philadelphia: Westminster Press.

Fontaine, Carole R. 1982. *Traditional Sayings in the Old Testament.* Sheffield: Almond Press.

Fox, Michael V. 1989. *Qoheleth and His Contradictions.* Sheffield: Almond Press.

——————. 1993. "Wisdom in Qoheleth." In *In Search of Wisdom: Essays in Honor of John G. Gammie.* Edited by Leo G. Perdue et al. Louisville, Ky.: Westminster/John Knox Press.

Gordis, Robert. 1968. *Koheleth—The Man and His World: A Study of Ecclesiastes.* 3d ed. New York: Schocken Books.

Hubbard, David Allan. 1976. *Beyond Futility: Messages of Hope from the Book of Ecclesiastes.* Grand Rapids: Eerdmans.

Humphreys, W. Lee. 1985. *The Tragic Vision and the Hebrew Tradition.* Overtures to Biblical Theology. Philadelphia: Fortress Press.

Loader, J. A. 1979. *Polar Structures in the Book of Qoheleth.* Beihefte zur Zeitschrift für die alttestamentliche Wissenschaft 152. Berlin: Walter de Gruyter.

Murphy, Roland E. 1981. *Wisdom Literature.* Grand Rapids: Eerdmans.

——————. 1990a. "The Sage in Ecclesiastes and Qoheleth the Sage." In *The Sage in Israel and the Ancient Near East.* Edited by John G. Gammie and Leo G. Perdue.

_____. 1990b. *The Tree of Life: An Exploration of Biblical Wisdom Literature*. The Anchor Bible Reference Library. New York: Doubleday.

Perdue, Leo G. 1994. *Wisdom and Creation: The Theology of Wisdom Literature*. Nashville: Abingdon Press.

Scott, R. B. Y. 1965. *Proverbs, Ecclesiastes*. The Anchor Bible. Garden City, N.Y.: Doubleday.

Sheppard Gerald T. 1980. *Wisdom as a Hermeneutical Construct*. Beihefte zur Zeitschrift für die alttestamentliche Wissenschaft 151. Berlin: Walter de Gruyter.

Whybray, R. N. 1989. *Ecclesiastes*. New Century Bible Commentary. Grand Rapids: Eerdmans.

Wright, Addison G. 1968. "The Riddle of the Sphinx: The Structure of the Book of Qoheleth." *Catholic Biblical Quarterly* 30:313–34.

_____. 1980. "The Riddle of the Sphinx Revisited: Numerical Patterns in the Book of Qoheleth." *Catholic Biblical Quarterly* 42:38–51.

6

Song of Songs

Introduction

> All the world is not worth the day that the
> Song of Songs was given to Israel; all the
> *Kĕtûbîm* [writings] are holy but the Song of Songs is
> the holy of holies. (Mishna Yadaim, 3:5)

TWO NOTABLE STUDIES OF THE SONG OF SONGS (Exum, 1973:47; Gordis, 1974:1) begin with this rabbinic quote, which both represents the reverence in which its advocates have held the book and, for the sake of its skeptics, justifies its inclusion in the canon of Sacred Scripture. The book itself has generated considerable controversy regarding its literary integrity, its genre, its structure, and its interpretation. Some scholars contend that it is really an anthology of discrete poems (Landsberger, 1954). Today, most believe that the eight chapters should be interpreted as a unit, albeit one composed of several different poems. Neither opinion adequately addresses all of the questions about the book's composition, yet some view must be cautiously espoused if one is to engage in critical analysis of the entire received text. For the sake of such analysis, this study presumes some form of literary unity that was present prior to any kind of final canonical editing.

Although there is general agreement about the erotic nature of this lyric poetry, the overall literary character of the book influences the way this erotic poetry is to be understood. The Song has been interpreted in basically four ways: allegorically (Robert, 1963); as a cultic reenactment (Pope, 1977); as a dramatic performance (Pouget and Guitton, 1948); and as a collection of love poems (Murphy, 1990). Each of these interpretive approaches reveals different facets of the literary quality of the book and opens up possibilities for understanding its message.

The book does in fact contain certain features that lend themselves to one or another of these approaches. For example, the marriage metaphor used to characterize first the love relationship between YHWH and Israel (Isa 54:5; Hos 2:14-20) and later Christ and the church (2 Cor 11:2; Rev 19:6b-8) provided a precedent for an allegorical interpretation of the Song. Instances in this book of parallels with the vocabulary and themes of ancient fertility rituals persuaded others, however to look for literary origins in the sacred marriage rites of Damuzi/Inanna (Hebrew Tammuz/Ishtar). Still others saw the absence of a narrator and the inclusion of what seem to be refrains and choruses as evidence that this is really the script for a drama. Finally, the similarity between these poems and some Egyptian love poems led many to conclude that the Song of Songs was made up of lyric love poems, some of which, quite similar to the style of the Arabian *wasf*, recount the physical charms of the loved one while others describe erotic longing.

This ambiguity in explanation has led some interpreters to maintain that any supposed structure that is advanced is really brought to the book by the commentator rather than found within the text itself. Interestingly although the first and preferred method of interpretation of most of the Bible traditionally has been the literal approach, the opposite has been true with regard to this book. It seems that much of the sexual imagery has been either so explicit or so suggestive as to offend the sensitivities of many of the faithful. This point and the fact that there is no mention of God in the entire book have brought some to believe that the poems originally were secular love songs. Therefore, until recently, most commentators presumed that the poems were not to be understood literally but must have some concealed religious meaning. (A comprehensive treatment of the history of the Song's interpretation is found in Pope, 1977:89–229.)

There is even more variance in determining the structure of the book. Divergences regarding the decisive criteria have yielded various literary designs and enumerations of the poems. The number has ranged from twelve to fifty-two, the median being about thirty (Elliot, 1989:20). While the composition of the book is not the principal concern of this study, a decision regarding its literary structure is the first step in any serious analysis. The critical reading adopted here will be facilitated by the following division: 1:1; 1:2—2:7; 2:8—3:5; 3:6—5:1; 5:2—6:3; 6:4—8:4; 8:5—14.

The Book

The Song of Solomon

The superscription (1:1) performs several significant functions. It identifies the book's genre as a song. The singular form of "song" indicates that in the final analysis the book does indeed possess literary integrity. Literally, the superscription reads: "The Song of Songs, which is Solomon's." The Hebrew construction of the superscription lends itself to two different meanings. Either this song comes from the mouth of Solomon, or it in some way belongs to him. Since, as will be seen in what follows, the poems relate the woman's perspective not the man's, the phrase must be understood in the latter sense. Thus, the superscription indicates that the book is somehow Solomonic. Most likely it accords authoritative Solomonic legitimation to the message of the book.

The Hebrew form of *šîr haššîrîm* ("Song of Songs") suggests that the phrase is less the title of the book than it is a superlative construct intended to set this song apart from all other songs. Given the apparent uneasiness of many commentators concerning its interpretation, it is unlikely that the superlative character of the book stems from its erotic content. It was probably considered exceptional because it is attributed to Solomon. This explanation just begs the question, however. Why would a collection of love lyrics be accorded Solomonic legitimation? Was this the only way for it to garner official approval? And did the tradition about Solomon's wives and concubines (1 Kgs 11:3) invite such a link? But why include it in the first place? Answers to these questions abound. However one explains these historical issues, the love poems now enjoy not only canonical status but also Solomonic legitimation. This means that their message is considered authoritative.

The first unit (1:2—2:7) consists of a lyric speech by the woman (vv. 2-7) and a series of poems wherein the couple proclaim their mutual admiration (1:8—2:7). The shift between second and third person (1:2), a poetic device known as *enallage*, is less confusing than is any attempt to determine with certainty the identity of the voice at each point in the unit (for example, who is speaking in 1:8, the man or the daughters?). The closing refrain (2:6f.) includes a solemn adjuration directed to the daughters of Jerusalem. The second unit (2:8—3:5) ends with the identical adjuration (3:5). Here the woman's lyric includes a poetic reminiscence of an encounter with the man (2:10-14). The third unit (3:6—5:1) begins with a segment that is clearly independent but difficult to ascribe with certainty to a particular voice (3:6-11). This is followed by a *wasf*, a tribute to the beauty of her body (4:1-7), and an admiration poem (4:8—5:1), both from the man. The fourth unit (5:2–6:3) consists of narrative and dialogue. The woman relates an encounter with the man (5:2-7) and then praises his charms, employing the *wasf* (5:10-16) and some garden imagery (6:2-3). The fifth unit (6:4—8:4) consists of several different genres ascribed to the male voice (6:4—7:10a[9a]) and an amorous reply of the woman which closes with an adjuration (7:10b[9b]—8:4). If any part of the Song can be called a collection of disparate poems, it is the final unit (8:5-14). It has no continuity from one part to the next, nor is the specific voice always identifiable. The high point of the Song is found in vv. 6-7. The book itself ends on such a strange note that some believe the real ending has been lost.

Form critical study has provided genre classification that can assist in understanding this rather complex literary creation. The material can be identified as: poems of yearning (1:2-4; 2:6; 7:9b-10[8b-9]; 8:1-3); self-descriptions (1:5-6; 8:10), poems of admiration (1:9-17; 2:3; 4:9-15; 6:4-5a; 7:8); accounts of an experience (2:8-10a; 3:1-5; 5:2-8; 6:11-12; 8:5b); characterizations of the physical charms of the loved one, similar to the Arabic *wasf* (4:1-7; 5:10-16; 6:5b-7; 7:2-8[1-7]); invitations to tryst (2:10b-14; 4:8; 5:1; 7:12-14[11-13]; for different classifications see Gordis, 1974:35f.; Murphy, 1981:101–3; Fox, 1985:271–77).

The Song of Songs is unique in that it is the only book of the Bible to have all of its content in the form of speeches; there is no straightforward narration. This direct speech, a feature that provides a better insight into the disposition of the speaker than does mere narrative reporting (Alter, 1981), opens the book to analysis through an examination of the characterization revealed through the lyrics (cf. Fox, 1985:253–66). The major speakers are the woman and the man. In addition to these lovers, other gender-identified groups include the daughters of Jerusalem, the watchmen, and the woman's brothers.

The Lovers

The woman in the Song of Songs is identified as the Shulammite, perhaps the feminine form of the name Solomon (7:1[6:13]). Some translations refer to her as a girl or a maiden in order further to portray her presumed unmarried state. The connotation of youthfulness carried by these nouns also suggests immaturity, however, a trait that conflicts with the book's depiction of the woman. Refuting her brothers' impression of her (8:8), she describes herself as full-figured (8:10). Furthermore, she is quite independent of societal restraints, in contrast to women in a patriarchal society. While she may be rather young, this is a mature woman, not a naive girl.

Although the Song is a tribute to mutual heterosexual love, the principal frame of reference is the amorous disposition of the woman. Her words open and close the Song and her voice is dominant throughout (cf. Trible, 1978:144–65). She utters most of the poems of yearning (1:2-4; 2:6; 8:1-3; 7:9b-10[10b-11] is an exchange between the lovers). She is the one who is portrayed as lovesick (2:5; 5:8), longing to follow her beloved should he bid her come with him (1:4), and she is the one who celebrates their mutual belonging (2:16-17; 6:3). She takes the initiative, seeking him both in the privacy of her room (3:1; 5:6b) and in the public streets of the city (3:2; 5:7). Her concern to protect their love from public scrutiny and the possibility of criticism (1:7; 8:1) does not prevent her from venturing out, alone at night, in search of him, even jeopardizing her own safety. She is neither slow to speak erotically about their union (1:2,4,13; 3:4) nor embarrassed by the tit-illating language that he uses to describe her body (4:5-6; 7:2-10a[1-9a]). Clearly the woman depicted in the Song is driven by love, not inhibited by social opinion or some narrow sense of sexual propriety.

The family relationships of the woman should be noted. Nowhere does the book refer to her father. Her brothers seem to have assumed responsibility for her (1:6; 8:8), a practice quite common in patriarchal societies. She does not appear to agree with their perception of her degree of maturity, however, nor with the overbearing nature of their attempts at supervision. In fact, her behavior indicates that she disregards any restraint they place on her. If there is a prominent family member, it is her mother. The Shulammite herself is acclaimed "the darling of her mother" (6:9). Her siblings are not even called brothers. Instead, they are identified through their maternal relationship; they are her mother's sons (1:6; 8:1). Furthermore, one of the places where she would tryst with her lover is her mother's house (3:4; 8:2). One might say that this is not unusual, since women's concerns and activities are often restricted to women's worlds and quarters. Rendezvous in vineyards and excursions into city streets and squares, hardly private and secluded places, suggest however, that this woman had access to a broader world.

The Shulammite's description of the charms of her lover and the plea-sures of their lovemaking, though often symbolic, is quite provocative. Her beloved is comely and agile like a young stag, renowned for its sexual prowess (2:8-9, 17; 8:14). The beauty of his body is extolled part by part from his head to his thighs (5:10-15 [a *wasf*, cf. Falk, 1990:125–35]). She rhapsodizes about the impassioned delights they experience that intoxicate like wine (1:2; 2:4; 7:9) and about those that can be savored like one savors luscious fruits (2:3; 4:16; 7:13). She relates how various luxurious aromas enhance the ardor of their passion (1:3, 12-14; 6:2). Sensuous figures of speech such as these not only evoke vivid images but can arouse desire as well. This woman is not intimidated by eroticism.

The words of the man are either in answer to the woman's questions or in dialogue with her. They provide the reader with a glimpse of the woman as perceived by her companion in love. His first words acclaim her as beau-tiful (1:15; also 2:10b, 13; 4:1, 7; 6:4, 10; 7:6), the fairest among women (1:8; also 5:9; 6:1). No other woman can compare with her (2:2; 6:8-10); her beauty is unblemished (4:7). The jewelry that adorns her makes her resplen-dence rival the most ornate of Pharaoh's chariot horses (1:9-11). Her eyes have enraptured her lover (4:9; 6:5), even though they are as gentle and innocent as doves (1:15; 4:1). Every part of her body is comely (4:1-5; 6:5b-7; 7:2-6 [*wasfs*]; also 7:7-9a), and her voice is sweet to the ear (2:14). The man compares her to a garden that is fruitful yet inaccessible to all but himself (4:12-15; 5:1; cf. Landy, 1983:188–205). This is a man who has been smitten by love. His interest in the woman is certainly erotic, but there is no indication that he desires her merely for his own pleasure. The desire described in these poems is mutual, seeking mutual fulfillment. The woman is not being used; she is being loved.

The character of the other people mentioned in the Song also points out the prominence of the Shulammite. They are directly involved only with her and not with the man. The daughters of Jerusalem act as a kind of foil for the woman. Since there are no soliloquies in the Song, she is most likely addressing them when it is clear that she is not speaking to the man (Fox, 1985:253–66). They pose questions (3:6; 5:9; 6:1) to which she provides answers, thus facilitating the forward movement of the dialogue. She appeals to them not to judge her by the darkness of her complexion (1:6), not to interrupt the couple's lovemaking (2:7; 3:5), and to tell the man that she is sick with love for him (5:8). Her brothers, with their misconceptions, provide an opportunity for her to assert her independence of their inhibiting control. The watchmen, the protectors of the city, only briefly encounter the woman, whom they too misunderstand and treat inappropriately. It is apparent that the Song is a celebration of heterosexual love, principally from a woman's point of view.

The Tryst

The Song moves from the experience of intense longing to that of blissful enjoyment, and then to longing once more. The woman seeks her absent lover and finds him, only to lose him and seek him again. The lovers are separated from each other, are joined in an ecstatic embrace, and are then apart once again. This alternation between presence and absence, possession and loss, exhilaration and dejection accurately characterizes the ebb and flow of human love with its various combinations of desire, anticipation, and consummation. Everything about this love is mutual (Fox, 1985:305–10). Both the woman and the man move from one emotion to the other. At times she is the initiator, at other times she is reserved. He is variously the object of her search and a forceful suitor. Neither of the lovers has to be cajoled. The tryst is an encounter sought and enjoyed by both the woman and the man.

The trysts take place in several locations: cultivated orchards (2:3; 6:11; 8:5), gardens (4:16—5:1; 6:2), and vineyards (7:12); natural fertile settings (2:16; 6:3; 7:11); and enclosed chambers (2:4; 3:4; 5:2-6; 8:2; cf. Fox,

1985:283–88; Falk, 1990:137–43). Each one of the natural sites is lavish with fruits and the possibility of continuous fertility. In each case the reference to fertility has less to do with progeny, the fruits of sexual fecundity, than with ongoing sensual satisfaction. Not only do these sites promise ample comfort and natural charm, they also provide a modicum of privacy. It is not clear whether actual locations are intended or veiled sexual allusions are being made. There is no reason to choose one interpretation over the other, however. Since the Shulammite herself is explicitly referred to as a garden (4:12, 15) and the man is compared to a thriving apple tree (2:3), these references can be understood both literally and figuratively, thus giving the poems a richness that only a multilayered composition can boast.

The rooms that lend themselves to lovemaking include a wine house (2:4) and a room in the home of the Shulammite's mother (3:4). Once while she was sleeping, her lover came to her own chamber, but she was slow to admit him and he quickly withdrew (5:2-6). It is quite logical that such rooms as these should be the setting for love. The wine house promotes the image of the vineyard already mentioned. Besides the notion of intoxication, it denotes fruitfulness and maturity, characteristics of the lovers that have sexual connotations.

The room in her mother's home is described as the place where her life began, an allusion to newness but also heavily laden with sexual significance. The description of the exchange that took place at her own sleeping chamber is quite provocative. He intends to enter and consummate their love. Some believe that the passage actually describes coitus (cf. Pope, 1977:519:4–6; Fox 1985:310–15). The fact that the man seems to have immediate access to her room should be noted. Whether the reference is to an actual room or is a euphemism for genitalia, the only thing that hinders his entry is her delay in making herself accessible to him.

Each trysting place clearly is steeped in sexual allusions. Interestingly, it is the woman who speaks about the site of the rendezvous, not the man. When he does invite her to come away with him, it is to join him. No intimate trysting place is ever mentioned by him (2:10b, 13b; 4:8). He appears to be preoccupied with her beauty and his delight is in her charms rather than with the details of their meeting place.

Another feature of the Song that bespeaks the vibrant surging of the powers of fertility is the season of the year suggested by the poem's vivid imagery. Near Eastern winter, the rainy season, is over; spring has arrived. An abundance of flowers appears; the vines are all in blossom (2:11-15; 6:11). There is a freshness and innocence to nature, just as there is freshness and innocence to the love that has captivated this couple. The man may not have been concerned about the *place* of the tryst, but he is the one who declares that the *time* for love has come (2:11-14). This suggests that he has interest in when love-making occurs, while she is attentive to where it takes place.

The passion of the Shulammite is not indecent, but neither is she demure about it. She enlists both the watchmen and the daughters of Jerusalem in her ardent search for her love. The places of rendezvous may afford the lovers privacy, but they are not secret spots, unknown to others. Although she does not speak explicitly to the men regarding these locations, she is quite open about them to the women (2:4,16; 3:4; 5:2-4; 6:2-3, 11; 7:10b-12[9b-11]; 8:2, 5b). In fact, the latter may have planned to expedite love by awakening desire in some way, for she pleads with them to allow love to take its natural course without any stimulation or interference (2:7; 3:5; 8:4). If by chance they should come upon her lover, however, they are free to tell him of her longing for him. In fact, she asks them to do this for her (5:8). In this way, the daughters of Jerusalem do play a role, if only an indirect one, in bringing the lovers together.

Clearly this couple has already experienced the pleasures of lovemaking. He has lain on her breast (1:13), been encircled in her embrace (3:4), and been aroused by her (8:5). As already stated, the relationship between the woman and the man is one of mutual desire and enjoyment. Neither one of the lovers nor the couple itself fits a gender-determined stereotype. They are fiercely committed to each other and to no one else. The two use much of the same colorful and provocative imagery to describe each other and the love they share. They have known some form of sexual union (2:16; 6:3) and have both relished the enjoyment that came from it (2:3; 4:10-11). Not only is this clearly stated throughout the Song, but it is implied by the use of metaphors of eating and drinking (1:2, 4; 2:3; 4:10-11, 16—5:1; 8:2).

The titles of endearment employed in this book are telling. The Shulam-mite uses straightforward language, consistently calling him "my love." Once she uses "friend" in a parallel construction with that term of affection, thus signifying the connotation of intimacy carried by the word *friend*. He calls her "friend" (1:9, 15; 2:2, 10b, 13; 4:1, 7; 5:2; 6:4), "bride" (4:8, 9, 10, 11, 12; 5:1), "sister" (4:9, 10, 12; 5:1, 2), and "dove" (2:14; 5:2; 6:9). He fur-ther refers to her as "perfect one" (5:2; 6:9), "beautiful one" (2:10b, 13), and "noble daughter" (7:2[1]). Clearly, these are all pet names that express his affection for her. Since the poem itself contains no indication that the cou-ple is married or planning to do so, the term "bride" is probably merely an expression of intimacy. "Sister," also a term of endearment, should not be limited to a reference to consanguinity, and "dove" evokes the image of a lovebird. Descriptive phrases are also epithets. "Perfect one" is always in a literary construction with the word "dove" and might be intended as a hen-diadys; "beautiful one" addresses the way the man frequently speaks about his love; and "noble daughter" may be a reference to the identification of the woman as a Shulammite (the feminine form of Solomon). It also corresponds to some of the royal imagery found throughout the Song, imagery that can simply allude to the noble character of all human love.

While the book certainly applauds the glories of lovemaking, more importantly, it celebrates the depth of the commitment shared by the woman and man. Chapter 8:6-7 has been described as the high point of the entire Song. The seals mentioned there may refer to apotropaic charms that were often worn around the neck or on the arm. The Shulammite asks that her lover allow her to be for him just such an amulet, a prominent sign of the love that they share. She maintains that their love possesses a force that can easily rival the power of death and Sheol, the place of death. It can even withstand the chaotic primal waters. Neither death nor chaos is a match for the love that joins these two. No power from the netherworld and no treasure from this world can compare with the strength and the value of love.

Rhetorical Function

Everything about the Song extols heterosexual passion. It celebrates erotic love, portraying the longing of the woman and the man as unrestrained yet beyond reproach. All the senses are awakened, attuned to the object of their desire. The imagery that describes both the craving and the pleasure savored when that craving is satisfied is sensuous yet not lascivious. Nothing in this portrayal suggests impropriety or overindulgence. If anything, it characterizes heterosexual passion as noble and mutually self-transcending. The superscription, according Solomonic authority to the message of the book, legitimates sexual longings, passionate pursuits, and sensual gratification.

The depiction of this complex and irresistible human drama is viewed from the perspective of the woman. Her own words depict the love as captivating, as alternately energizing and expending, as refreshing and intoxicating. The self-disclosive character of the poems immediately engages the reader, who is thereby brought into the intimacy of love's attraction. From this vantage point, the devotion, courage, and determination of the young woman can be clearly seen and totally supported, and anyone who seems to place obstacles in her path is viewed with suspicion.

The unabashed love of the woman authenticates female passion and erotic assertiveness, and the desire that she engenders in her lover bespeaks her sexual attractiveness. Women will be affirmed by this positive depiction of their sensuality. While men too appreciate being considered desirable, their acceptance of sexually assertive women may depend largely upon the type of the gender roles to which they subscribe. The judgment placed on the

woman's behavior may say more about the interpreter than about the Shulammite herself. Whatever the reader's point of view, these poems presume
that the demeanor of the woman is honorable.

The fact that the Shulammite is portrayed as sexually assertive does not
imply that the man is thereby passive: on the contrary. Overcome by her beauty (1:9-11, 15f.; 4:1-7, 9-15) he goes in search of her (2:8f.) for the purpose of
making love with her (5:2). Sometimes he invites her to come away with him
(2:10—13; 4:8); at other times he leads her to a trysting place (2:4). He
appears to be neither threatened by her independence nor dominated by her
assertiveness. He enkindles in her the same passion that she inspires in him.
The mutuality of their devotion will appeal to both men and women. The
poems do not disclose how the love originated or whose passion launched the
amorous adventure. They narrate its unfolding, and they do so in a way that
has touched the sensitivities of women and men down through the centuries.
The Song of Songs remains the prototype of heterosexual yearning and a
measure of the lengths to which lovers will go in order to be united.

Unmasking the Powers

The liberationist reading of the Song of Songs next examines the issues of
race or ethnic origin, class, and gender in order to discover the underlying
bases of power. The Song of Songs is remarkably lacking in ethnocentric
prejudice; in fact, the reverse is true. It shows knowledge of and appreciation
for the grandeur and abundance of lands other than Israel. It refers to the
tents of Kedar (1:5); the cedars (3:9; 5:15), scent (4:11), mountains (4:8),
and streams (4:15) of Lebanon; and the pools of Heshbon (7:4). It even
acknowledges the opulence of its ancient enemy, Egypt (1:9). By using this
natural beauty or cultural splendor in praise of the charms of the lovers, the
Song celebrates features of those countries as well.

A good bit of debate surrounds the nature of the darkness of the
woman's skin (1:5f.). In other places of the Bible the Hebrew word *šāḥar*
denotes the color black (5:11, also Lev 13:31, 37; Zech 6:2, 6), and so there
is no reason to translate it differently here. At issue is whether black refers
to skin tone or to race. Most commentators opt for the former (Murphy,
1990:126, 128; Fox, 1985:101f.; contra Pope, 1977:307–22; an example of a
different position is found in Copher, 1991:149). This is supported by the
text itself, which explains the woman's dark color as the result of exposure
to the sun (1:6). She compares her blackness to the goat-haired tents of
Kedar as well as to the curtains that hung in the wilderness tabernacle (cf.
Exod 26:1-13; 36:8-17), anachronistically ascribed to Solomon. These both
clearly refer to color.

Though this may not be a reference to racial origin, some sort of discrimination still seems to exist here, for the woman defends her dark coloring. This may reflect a class bias. Unlike the sheltered women of the elite (the daughters of Jerusalem?), the lower-class status of the Shulammite requires that she tend the vineyards, thus exposing herself to the scorching rays of the sun (Fox, 1985:101f.; Falk, 1990:168f.). The favorable depiction of the Shulammite indicates that the author explicitly disavows any class bias of which the daughters may have been guilty. This does not mean, however, that the poems do not show subtle partiality toward affluence. While much of the luxuriant imagery is drawn from the lush abundance of nature (for example, fruits [2:3; 4:16; 7:13] and aromas [1:3, 12-14; 6:2]), some of it sketches the kind of extravagance that only money can buy (such as, a house of cedar and cypress [1:17] and reinforcements of silver and cedar [8:9]). The elegance described may be only figurative, the kind of hyperbolic overstatement lovers are prone to use when singing the praises of the beloved. Nonetheless, the fact that aspects of the romance are characterized in terms of material prosperity suggests that wealth is the standard after which value is described.

A specific example of this bias can be seen in the allusions to royalty. The woman refers to her lover as king (1:4, 12; 7:5) and is herself described as a queen (7:1). Because Solomon and his riches are explicitly mentioned several times (3:6-11; 8:11f.), some interpreters conclude that the poems describe an actual romance between that Israelite king and some foreign maiden. More than likely, the references reflect a common Near Eastern custom of ascribing royal personae to every bride and groom. Although these poems could well have been sung during a marriage celebration, there is no evidence within the Song of Songs itself that this couple is married or even planning to marry in the future. Instead, the poems suggest that human love itself possesses a dignity and splendor that are nothing less than royal. As commendable as this metaphor may be, its use does create the impression that dignity and splendor belong to royalty, and those who possess them are some kind of cryptoroyalty. This is clearly a class bias.

Another image that could be understood as a reference to royalty is the representation of the man as a herder of flocks (1:7, 8; 2:16; 6:2, 3). While on the one hand this occupation could mark him as a member of the peasantry, on the other hand it can identify him as a monarch. Ancient kings were frequently portrayed as shepherds, who were responsible for the protection and well-being of their people (their flocks). Whether this royal imagery is understood literally or figuratively, it suggests a measure of excellence that at heart contains a class bias.

Allusions to elegance include mention of the woman's jewelry and reference to the prodigality of nature. Whether the finery that embellished the woman was part of wedding apparel or merely customary accessories, her ornaments are compared to the lavish adornment of Pharaoh's chariot horses (1:9-11) and a point made about the seductive quality of her jewelry (4:9). In both cases, flashy decoration is the measure of value. In fact, it is only in the celebrated poem praising the strength of love ("love is strong as death, passion fierce as the grave" [8:6]) that the insignificance of wealth is acknowledged: "If one offered for love all the wealth of his house, it would be utterly scorned" (8:7). Even if this is a veiled allusion to some kind of bride-price (Murphy, 1990:198), the statement unmistakably asserts that love is beyond the power of wealth.

Comparing the delights of lovemaking and the appeal of the lovers with the succulent tastes of exotic fruit and the hypnotizing aromas of rich nard, spices, and woods (1:2f., 12-14; 2:3f.; 4:9-16; 6:2; 7:9, 13) appeals to the abundance that nature yields. The generosity of nature is not conditioned by the socioeconomic status of people. The luxuriance that is depicted here, however, is a facet of the natural world normally accessible only to the prosperous.

The gender depiction of this book is quite remarkable. The sexual activity of the woman is neither suppressed nor supervised. She is self-assured in pursuit of her lover. Her desire, which is both unabashed and observable, is neither repressed nor manipulated by an overseeing man. While it is noteworthy that she acts in this way, it is even more significant that no one and nothing in the Song suggests that she should be censured for such an attitude. Despite this, an underlying gender bias still exists, evident in the nature of the imagery that characterizes the individual lovers.

The Song of Songs is a treasure trove of luxuriant nature imagery that appeals to sight and taste and smell. It is also replete with metaphors drawn from creation that enhance the account of the passion shared by the woman and the man. Chief among these metaphors are vineyard, garden, and gazelle. It is clear that usually the reference is to an actual vineyard (1:6, 14; 2:15; 7:12; 8:11). In most cases the spot is somehow related to the human romance that is being played out. The vineyard is either a place of trysting, or its yield is a sign of the fruitfulness of the love. However, twice the Shulammite speaks of her own vineyard (1:6; 8:12). Most interpret this reference metaphorically, believing that in these instances the vineyard is really the woman's own sexuality (Pope, 1977:326; Fox, 1985:102; Murphy, 1990:128).

The garden is also difficult to interpret in each instance. In some cases the word is clearly used metaphorically, characterizing the woman (4:12, 15, 16). In other passages (4:16; 5:1; 6:2; 8:13) the referent is not clear. An actual garden may be intended, or the initial metaphorical sense alluding to the woman may carry over into the remaining citations. Though different in themselves, these two metaphors (vineyard and garden) carry similar connotations. Both are fertile, cultivated, circumscribed lands, which produce yields that gladden the human heart. Their literal meanings describe the productivity of love; their common metaphorical meaning symbolizes the fertility and desirability of the woman.

The gazelle is an animal known for its beauty, agility, and sexual potency. As with the other metaphors, the exact meaning carried by this term is difficult to determine. The word is used in reference to the man as well as to the breast of the woman. Several commentators believe that, when used in the adjuration to the daughters of Jerusalem, it is really a circumlocution that avoids using the name of God (see Pope, 1977:385f., 390).

Although these metaphors are in themselves all quite complimentary, together they reveal a definite gender bias. The woman is identified as a vineyard and as a garden, both fertile, cultivated, circumscribed lands planted and cared for by another. This identification may be ambiguous when it comes to the vineyard, but it is quite clear in the case of the garden. The woman is a lavish but locked garden, which her beloved alone can enjoy. The man, on the other hand, is likened to a gazelle, bounding freely over the mountains, beholden to no one. These metaphors clearly suggest asymmetric gender expectations.

Into the Looking Glass

After carefully looking at the text with an eye to the issues of race or ethnic origin, class, and gender, the reader can engage the biblical text as a mirror and then as a door through which to step into a new way of perceiving the issues themselves. In other words, the revelatory power of the Bible can be tested. We might think that the possibilities are quite limited because the Song of Songs deals with only one major theme, heterosexual love. If we remember, however, that a liberationist approach is really critiquing a worldview, a worldview that leaves its footprints behind wherever it has been, we will detect traces of this worldview in everything that it has touched.

References to Solomon, Jerusalem, the land of Israel, and the nations that surround it clearly identify the Song of Songs as Israelite literature. Despite its clearly defined origin, the book contains no ethnocentric bias. In fact, it contains more positive mention of places outside of Israel than of those within the borders of the nation. This mention is found in the comparisons of the charms of one or both of the lovers with natural splendor or abundance. The poems do not discriminate between the grandeur of one country and another. Instead, they appreciate the majesty of creation wherever it is found. This universalism even includes nations that were once mortal foes of the people (Egypt [1:9] and Damascus [7:4]).

Narrow ethnocentricity can blind us to the wisdom, goodness, or beauty present in another culture or another land. While racial or ethnic pride is both normal and laudable, racial or ethnic bigotry is divisive and can seriously cloud our judgment. It can lead us to make sweeping categorizations and to relegate people to restrictive stereotypes. When we scorn people, we often devalue what they hold dear; we criticize their customs and mores and we disdain what they possess. Such bigotry originates not only from distorted nationalism but also from the kind of ignorance that is linked with xenophobia. The Song of Songs contains none of this; rather, it manifests an appreciation for beauty wherever it is found.

The fact that the poems embody figures of speech that include such references indicates that the poets had knowledge of certain features of these foreign lands. They may have been able to contemplate the heights of Mount Hermon without leaving the northern districts of Israel, but references to Lebanon's cedars (3:9; 5:15) and scents (4:11) suggest some form of travel or trade or both. The same is true with regard to knowledge about the bedouin tents of Kedar (1:5). Someone had to have had contact with this nomadic tribe. The poets responsible for these verses were not isolationists.

Perhaps the most extraordinary allusion is to the panoply of Egyptian chariot horses. Given the antagonistic relationship that usually existed between Israel and Egypt, and the role that Pharaoh's chariots played in this hostility, the inclusion of this comparison and its lack of even the slightest condemnation is quite remarkable. This may suggest something about the dating of the poems, but the absence of any nationalistic barb should be noted. Natural beauty and cultural elegance are not the exclusive properties of only one or another people. They characterize every locale and every society and these poems recognize that fact.

The metaphorical nature of much of the description and many of the allusions in the poems prevents us from identifying with certainty the social status of the lovers. This makes a biblical critique of class preference somewhat tenuous. Nonetheless, the final poem, which exalts the depth of love, unmistakably asserts that love transcends not only the power of death and the grave but also the influence of wealth (8:6f.). This assertion, which many maintain is the high point of the book, can function as an internal interpretive key to the understanding of the imagery used to characterize the love depicted elsewhere.

Because it is clearly asserted that all the riches of the household cannot compare to the excellence of love, one may legitimately suggest that the metaphors of comparison found within the book should be interpreted figuratively rather than literally. In other words, the metaphors that suggest wealth (such as, houses made with cedar [1:17], battlements of silver [8:9]) should be considered figurative expressions characterizing the intrinsic value of the referent and not literal descriptions of its material makeup. Thus the luxuriance depicted represents the grandeur and abundance of the private world inhabited by all lovers, regardless of their social class.

The riches of the prosperous are, in fact, the riches of the land. The precious metals, the fragrant nard, the luscious fruits are all the harvest of the earth, brought forth freely with no thought of social restriction. The earth itself is prodigal, and the extravagance of the imagery of the Song illustrates this. From it springs the heady aromas, the enthralling visions, the delectable tastes, the captivating sounds, and the gratifying tactile sensations portrayed in the poetry. In order to extol their passion, the lovers call on elements from the natural world. They can do nothing else, for everything beautiful, everything enchanting, everything satisfying comes through the wonders of creation. The glorification of the physical charms of each of the lovers can only be done through figures of speech drawn from nature (Landy, 1987:308), for that is the only source of imagery available to them or to us. This is an excellent example of the affinity that exists between human beings and the rest of natural creation.

In the Song of Songs, the natural world is not merely the stage upon which the drama of heterosexual love is played, the props of which can be set up and dismantled once a scene is completed. Rather, human love is an expression of the natural world. It is born because of it and as a part of it. It is an aspect of the allurement that is at the heart of the macrocosmic universe (Swimme, 1984:41–52). Lovers look into each other's eyes and there glimpse the passion of creation. As they applaud each other's body (the tenor of the metaphor) employing figures of speech, the lovers are also enhancing their appreciation of the world (the vehicle of the metaphor) with the eyes of love. That is the way metaphors function (Richards, 1971:96). As they describe their experience of each other's body, they are investing their experience of creation with the love that has left them spellbound.

The Song of Songs refutes the gender-identification of certain roles and behaviors. It declares that the assertiveness of love can be found in the heart of a woman as well as that of a man, and that both women and men fantasize about the physical attributes of the other. It depicts heterosexual attraction, the pursuit that it arouses, and the ecstasy that its consummation effects as characteristic of both lovers. Again and again it notes motivation that emanates from the heart as opposed to acquiescence to external pressure. Since the roles that we enact in the drama of love correspond to the roles that we assume in social interaction, such a shift in gender-identification is bound to have wide-ranging repercussions.

Love as Strong as Death

In its description of the glories of human love, the Song of Songs is replete with nature imagery. Nevertheless, the most powerful statement made about love is found in its comparison with death (8:6f.). In the midst of so many sensuous allusions, this metaphor is jarring; in a collection of poetry that celebrates life, this comparison is chilling. And yet, it is not out of place in this passage, which is considered the culmination of the entire book. If the lavish poetry has left anyone imagining that love is mere emotional infatuation or physical excitement, the testimony of these verses dispels such misconceptions. We all know that there is no force on earth that can withstand the power of death. It is fierce and all-consuming. It is not bound by social restrictions. It does not discriminate between the rich and the poor, the young and the old, the powerful and the vulnerable. It brings every human consideration down to the fundamental facts of life. Death has the final word. If love is strong as death, then it must possess comparable strength and fierceness, it must be unquenchable and inestimable.

The poems themselves show that the passion shared by the lovers is indeed fierce and all-consuming. It enabled them to withstand personal disapproval (1:6) and restrictive social pressure (5:7; 8:1). Despite the opulence of the imagery, the social status of the lovers is not certain, leaving the description to be applied impartially to any loving couple. Finally, every other human consideration plainly pales in the face of love; nothing can really compare with it and no amount of wealth can procure it. Experience has shown that the bonds of love can even endure beyond the grave. It may well be that love is even stronger than death. When all is said and done, love of itself and in itself is the fundamental fact of life.

If the Song of Songs is to be considered wisdom teaching, as its place within the canon would suggest, just what message does it advance? Decisions about the literary character of the book will influence the way this question is answered. If the book is considered an allegorical depiction of the love relationship between YHWH and Israel, Christ and the church, or God and the individual soul, the message will probably include some aspect of covenant theology. If it is thought to be a cultic reenactment, the teaching will likely touch liturgical matters. If it is seen as a stage performance, the narrative will say something about situations, whether biblically founded or dramatically imaginative, from the life of Solomon.

This study has read the Song of Songs as a collection of lyric love poems, some of which recount the physical charms of the loved one while others describe erotic longing. Accordingly, the wisdom teaching concerns one form of human love. It seems clear that the approving portrayal of the romance reaffirms the nobility and mutuality of passion. It also exemplifies the self-forgetfulness that love engenders and the creative potential that it offers. The style of the depiction of this love leads one to conclude that it is as natural and resplendent as the world of creation. In the wisdom tradition, the experience of life is the great teacher. In the Song of Songs, fearless and undivided love is the greatest experience of life.

Works Consulted

Alter, Robert. 1981. *The Art of Biblical Narrative.* New York: Basic Books.

Clines, David J. 1994. "Why Is There a Song of Songs and What Does It Do to You If You Read It?" *Jian Dao: A Journal of Bible and Theology* 1:3–27.

Copher, Charles B. 1991. "The Black Presence in the Old Testament." *Stony the Road We Trod.* Edited by Cain Hope Felder. Philadelphia: Fortress Press.

Elliot, M. Timothea. 1989. *The Literary Unity of the Canticle* (European University Series 23). Bern: Peter Lang.

Exum, J. Cheryl. 1973. "A Literary and Structural Analysis of the Song of Songs." *Zeitschrift für die alttestamentliche Wissenschaft* 85:47–79.

Falk, Marcia. 1990. *The Song of Songs.* San Francisco: Harper.

Fox, Michael V. 1985. *The Song of Songs and the Ancient Egyptian Love Songs.* Madison: University of Wisconsin Press.

Gordis, Robert. 1974. *The Song of Songs and Lamentations.* Revised and augmented edition. New York: KTAV.

Landsberger, Franz. 1954. "Poetic Units within the Song of Songs." *Journal of Biblical Literature* 73:203–16.

Landy, Francis. 1983. *Paradoxes of Paradise: Identity and Differences in the Song of Songs.* Sheffield: Almond Press.

——————. 1987. "The Song of Songs." In *The Literary Guide to the Bible.* Edited by Robert Alter and Frank Kermode. Cambridge: The Belknap Press of Harvard.

Murphy, Roland E. 1981. *Wisdom Literature.* Grand Rapids: Eerdmans.

——————. 1990. *The Song of Songs.* Hermeneia. Minneapolis: Fortress Press.

Pope, Marvin H. 1977. *The Song of Songs.* The Anchor Bible. Garden City, N.Y.: Doubleday.

Pouget, Guillaume, and Jean Guitton. 1948. *The Canticle of Canticles.* 2d edition. Translated by Joseph L. Lilly. New York: Declan X. McMullen.

Richards, I. A. 1971. *The Philosophy of Rhetoric.* Oxford: Oxford University Press.

Robert, André, Raymond Tournay, and André Feuillet. 1963. *Le Cantique des Cantiques.* Paris: Études Bibliques.

Swimme, Brian. 1984. *The Universe Is a Green Dragon: A Cosmic Creation Story.* Santa Fe: Bear & Company.

Trible, Phyllis. 1978. *God and the Rhetoric of Sexuality.* Overtures to Biblical Theology. Philadelphia: Fortress Press.

Weems, Renita. 1992. "Song of Songs." In *The Women's Bible Commentary.* Edited by Carol A. Newsom and Sharon H. Ringe. London: SPCK.

7

Wisdom of Solomon

Introduction

THE WISDOM OF SOLOMON, ALSO KNOWN AS the book of Wisdom, does not appear in the Protestant Bible because it was not included in the Jewish canon upon which the decision of inclusion was based. Considered apocryphal by Protestants, it is regarded as deuterocanonical by Catholics and included in their canon. It gets its name by inference. Although the author does not explicitly identify himself as Solomon, speaking in the first person he describes himself as such (7:5; 8:21; 9:7f.; cf. 1 Kgs 3:5-15). The book is a form of royal testament, instructions of a dead monarch to those who follow him in governance of the people.

The pseudonymity of the author can be demonstrated in several ways. First, in the Septuagint (the Greek version of the Bible), the book's linguistic form is natural and free-flowing, suggesting that it originated in Greek rather than Hebrew. Then, the ample vocabulary from Hellenistic anthropology, philosophy, psychology, medicine, and the popular Isis cult reveals an author who enjoyed an exceptional grasp of the learning of this culture, a culture that did not exist at the time of the Israelite king. In addition, several rhetorical devices found within the book resemble those developed by various Greek Cynic or Stoic philosophers (see below). These observations have led many commentators to suggest a Hellenistic origin of the book and to refer to its author as Pseudo-Solomon.

Unlike the Jewish wisdom instruction directed to "sons" (cf. Prov 1:8, 10, 15; 2:1; 3:1, 11, 21; 4:1, 10, 20; 5:1, 7, 20; 6:1, 3, 20; 7:1, 24; 8:32), this teaching addresses men who enjoy a certain social status, those who perform a very important role within the community (v. 1; cf. 6:1-4, 21). Whether this designation is merely a Hellenistic literary convention in preference to the

Jewish custom of address (Reese, 1970:111), or a feature that is characteristic of the tracts of kingship popular at the time and that advances the pseudonymous fiction of the book (Winston, 1979:101), the designation sets a different tone to the instruction from that found within early sapiential books.

Despite these Greek characteristics, this is nonetheless a Jewish book. The influence of Hebrew parallelism can be detected throughout (for example, 1:10-12), as can certain Hebraic figures of speech (for example, "integrity of heart" [1:1]). The description of God's care during the exodus is a kind of homiletic *midrash*, a method of Jewish interpretation that makes the biblical message relevant in new situations (cf. Reese, 1970:91–102). This kind of interpretation allows the law, restated as *halakah*, and narratives, retold as *haggadah*, to give faithful direction to a new generation.

In the past, the literary integrity of the book was questioned (cf. Winston, 1979:12–14). Today scholars generally agree on its structural unity. They have noted that a theme of one paragraph becomes the major focus of the next, and they have detected literary inclusions that serve to organize the material in a concentric manner (Reese, 1970:122–45). Although they agree on a three-part division of the book, they differ over the exact limits of each part and the subdivisions that comprise them. The following outline seems to enjoy the most support today: 1:1—6:21—Immortality as the Reward of Wisdom; 6:22—11:1—Solomon and the Quest for Wisdom; 11:2—19:22—God's Providence during the Exodus (Wright, 1967; Winston, 1979:9–12; Murphy, 1990:85f.; Perdue, 1994:293–318; for a slightly different view see Reese, 1970:90–116). In its final form, the book presents a coherent theology. God is encountered in the cosmos through Wisdom; eschatology is built into the cosmic structure and history illustrates that same structure (Collins, 1977:128). From the perspective of Pseudo-Solomon, creation is the matrix within which history and salvation are to be understood.

The book appears to belong to a form of Greek philosophical didactic exhortation known as protreptic, a method of argumentation that frequently included preoccupation with control of the universe, a critical attitude toward opposing philosophies of life, and a deliberate display of comprehensive knowledge (Reese, 1970:117–21). This rhetorical technique, an appeal to follow a meaningful philosophy as a way of life, lent itself to the purposes of this biblical author. Although the nations are not explicitly identified, the allusions within the book clearly point to animosity between the Israelites and the Egyptians. The arguments put forth by the author seek to encourage the Jews to cherish their religious tradition, illustrate the superiority of Jewish morality over that of the Greeks, justify the actions of God throughout the history of the Israelites, and impress the readers with the author's encyclopedic knowledge, thus legitimating his religious claims.

Within the book, the exhortation takes various Hellenistic rhetorical forms: the diatribe, a form of argumentation (1:1—6:11; 11); the sorites, a chain of syllogisms (6:7–21); the aporia, a statement of a philosophical problem to be solved (6:22—11:1); the aretalogy, a litany of virtues (7:22); the syncrisis, a Hellenistic form of comparison (chaps. 9–11). All of these forms facilitate the author's fundamental purpose, namely, to offer an authoritative polemic against the accomplishments of Hellenism which seemed so attractive to many of the Jews of the time.

The Book
Immortality: The Reward of Wisdom

The very first verse of this first section (1:1—6:21) sets the agenda of the entire book: "Love righteousness" (1:1). This verse and a second statement about righteousness form a kind of *inclusio* and set the verses off as a discrete section (1:1-15). The initial exhortation is followed by a series of consequences that flow from such a choice (vv. 2f.), chief among them being an intimate relationship with God and the inestimable gift of wisdom. This teaching clearly demonstrates the theory of retribution (for a form critical study of Wisdom 1–6 see Nickelsburg, 1972). At the very outset, the author carefully traces the differences between a life lived in righteousness and one marked by wickedness. Pseudo-Solomon even goes so far as to state that death, understood as separation from God (cf. Reese, 1983:31–35; Kolarcik, 1991), is invited onto the scene by sinners, who court it and draw it to themselves. God, on the other hand, made things that they might have being and thrive (vv. 10-14).

The teaching about immortality (*athanasía*) found here is remarkable. Although he is influenced by both the Jewish tradition of covenantal retribution and the Greek psychology of the immortal soul, Pseudo-Solomon's view of immortality is unique. Inheriting the Jewish belief in the relationship between righteousness and life and borrowing the Greek notion of immortality, he claims that "Righteousness is immortal" (v. 15). His argument develops in the following way: Israel believes that righteousness characterizes the relationship of human beings with the immortal God; therefore, righteousness too is immortal. Pseudo-Solomon's teaching about immortality can be simply stated: "Love righteousness" (v. 1), for "Righteousness is immortal" (v. 15).

This is the first biblical mention of the soul (v. 4), a concept from Hellenistic psychology that has become so much a part of both Western and Eastern thought. The reference introduces a feature of wisdom that is unconventional, namely, Wisdom's ability to enter into the souls of the righteous. (The special properties of wisdom are treated later in the book.) The text states that God does not delight in the destruction of life but made all things that they might endure, and that there is good in everything that has been made (vv. 13b-14). The theme of the integrity of creation will appear in other places within the book as well.

Another *inclusio*, possession of the wicked by death (1:16) and by the devil (2:24), marks a second unit. Pseudo-Solomon returns to the idea that sinners invite death, in fact, they make a covenant with it (cf. Isa 28:15). For this reason, they deserve to be its victims. In the diatribe that follows (2:1b-20), the sinners expound on their philosophy of life, a philosophy that bears great similarity to certain Greek thought but that diverges radically from the tradition of Israel. Although the brevity of life was a cause of distress for everyone, the claim that life itself is a chance event, as the Epicureans believed, and, contrary to Jewish hope, that it ends with no trace even in memory leads to a carpe diem attitude. This exhortation to enjoy the pleasures of life within our grasp sounds very similar to the teaching found in Qoheleth. Qoheleth acknowledged, however, that the pleasures come from the hand of God and were given out of divine munificence (cf. Eccl 2:24-25a; 3:12f., 22; 5:17f.; 8:15; 9:7-9). They are not to be seized at any cost, either to oneself or to others, as the hedonists described here suggest.

These self-indulgent allies of death even advocate disregard of others in the pursuit of gratification. Their attention turns first to those who are just and also needy, but it is not limited to them. They believe that no one should stand in their way, neither those in economic need, nor those devoid of legal rights, nor those lacking the strength to defend themselves. In fact, weakness of any kind is considered reason enough to be abused by others. This point of view has spawned the appalling adage: "Might makes right."

Disdain for the just one turns to abhorrence. They hate him because he found fault with their transgression of the law and their disregard for their religious training. These accusations suggest that the conflict described here is an internal one between those faithful to a religious tradition and those who have disowned it. The description of the plot of the wicked against this righteous person is reminiscent of both Isaiah (42:1; 52:13—53:12) and Psalm 22 (v. 9). Pseudo-Solomon allows these vile individuals to speak for themselves, to trace the contours of their own depravity, thus making clear to all the contrast between their corrupt philosophy and the moral superiority of the tradition of Israel.

Pseudo-Solomon maintains that the wicked disdain morality or social responsibility, championing lives of expediency that seek only enjoyment in the present. In his denunciation of them, he appropriates a concept from

Hellenistic philosophy and interprets it from the perspective of Jewish tradition. The Epicureans believed that incorruption (*aphtharsía*) was a divine quality, that rendered the gods invulnerable to disintegration. Jewish tradition holds that humankind was made in the "image of God." Thus, the author argues, though mortal by nature, as images of God human beings were meant to be incorruptible. Having already asserted that death entered the scene through human sinfulness (cf. 1:12), he elaborates on the Genesis account of human sin (Gen 3) and concludes that all of this was caused by the envy of the devil.

The first two chapters of the book expose the anthropology/eschatology of Pseudo-Solomon, demonstrating his reinterpretation of elements from both Hellenistic philosophy and the biblical tradition. Appropriating the Hellenistic concepts of soul, immortality, and incorruption, he has reread the Genesis accounts of creation and sin. It is important to understand the view presented here, in order to grasp the instruction that follows.

The central section of this opening diatribe (3:1—5:23) is quite long and carefully argued. Having selected three aspects of the Jewish teaching on retribution, namely, innocent suffering (3:1-12), childlessness (3:13—4:6), and early death (4:7-19), the author contrasts the fates of the upright with that of the sinners and in these contrasts reinterprets Jewish eschatology. He develops his argument in a very creative way. Though discrete in themselves, the three sections are woven together thematically, a secondary theme from one section becoming the major theme of the next. This is more evidence of the book's literary coherence.

One of the most troublesome questions that faced the later wisdom writers was the problem of innocent suffering (cf. Job and Ecclesiastes). Pseudo-Solomon's treatment of this issue flows from his previous teaching. He had claimed earlier that death is the consequence of sin. His teaching about righteousness (cf. 1:1, 15) comes into play here as he explains the death of the virtuous. The just are in a relationship with God that is not severed by death. They may in fact have suffered and endured physical death, as is the lot of all mortal humans, but this has not dissolved the bonds that united them with God. Instead, they are in God's hand and at peace (3:1, 3). Anyone who thinks otherwise does not understand the mystery of God's justice or the implications of covenant relationship. The righteous, on the other hand, placed their trust in this relationship, and it was their hope that was full of immortality.

The author does not minimize the suffering that the just endured but attempts to explain it as a test (cf. Job 1–2), which they passed with great integrity. These righteous will be rewarded with the grandeur that was concealed by their suffering (cf. Dan 12:3) and the honor denied them during the time of their tribulations (cf. Dan 7:18, 27). Now that their trials are over, they are with God, enjoying all that this means. By contrast, the plight of the wicked is sobering. They have derided wisdom and so they will be denied the blessings that are its fruits, specifically, prosperity, a harmonious family, and a distinguished progeny. The theme of progeny is developed further in the next section.

Children were considered a blessing from God (for example, the promise to Abram [Gen 15:2-6]). In a patriarchal society, offspring guaranteed, among other things, support in old age and assurance that the inheritance would be maintained and the lineage preserved. Since the woman's value was often determined by her ability to bear sons who would be able to fulfill these duties, barren women were looked upon with great disdain. They appear to have failed to fulfill their responsibility to the group—past, present and future (for example, Hannah [1 Sam 1:6]). Pseudo-Solomon dismisses this traditional understanding, claiming that genuine fruitfulness is a matter of virtue, not of procreation. If she is blameless, the barren woman will enjoy a kind of spiritual fecundity (cf. Isa 54:1). In like manner, if he has been faithful, the eunuch will be granted access to the (heavenly?) temple, an honor previously denied him (cf. Isa 56:2-5). Righteousness, not procreative ability, guarantees fruitfulness (3:15).

On the other hand, the wicked cannot rest secure in their progeny. The children they do have will not be a blessing to the group. They will either die prematurely or, if they do survive into old age, they will not be held in high esteem. The author concludes this initial contrast with a statement that appears to be quite innovative: it is better to be childless and upright than to have many descendants and lack virtue (4:1a). Once again, moral integrity is the governing value, one that will be remembered by God and by human beings.

Israel believed that human beings lived on in their descendants and in the remembrance of them in the memory of others. In this way the deceased enjoyed a kind of immortality. Pseudo-Solomon reinterprets this belief slightly, asserting that immortality is not in remembrance generally but in the remembrance of the integrity of that person. Those who survive the deceased hold that specific virtuous life in high esteem and aspire to imitate it, thus keeping its memory alive (4:1). The author does not elaborate on the implications of God's relationship with this memory; however, he has already attested to the immortality of righteousness. Perhaps this is what guarantees immortality to the memory. Whatever the case, for Pseudo-Solomon, immortality is not a purely human characteristic but is always somehow associated with God.

The premature ruin of the offspring of the wicked leads the author to a consideration of the third aspect, the problem of early death. The traditional view of retribution taught that the reward of righteous living was a long life and, conversely, the wicked die young. Pseudo-Solomon overturns this theological opinion and proposes another, one in line with the rest of his teaching on eschatology. In his earlier discussions of death (cf. 3:1-12) and childlessness (cf. 3:13—4:6), he argued that the ultimate value of a life is found in the degree of its righteousness. The same argument holds in cases of untimely death. The just are at peace after death, regardless of when in their lifetime it claims them, for it is goodness and not length of years that determines the quality of a life. In fact, goodness can be achieved in a short period of time. The author maintains that it may be precisely because of their virtue that the good die young (an allusion to Enoch? cf. Gen 5:21-24). In such cases, death comes to save them from the treacherous yet alluring designs of the wicked, designs that include fascination with sin and the frenzy of desire.

The author insists that the death of the just, even though it be an untimely death, should not in any way be deemed a form of retribution. It may actually be a condemnation of the wicked, who do not understand the ways of God but judge everything according to a bankrupt theory of retribution. In Pseudo-Solomon's view, not only will the lives of these wicked be condemned but their deaths will be followed by further disgrace. Their arrogance vanishes as they perceive the newfound boldness of the wise. In a speech that parallels an earlier monologue (5:3b-7; cf. 2:6-20), the wicked recognize the error of their previous assessment both of the predicament of the righteous and of the course of their own lives. They compare the futility of their own base pursuits, which have nothing enduring to show for themselves, with the blessings that the righteous receive from the hand of God.

The vindication of God is described in apocalyptic terms (5:16b-23). Apparently, all of creation serves as the battle array of the mighty Creator-God, who wars against and overturns the perverse in the name of justice. This description is more than vivid figurative expression. It is a characterization based on the cosmological conviction that history, human destiny, and eschatology are all bound up in the structure of the universe (Collins, 1977:128,134,142). Whatever happens in one sphere has repercussions in the others.

The first part of the book closes with the first clear example of the personification of Wisdom (6:12-20). The description is vivid and dynamic. Wisdom Woman is both the object of search and the one searching. Those who seek her wait for her, and she in turns waits to be found by them. Employing a sorites syllogism (vv. 17-20), the author shows how the desire for Wisdom leads one to God: desire leads to love; love persuades one to observe the law; observance of the law is the basis of incorruptibility; and incorruptibility brings one near to God. The teaching of this section ends where it began: one's incorruptibility and immortality rest on the quality of one's relationship with God.

Solomon and the Quest for Wisdom

The personification of Wisdom acts as a bridge connecting the first part of the book (1:1—6:21) with the second (6:22—11:1). Having described Wisdom as desirable, Pseudo-Solomon personally recounts his own longing for her and the steps he took to acquire her. He states his intent to describe the nature and origin of Wisdom, promising not to hold back jealously the secrets that have been revealed to him (a denunciation of the practice of the gnostic mystery cults?). Although the speech recites the glories of Wisdom, it is framed within an autobiographic recollection. In details reminiscent of an event in the life of Solomon (cf. 1 Kgs 3:4-14), the author describes how he himself acquired wisdom, thus identifying himself with the Israelite king.

Pseudo-Solomon's praise of Wisdom demonstrates his encyclopedic knowledge that encompasses the fields of ontology, cosmology, physics, astronomy, biology, botany, and esoteric information (cf. Winston 1979:172–77). In the end, he states that he not only knows about Wisdom, but it is precisely because of her that he knows at all. She, the crafter of all things, taught him about everything that she had crafted (7:22; cf. 8:6; 14:2; Prov 8:30).

Just as the world exists through Wisdom, so she is embedded in the world. Her cosmic nature is described most elaborately with twenty-one characteristics akin to those attributed to the Greek goddess Isis (7:22b-23) and with activities associated with the Hellenistic concept of the world soul (v. 24). Pseudo-Solomon would have her resemble, even surpass, any deity, demiurge, or supernatural force found in Stoic philosophy. She is an emanation of divine power, glory, light, and goodness, and she possesses powers that are ascribed to the God of Israel. It is Wisdom that enters holy souls (cf. 1:4), making them friends of God (cf. 7:14) and rightly disposing them for a loving relationship with God (vv. 27b-28). God's love referred to here is more than *philía*, the love of friendship; it is the pure love of *agapē*. Once again the author shows his ability to integrate concepts from two very different worlds of thought.

Pseudo-Solomon recounts how Wisdom has enriched his own life. Using imagery replete with sexual nuances, he characterizes her as a bride with whose beauty he was captivated from his youth and with whom he lived in marital intimacy (cf. Reese, 1970:41, n.45). He claims that, as a consequence of her own intimacy with God, who loved her with the love of *agapē* and allowed her to manage divine works, she has been favored in ways that both enhance her nobility and benefit those who embrace her. The account of his own experience with Wisdom clearly has a rhetorical function. The author moves from a personal testimony to a description intended to convince the readers that they too should desire her and seek her.

Whatever one desires, whether wealth, understanding, righteousness, or wide experience, Wisdom can impart it because she excels in all of these areas. In this remarkable portrayal, the author appropriates elements from Greek philosophy, specifically Plato's cardinal virtues of temperance, prudence, justice, and fortitude, and assigns them to Wisdom (8:7). The Greeks believed that these virtues could only be achieved through heroic human effort. Pseudo-Solomon maintains that they are actually the fruits of Wisdom's labor, probably the labor associated with childbirth. Wisdom brings forth these virtues in the hearts of those who love righteousness. With Wisdom as his life companion, Pseudo-Solomon possessed what he needed to rule wisely and successfully. The distinction of his reign would give him a kind of immortality; his memory would last forever (8:13; cf. 4:1). It is important to note that it is not his memory generally that will be immortal but the memory of the judicious character of his reign. Kinship with Wisdom also gives birth to pleasure, wealth, understanding, and renown, and so Pseudo-Solomon sought ways of making her his own (v. 18).

The author's account shows that his concept of immortality is closer to the thought of ancient Israel than to that of the Greek philosophers. Any possible immortality for human beings flows from their relationship with the righteousness of God rather than as a property of the human soul (Reese, 1970:62; Nickelsburg, 1972:179). Although the focus here is the king's union with Wisdom, an attendant at God's cosmic throne, Wisdom's marriage with God ensures the everlasting memory of anyone who embraces her.

The reference to the soul (8:19f.) is perhaps the most controversial passage in the book (Reese, 1970:80–86). It should not be presumed that Pseudo-Solomon believed in the preexistence of souls, for nowhere does he describe the soul as immortal or at any time enjoying an existence separates from the human body. Rather than detach body and soul and understand them as separate and independent entities, the author conceives of them as a unity (cf. 1:4, where soul and body are found in parallel construction; 9:15, where they appear to be interdependent). He apparently perceives the soul as the origin of personal moral decision. Thus, the integrity that flows from a noble soul results in an unsullied life.

Pseudo-Solomon's prayer for Wisdom (9:1-18; cf. 1 Kgs 3:6-9) consists of three strophes chiastically arranged (Winston, 1979:200f.). The first two

(9:1-6; 7-12) are identically structured appeals that include an address, a petition, a motive for the prayer, and a general observation. The last strophe (vv. 13-18) is a concluding reflection. Creation is the focus of the first petition, which addresses God as the creator who made all things and who placed humankind over the rest of creation. Fully aware of his own natural human limitations as a finite creature, Pseudo-Solomon pleads for Wisdom. Since she was with God at creation, she would understand the workings of that creation and would be able to assist him in the accomplishment of the responsibilities given to him by God. He fully admits that regardless of how successful one appears to be, everything is meaningless without the wisdom that comes from God.

The second petition concerns another God-given commission, the divine appointment of kingship. The author acknowledges that the people under his jurisdiction are the people of God, a people with whom God is in covenant and who, for that reason, are not to be mistreated. He also admits the obligation that he has to build a temple patterned after God's majestic cosmic sanctuary. Realizing the awesomeness of these responsibilities, he prays for Wisdom who was with God at creation and who knows the mind of God. She will be able to assist him in fulfilling the weighty duties of his royal estate.

The concluding reflection treats the human condition generally. Mortal human beings are incapable of understanding the counsel of God. They can hardly comprehend the things of this world, much less the things of God. Only those to whom God gave Wisdom ever knew what pleased God. This final statement is a clear summary of the fundamental teaching of the book: without the Wisdom that comes from God, one cannot know God's will. The prayer ends with a statement about the salvific function of Wisdom. Not only does she instruct, she also saves. This theme will prove to be very prominent in the remainder of the book.

In what functions as a transition into the final section of the book, Pseudo-Solomon briefly traces the early history of seven heroes of Israel (chapter 10). He shows how it was Wisdom who came to their aid in their great need and who saved them from their distress. The author makes a point of stating that Wisdom saves only the just. Many of the details of this recital are not found in the biblical accounts, but they do appear in some rabbinic versions (Winston, 1979:211–18). The fact that the heroes are not explicitly named suggests that the readers knew the stories well and could easily identify the characters. Pseudo-Solomon is not telling a new story; he is telling an old story in a new way.

It was Wisdom who acted as companion to the lonely Adam before the first woman was created, who lifted him up after his sin and enabled him to fulfill his commission to rule over creation. On the other hand, Cain perished when he rejected her. Wisdom guided Noah when the rest of the world suffered the punishment of Cain's sin, who gave Abraham the strength to follow God's command to sacrifice Isaac, and who saved Lot from destruction. Those who rejected Wisdom were left in ignorance; those who embraced her were saved by her. She saved Jacob from the anger of Esau, guided him to success, and preserved him from harm. She also rescued Joseph from the deadly scheme of his brothers, was with him in his imprisonment, and led him to a position of prominence in Egypt. Wisdom delivered the people from bondage and enabled Moses to stand strong against the power of Egypt. She led the people out at night and took them through the sea, defeating Pharaoh's armies. Finally, Wisdom herself opened the mouths of the dumb so that the people could sing praise to God. This recital of Wisdom's feats is not history; it is theology. It interprets events from Israel's sacred memory from a very particular point of view. Such theological recounting is the subject of the final section of the book.

God's Providence during the Exodus

At first glance it appears that the wisdom theme that has played such a major role in earlier parts of the book ceases to be prominent in this third section (11:2—19:22). The contrary is true. This midrashic reflection on some of the exodus events shows how Wisdom actually directed the course of history. The section consists of five syncrises, contrasts that compare the plight of the Israelites with that of the Egyptians (cf. Wright, 1967:177; Murphy, 1990:90f; Perdue, 1994:294; for seven contrasts see Reese, 1970:98–102; Winston, 1979:227). The contrasts themselves function in several different ways. Most obviously, they demonstrate how God rewards the righteous and punishes the wicked. A closer look shows that what acts as the agent of Israel's blessing is as well the means of Egypt's chastisement (11:5, 13). Finally, the punishment is frequently effected through the very things by which one sins (11:16). This is a reflection on God's preference of Israel over Egypt, a lesson not to be lost on the author's own contemporaries (Alexandrian Jews who are being seduced by the Hellenistic culture?).

The first syncrisis develops the theme of thirst in the wilderness. It begins with the Greek word *anti*, "instead of" (11:6; cf. 11:15; 16:2; 16:20; 18:3), and compares the plague that water-turned-blood of the Nile was for the Egyptians with the boon that the spring from the rock was for the Israelites. In this experience the Egyptians suffered a twofold punishment, having been plagued with the polluted water and further distressed by the knowledge of Israel's good fortune in the wilderness. The second syncrisis (11:15—16:15), which develops into a very extensive digression, both begins and ends with *anti* (11:6; 16:2). It compares the way the Egyptians were plagued by certain small animals while the Israelites were fed by other small creatures (16:1f.), and it states a secondary theme (11:15f.), the manner in which the very agents of Egypt's sin, the reptiles and insects that were worshiped in that land, turn on the people as blight and pestilence.

Mention of Egypt's theriomorphic (animal-form) worship is the occasion of the first digression. It discusses theodicy, the question of divine justice, under two different but related themes: God's power and mercy (11:17—12:27); and idolatry (13:1—15:19). As creator, God can employ everything within creation to serve as an instrument of punishment; but God's chastisement is measured according to the seriousness of the offense. In other words, while God's justice exacts recompense, God's mercy demands restraint. In fact, God can be compassionate precisely because God is all-powerful. As omnipotent creator, God disciplines reprobate creatures; as compassionate creator, God is lenient in punishing, for God created out of love and continues to love even in the face of human transgression. Both divine punishment and divine forbearance look to the repentance of the sinner and thus are intended to be instructive disciplines. The love of God is universal because the incorruptible spirit of God, which is in all things, is the cause of God's love for all creation (12:1). This is not a totally new concept, since the author has already declared that the spirit of God fills the whole earth (cf. 1:7), and that God is incorruptible (cf. 2:23).

The author insists that God's compassion was extended to all, even the Canaanites who inhabited the land before Israel arrived, and who engaged in repulsive ritual practices. God did not strike them down immediately, but instead afflicted them little by little so that they had opportunities to repent and reform. Even with these unrepentant unbelievers God was merciful, and this not out of any weakness but because of God's own undisputed power, which manifests itself not in unrestrained force but in requital that is just. With this discussion, Pseudo-Solomon leads the believer from a description of the power of God, which is grounded in the fact that God is creator of all, to the realization that this power is best demonstrated in divine mercy. He then offers God's deeds as an example for God's people to follow. They are to act toward others with the same kind of consideration (12:19).

Pseudo-Solomon also condemns idolatry (13:1—15:19), beginning with an attack on the worship of nature. Although it is admirable to appreciate the beauty and wonders of the natural world, it is foolish to worship the creature and not the creator who fashioned nature so marvelously. The author seems to attribute goodwill to those who err in this way; at least they showed an appreciation of the works of God. They are still guilty, however, for the very insight that brought them to an appreciation of nature should have led them to revere the creator. Here again is a reversal; intelligence, the very trait that could have won them praise, has brought their denunciation. They should have known better.

Much worse than those who worship nature, God's handiwork, are those who bow down before lifeless idols made by human hands. Pseudo-Solomon not only condemns such practices, he ridicules them. With biting irony, he demonstrates the foolishness in turning to dead wood for life, guidance, or prosperity. The example from navigation, which illustrates the folly in worshiping wood, leads into a testimony to God's provident guidance and the role that Wisdom played in creating a seaworthy vessel. The author contrasts the ruin brought on those who turn to carved idols with the protection through the agency of wood granted to those who trust in God (a reference to Noah and the ark?).

According to Pseudo-Solomon, the potter is even more despicable than the woodcarver. The latter's sin may have begun as error, but the former knew from the start that evil was being devised and engaged in it anyway, and all for the sake of profit. Idols may have originated at moments of human vulnerability and uncertainty and not at times of vitality and insight; nonetheless, the author condemns their worship. They were considered divine, even though they could not claim incorruptibility (a divine characteristic according to the Epicureans). Though empty of divine significance and lacking any supernatural power, they are contemptible because they still act as stumbling blocks to those foolish enough to be attracted to them.

Pseudo-Solomon draws a contrast between false worship with its dire consequences and fidelity to the God of Israel with the blessings that follow. He describes God in terms reminiscent of the Sinai covenant (15:1; cf. Exod 34:6), and the people to whom the author belongs are those who did not embrace dead gods made by human hands but who have been faithful to the God of Israel. Being faithful, they have lived lives of righteousness, which is the root of their immortality (15:3). Once again we see how human beings have a share in immortality through righteousness which is immortal (cf. 1:15; 4:1, and so forth).

The remaining comparisons are quite straightforward. The third syncrisis (16:16-23) describes how the heavens poured down both water and fire and how these consumed the fruits of the land of the Egyptians. In contrast (*anti*, v. 20), the same heavens opened up and rained manna, which sustained the Israelites in their need. The fourth syncrisis (17:1—18:4) contrasts the plague of darkness that befell the Egyptians with the pillar of light that led the Israelites to safety. The fifth and final syncrisis (18:5—19:21) describes how the Egyptians' decision to massacre the sons of the Hebrews reverted onto their own sons. Once again Pseudo-Solomon shows how God turns things around.

In the fourth syncrisis Pseudo-Solomon demonstrates the breadth of his knowledge. Sinners may have presumed that darkness would veil their evil deeds, but they soon discovered that it actually threw them into a state of terror. The author describes the fear that overwhelms the wicked, weaving together themes from legends that grew out of the Exodus narrative as well as data gleaned from Hellenistic psychology. The Egyptians were paralyzed by the darkness. On the other hand (*anti*, 18:3), the Israelites advanced in the light provided by the pillar of fire. This comparison moves the discussion of darkness/light to the metaphorical plane. Those who preferred the darkness of ignorance and had imprisoned the children of God deserved the terror of the night, while those who would bring the brilliance of the law to the world fittingly walked in light.

Initially Egypt had agreed upon Israel's safe departure, but then it revoked this permission and pursued God's people with a vengeance. This pursuit was to no avail, for even nature worked to save the Israelites and punish their pursuers (16:24-29). It should be noted that these are not miraculous events being described. Nature protected and provided for God's people according to its own law (19:6-13), as if reward of the righteous is built right into the structures of the universe. The distinctiveness of Pseudo-Solomon's creation theology should not be overlooked. Clearly, he follows the creation narrative of the priestly tradition (Gen 1:1-2:4a) in his teaching about creation. In a bold move, however, he has used this same tradition here to describe salvation (Vogels, 1991). The exodus event is not viewed as a military feat but as a refashioning of nature (19:6). Even the sequence of this description follows the pattern of the creation narrative rather than the book of Exodus. The book of Wisdom makes a unique contribution to creation theology. Instead of moving from salvation to creation, it begins with creation and moves to salvation. In fact, the book itself begins and ends with affirmations of God's creative purpose: "He created all things that they might endure" (1:14); "The whole creation was fashioned anew, so that your children might be preserved unharmed" (19:6).

Rhetorical Function

From beginning to end, the Wisdom of Solomon is an exhortatory discourse. Like other wisdom works, it champions a particular way of life, but it also condemns, even derides, all others. Furthermore, the worldview that it espouses is clearly particular to one specific people, and the philosophy that it denounces can be easily identified with another national group. Thus, the exhortation acts as a political polemic that is argued both in individual and national contexts.

At the very beginning of the book, where the anonymous wicked are pitted against the unnamed just, Pseudo-Solomon reveals the intercommunal character of this polemic. The righteous are those who have remained faithful to traditional teaching, and the sinners are those who have strayed from it (2:12). The dispute may be among compatriots, but the real conflict is between the religious tradition of one people and the philosophy of another. The accounts found within the book, both of individuals and of the nation as a whole, exemplify this. All of the arguments describe the ethnocentric source of true Wisdom and the destiny of those who have found and embraced her as well as of those who have not. Furthermore, the ethnocentricity described here is given divine legitimation. In fact, according to this version of the story, it originated out of God's preference of one people over all others.

The author, who has obliquely identified himself as the renowned Israelite king, goes to great lengths to show that he himself excels in all of the philosophical and scientific disciplines cherished by the rival culture. Moreover, he possesses such excellence not through any human accomplishment of his own, as his antagonists might suggest, but as a gift bestowed on him in view of his fidelity to the religious traditions of his ancestors. He first argues that the love of righteousness brings wisdom, and then he demonstrates the truth of this tenet in his own life.

Unquestionably, the author lives in a pluralistic society, where traditional values do not enjoy the prominence they may have had in earlier times. Opposing views challenge former ideological hegemony; the accomplishments of other cultures rival, even outclass, traditional values and practices. By its very nature the syncrisis sets up a polemic. Pseudo-Solomon uses this Hellenistic form of comparison to interpret some of the incidents that made up the foundational tradition of his faith, the exodus event. In his testimonies, he shows that not only is Wisdom found in the teachings of his tradition, but she actually directed the destinies of his ancestors. In contrast, the religious inclinations of the rival culture led to senseless and despicable idolatry as well as military defeat and political collapse. Through such argumentation, the author seeks both to dissuade vacillating compatriots from rejecting the faith of their youth and adopting the opposing worldview, and to persuade the apostates to return to the source of true wisdom.

The diatribes of Pseudo-Solomon can be heard and understood in various ways. The most traditionalist members of the community will be reaffirmed in their commitment to ancestral values. More than this, they might also assume a self-satisfied attitude of religious superiority, an attitude quite easily developed by those convinced of their special status as "chosen people." This superiority might also be directed judgmentally toward any members of the community who have drifted away from religious practice or who have deliberately abandoned their faith.

Those who have already made the choice in favor of the opposing culture might hear the arguments of this book in a different way. They are being censured for their religious disloyalty, and the merit of their choice is also being challenged on cultural grounds. The first part of the book repeatedly identifies them as wicked and foolish. By forsaking their faith, they have relinquished any claim to wisdom itself. By rejecting immortal righteousness associated with the law, they have made a pact with death. Although this denunciation might be heard as the harsh but empty censorship by a tradition that no longer exercises any influence over their lives, most likely it was intended to bring these straying members back to their senses.

In addition to the religious condemnation, their cultural discretion is questioned. The rival society may boast indisputable intellectual and aesthetic achievements, but the principles upon which it is established are ignoble and impermanent. Both their empty idolatrous religion and their futile history give evidence of this. Besides this, any authentic cultural achievements can be found within and even outdone by the traditional beliefs of Israel. In other words, they have left the best for something inferior, and Pseudo-Solomon's arguments are meant to convince them to return.

Most commentators think that those who were wavering in their devotion were really the intended audience of this instruction. For their sake, the author sketches the superiority of the religious tradition in unmistakable lines and bold colors while portraying the opposing culture as deceptive and its religious practices as ignoble. The contrasts posed are striking; there is no comparison. One worldview is able to realize the longings of the human heart, the other can only make empty promises. One society has always been under the watchful care of the creator, the other has been the victim of ravaging natural disasters. Those who are wavering in their faith should not be deceived by appearances, as were the enemies of God's people in the past. Fidelity to ancestral faith is the only way to wisdom.

Finally, there were probably many people in the community like Pseudo-Solomon himself who, while committed to traditional teachings, showed great facility in the language and thought world of the Hellenistic culture. These people would have been able to move back and forth between different worlds, because in many ways they belonged to both of them, as often happens in a pluralistic society. They would have respected the author's sophisticated education as well as his insight into his faith. He is the kind of teacher that they would turn to for direction in reinterpreting that faith in a new cultural context. Like the traditionalists described above, they would be reaffirmed in their faith, but with an appreciation of new cultural expressions. They would understand why so many would be attracted by the accomplishments of that culture, but they would also be aware of its pitfalls. The Solomonic authority given to the teaching of this author legitimates cross-cultural recontextualization.

Unmasking the Powers

Although human finitude limits the perspective through which all reality is viewed, this point does not thereby negate the value of the religious insights gained. Nonetheless, it is important to recognize and deal with these limitations lest we misjudge the scope and character of the insight. For this reason, the issues of race or ethnic origin, class, and gender will now become the focus of the critique of this biblical book.

In the first place, the ethnocentricity of this book is striking. In fact, it is not merely a characteristic of the work but its primary focus. From start to finish, the author is intent on demonstrating the superiority of his own religious tradition, and he does this at the expense of a culture that appears to him to have posed a real threat to the commitment of his compatriots. Not content to deride this threatening culture which was contemporary to himself, he ridicules another nation and culture with whom his ancestors interacted in times past. He does this in order to show that the people to whom he belongs have from their inception been God's special people, and their religious beliefs and practices have always been superior to the beliefs and practices of all others.

The notion of having been specially chosen by God has been at the core of Israel's self-perception from the very beginning. At times this belief has brought the people to their knees in awe and humble gratitude (cf. Exod 19:3-8). At other times it has led them into attitudes of arrogance and false confidence (cf. Jer 7:1-15). In the Wisdom of Solomon such ethnic bias may well be a defensive reaction to a perceived threat to cultural survival, a threat arising out of a sense of vulnerability rather than superiority. Even if this is the explanation of their self-understanding, their ethnic bias must be recognized for the chauvinism that it is.

The underlying intolerance present in the teaching of this biblical book is not merely leveled at those who are outsiders to the culture of the author; there is a class prejudice within his own society as well. This bias manifests itself in several ways. The exhortations of the book are purportedly addressed to the leaders within the society (1:1; 6:1-9, 21). The author seems to hold these rulers responsible for leading the entire people to faithful observance of the traditional values and customs. The literary form of the book suggests that it is an exhortation of one ruler to several other rulers. The general population appears to be objects described or referred to within the exhortation, rather than subjects to whom the admonitions are addressed. The practice of leaders deciding for and speaking in the name of the populace indicates class bias.

Another sign of class preference can be seen in the characterization of Pseudo-Solomon. He describes himself as being privileged from birth (8:19f.), a privilege that apparently afforded him access to the social circles of the powerful. Though access did not guarantee him any degree of esteem within these circles, he did gain the respect of others (8:10f., 14f.) after God had freely granted him wisdom (8:21). Having first been chosen to rule (9:7), with wisdom he could now do so in a way beneficial to the people (9:12).

Pseudo-Solomon was doubly blessed. He enjoyed the privilege into which he had been born and, because God had particularly favored him with wisdom, he had status within the circles of power. Although his social station did not ensure him respect, those who themselves enjoyed social status esteemed him. They seem to have been the arbiters in this court of honor. This indicates class exclusivity.

The gender bias of the book is unmistakable. In the first place, God is not only characterized as a male deity but is identified as father (2:16; 11:10; 14:3) and as king (11:10). Throughout the exhortation to righteous living, reference and examples are generally androcentric, describing the roles played by fathers (12:6; 14:15; 18:6, 9, 24) and sons (9:6; 12:19, 21; 16:10, 26; 18:4, 13). The covenant was promised to ancestral fathers (12:21; 18:22), and the righteous are called "sons of God" (2:13, 18; 5:5). In line with this, God is addressed as "God of my fathers" (9:1). Furthermore, when the history is retold, only stories of male heroes are included. All of this reveals the gender bias that relegates women to a state of invisibility and ignores their involvement in the history of the people.

In the midst of this male preference, other passages reflect a degree of gender balance. Without exception, the word used to refer to all people is the gender-inclusive term *ánthrōpos*, which is best translated "humankind" and not "man" as so many English versions render it. Another example of gender balance is found in Pseudo-Solomon's comparison of the value of righteousness versus the blessings of children (3:13f.). There he argues that neither the childless woman nor the eunuch is to be scorned for producing no progeny. Instead, the blessedness of both woman and man is found in their virtue.

The figure of Woman Wisdom looms large in this book, which draws the characterization with the same contours as in the corresponding figure found in Proverbs. She is intimately associated with God, coming forth from God, almost godlike herself (cf. Prov 8:22-31). In Pseudo-Solomon's embellished portrait, she also possesses features comparable to those of Isis, the Hellenistic goddess of culture and the benefactor of humankind (7:22b-23), as well as characteristics of the world soul (7:24). The implication of this similarity should not be overlooked. Throughout the book, Pseudo-Solomon insists that real Wisdom is found only in Israel. This assertion supports his claim that his own religious culture is far superior to that of Hellenism. By attributing Isiac characteristics to Woman Wisdom, he is suggesting that she, rather than Isis, is the source of culture. Thus Israel is indebted to Woman Wisdom of its own tradition for the treasures of culture.

Pseudo-Solomon also states that like a fruitful mother, Woman Wisdom engendered all good things, including health, prosperity, and prestige (7:12). Although in praising wisdom the author employs a stereotypical maternal image, this mother brings forth the kind of beneficence that traditionally comes from God, and so the traditional image is not as restrictive as at first it might seem.

As affirming of women's reality as this characterization of Woman Wisdom may appear to be, its rhetorical function within the book cannot be overlooked. The primary interest of the author is not the female representation of wisdom but insistence on the preeminence of the religious tradition of Israel, a tradition that is unquestionably androcentric, disparaging of women and relegating them to invisibility. The female personification of wisdom, along with almost every other theme in the book, serves the androcentric goals of the author's ethnic chauvinism.

Into the Looking Glass

Once the instructions of Pseudo-Solomon have been critiqued from an advocacy stand sensitive to issues of race or ethnic origin, class, and gender, the revelatory power of the word of God can next be directed to these very issues. If the biblical message is to function for the reader as a mirror and as a doorway to a new world, the message of Pseudo-Solomon must be able to challenge the very bias out of which it was written. If it is truly to function as the word of God for us today, a new world must be made available to the contemporary reader.

The analysis of the book has revealed the extent to which Pseudo-Solomon has employed Hellenistic literary forms and methods of argumentation. In the first part of the work, he uses the diatribe to show that righteousness, a characteristic of fidelity to the Israelite religious tradition, is immortal. In the second part, he uses another Hellenistic strategy, the sorites, to argue that true Wisdom is found only in Israel. The syncrisis is a major technique used in the third part to contrast the fortunes of the Israelites with those of the Egyptians.

Throughout the book, the methods and the content of his argumentation reveal a man who is well versed in many areas of the very culture that he is denouncing. Pseudo-Solomon may be a faithful Israelite, but he is thoroughly acculturated into the Hellenistic world. Its language is his own as are its figures of speech and techniques of expression. From this, one can conclude that he is not opposed to Hellenism in itself. What he decries is the perverse accommodation of basic traditional Israelite religious values and beliefs to elements of the competing Hellenistic worldview that has captured the imagination of those weak in the faith of his forebears.

Cultural values are seldom devoid of religious meaning. Consequently, when they are challenged or spurned the religious underpinnings of the culture are threatened. This frequently happens when one culture encounters and interacts with another. A cultural crisis ensues. In the face of this, traditionalists frequently call for withdrawal from everything foreign that might jeopardize religious identity and practice (cf. Deut 7:1-11; Ezra 10:3-4; Neh 10:29-31). Such a course of action might be possible in a monocultural situation, when the introduction of new ideas can be controlled and the process of accommodation can be regulated. Such control and regulation are not always possible, however. In such cases the culture will have to deal with what it perceives as a danger to its integrity. If it is not to be absorbed by a commanding alien worldview, it will have to reinterpret its identity and way of life in new yet faithful ways.

Pseudo-Solomon found himself in just such a situation. He was not a rigid traditionalist but a revisionist who found ways of reinterpreting his religion within the context of the new Hellenistic cultural setting. He called for fidelity, not merely by clinging to former ways but by accommodating to the dominant society while condemning whatever within it was incompatible with the precepts of his faith. Although he directed the specifics of his message toward his own compatriots, the character of the instruction exemplifies the twofold process of theological reinterpretation and development. His own ethnocentric bias was not so rigid as to prevent this from happening.

Pseudo-Solomon describes his humble origins and identifies himself with all other human beings (7:1-6). Like everyone else, he is mortal, a child of the earth. He was born into the world like the rest, and he will pass out of it as do others. In this respect all are the same. There are no ethnic or racial privileges here. His ethnocentricity is further modified. He states that God's mercy extends to all, because God loves everything that God has created

(11:23—12:1). This includes even the early inhabitants of the land of Canaan, whose punishment by God was a form of discipline intended to bring them to their senses and move them to relinquish their abominable religious practices (12:2-10). Even though elements of the culture are condemned, other nations are still seen as created and loved by God.

The question of punishment brings up the matter of retribution. Unlike other teachings about reward and punishment, the Wisdom of Solomon seldom identifies them with economic prosperity or the lack thereof, characterizations normally associated with class distinctions. Instead, the author describes the punishment of the enemies of Israel as the reverse of God's providential care of the chosen people and depicts reward and punishment as either national salvation or national affliction. While this appears to be an ethnic bias, the punishment is meted out because the Egyptians oppressed God's people and not merely because they were a different nation. This is substantiated by the text itself, which states that God's mercy sought to bring them to repentance (11:23—12:2).

Without denying the privilege that was his in the possession of wisdom, Pseudo-Solomon clearly states that Woman Wisdom herself is more valuable than scepter and throne or riches of any kind (7:8f.). He declares that wealth and the advantage that it typically claims are like sand in comparison to wisdom. In a very real sense, Pseudo-Solomon is here democratizing the possession of wisdom. It was not his royal status that gained him this matchless treasure, it was his prayer and devotion. By implication, anyone with the same religious devotion can receive from God the same incomparable blessing. In fact, this is the very point of the argument of the entire book: Wisdom, the most cherished treasure of all, is available to anyone who is faithful to the religious traditions of the ancestors, regardless of social or economic status.

Finally, despite the apparent class bias, the privilege described in the book is qualified in another way. Those in positions of authority, and this would include Pseudo-Solomon, may wield power in the social and political arenas, but they are no match before the might of God (12:14). By itself this acknowledgment may not appear to undermine class bias, but other elements of this instruction blunt the edge of privilege. Together they constitute a significant modification. First, there is the insistence upon the commonality of all human beings as mortal creatures of God. Coupled with this is the assertion that all who pray, regardless of their social class, can be granted wisdom. Finally, retribution is not described in terms of material prosperity and station. All of this suggests the subversion of class privilege.

Although it is very difficult to redeem the book from its inherent gender bias, certain elements within it might reflexively challenge its prejudiced view. Pseudo-Solomon maintains that blessedness is determined by the quality of one's virtue, not by one's reproductive ability. One of the measures used for judging a woman's value is here thrown into question in two distinct ways. First, women, and for that matter men as well, are perceived as something more than procreators. Second, women and men are both judged by the same standard, and that standard is not genetically determined. In other words, biology is *not* always destiny.

The image of Woman Wisdom as a fecund mother (7:12) lends itself to feminist reinterpretation in two ways. If in a metaphor, the tenor and the vehicle reinterpret each other, then one can argue in the following way. First, the fecund mother brings forth fruits that normally come only from God. Therefore, *she* is godlike. Second, if being thus fruitful is godlike, then one can say that God is like a fruitful mother. Thus, not only is this fruitful mother godlike, but it is precisely in her being a fruitful mother that she is so.

Pseudo-Solomon incorporates properties of Isis, the Hellenistic goddess of culture and the benefactor of humankind, into his depiction of Woman Wisdom. Although the expertise and artifacts of this culture were generally ascribed to the men, the deity from whose bounty the skills flowed was characterized as female. Thus one can say that in one sense the magnitude and grandeur of the culture is ascribed to the proficiency of men and in another sense to that of women. In other words, women and men together are the artisans of their culture.

The cosmological perspective of Pseudo-Solomon cannot be overlooked. As stated earlier, this author unmistakably moves from creation to salvation, the natural world itself acting as the agent of God's saving power. The apocalyptic imagery used to describe the punishment of the wicked (5:16b-23) depicts God as the cosmic warrior arrayed with all of the powers of creation in mortal combat against the evil brought into the world because of sin. Because it conforms to the order created by God, the universe is on the side of righteousness (16:17c). Each syncrisis demonstrates this. It also shows that a corresponding affliction befell the enemies of Israel in order to retain the natural balance in creation.

There is a difference between Pseudo-Solomon's rendition of Israel's salvation and the version found in the books of Exodus and Numbers. These books see the acts of nature as miracles, acts of direct divine intervention. Pseudo-Solomon sees creation as working according to its natural laws (19:6), as if reward and punishment were built into the very structures of the universe. More than this, Israel was saved because creation was fundamentally renewed. Both at creation and during the exodus first darkness covered everything (Gen 1:2; Exod 14:20), then dry land appeared (Gen 1:9; Exod 14:21). In Pseudo-Solomon's account, creation may have been transformed, but its transformation happened according to its own natural laws.

Love Righteousness

The Wisdom of Solomon is a book about fidelity, Israel's fidelity to its religious traditions and God's fidelity to Israel. Each of the three divisions of the book demonstrates a different aspect of this fidelity. The first part explains how God's enduring faithfulness to the covenant makes immortality of each covenant member possible. Because God is faithful, the bond that unites God to those who have been loyal to their covenant commitment will survive death. The second part claims that true wisdom is found in the religion of Israel, and one will attain this wisdom only through devotion to that religion. This does not necessarily mean that one must practice this faith as it was practiced in the past. Reinterpretation can be done, but the essence of the faith must be preserved and heeded. Finally, aspects of Israel's history are recounted in a way that exemplifies God's steadfast providence. This is done in order to persuade the people to hold fast to their commitment. They should be faithful because God is faithful.

Behind the ethnocentric posturing of the author is the conviction that not only can his religious tradition stand firm in its pristine form in the midst of a foreign culture, but it is flexible enough (this means universally applicable) to adapt to that new culture without losing its basic religious force and meaning. The Wisdom of Solomon demonstrates two of the central features of a living tradition, namely, continuity and discontinuity. Rooted in the past, it struggles in the present to be open to the future. It rearticulates key religious concepts through the employment of current ideas and techniques of expression. It retells its founding story in a style contemporary to the new generation of believers. Most strikingly, it shows how the new culture can actually open the tradition to development in ways its initial worldview could not.

The Wisdom of Solomon is a guide for intercultural experience and life within a pluralistic society. It may not provide specific direction for such living, but it is testimony to its possibility. It is a summons to both loyalty and adaptability, two traits so necessary for life in a multicultural situation. It calls for and gives evidence of a loyalty that is adaptable and an adaptability that is loyal.

Works Consulted

Collins, John J. 1977. "Cosmos and Salvation: Jewish Wisdom and Apocalyptic in the Hellenistic Age." *Harvard Review* 17:121–42.

Kolarcik, Michael. 1991. *The Ambiguity of Death in the Book of Wisdom 1–6.* Roma: Editrice Pontificio Instituto Biblico.

Murphy, Roland E. 1990. *The Tree of Life.* Anchor Bible Reference Library. New York: Doubleday.

Nickelsburg, George W. N. 1972. *Resurrection, Immortality, and Eternal Life in Intertestamental Judaism.* Cambridge: Harvard University Press.

Perdue, Leo G. 1994. *Wisdom and Creation: The Theology of Wisdom Literature.* Nashville: Abingdon Press.

Reese, James M. 1970. *Hellenistic Influence on the Book of Wisdom and Its Consequences.* Rome: Biblical Institute Press.

_____. 1983. *The Book of Wisdom, Song of Songs.* Old Testament Message. Wilmington, Del.: Michael Glazier.

Vogels, Walter. 1991. "The God Who Creates Is the God Who Saves: The Book of Wisdom's Reversal of the Biblical Pattern." *Église et Théologie* 22:315–35.

Winston, David. 1979. *The Wisdom of Solomon.* The Anchor Bible. New York: Doubleday.

Wright, Addison G. 1967. "The Structure of the Book of Wisdom." *Biblica* 48:165–84.

8

Sirach

Introduction

L IKE THE WISDOM OF SOLOMON, Sirach belongs to the Deutero-canonical/Apocryphal listing of biblical books. It is one of the few biblical books actually written by the ascribed author, "Jesus son of Eleazar son of Sirach of Jerusalem" (50:27). He provides the reader with some interesting autobiographical information. He was a teacher (24:30-34; 33:16-18) who did extensive traveling (34:12-13). Apparently he was associated with some kind of a school, a "house of instruction" (51:23). His panegyric on Simon (50:1-21), most likely Simeon II, the high priest from 219–196 B.C.E., helps to date the original work around 180 B.C.E.. A later preface to the book was written by his grandson, who translated the teachings of this Jewish sage into Greek so that, as his grandfather intended (33:16-18), they might be included with the other wisdom writings so translated.

The Greek version of the book survives in two different forms. The Hebrew text was lost until the nineteenth century, when about two-thirds of it was found in a Cairo genizah, a medieval synagogue room where discarded manuscripts were stored. More recently, other fragments have been found at Qumran and Masada. These fragments substantiate the authenticity of the Cairo document (Skehan and Di Lella, 1987:51–62). This multiplicity of manuscript evidence explains the disparity, both in content and in chapter and verse identification, that one finds among the versions available today. (The numbering of the critical edition of the Septuagint will be followed here.)

The book itself is known under several titles: Sirach, the Greek version of the author's name; The Wisdom of Ben Sira, from the Hebrew spelling; Ecclesiasticus or "church book" from the Latin Vulgate. The latter title dates back to Saint Cyprian and may derive from the book's extensive use as a resource for early Christian catechesis (Murphy, 1990:67).

Sirach's own canonical status is disputed. Although it was originally written in Hebrew and in Jerusalem, the Pharisees who determined the list of sacred writings omitted it from their collection. They may have done so because Ben Sira challenged some of the theology that these Pharisees espoused, such as retribution in an afterlife. Despite this fact, many subsequent rabbis quoted passages from the book as Scripture. Protestants who adopted the Jewish listing consider it apocryphal, while Roman Catholics regard it as Deutero-canonical.

It is clear that in content, basic structure, and choice of literary genre Ben Sira was particularly influenced by the book of Proverbs (Skehan and Di Lella, 1987:43; Murphy, 1990:70f.). Not content with citing a specific proverb, Ben Sira would develop it and explain its implications for his own day. In this way, he preferred the longer instructional form to the simple proverbial sentence. Like Proverbs, Sirach begins with a hymn to Woman Wisdom (Prov 1–9; Sir 1:1-20) and ends with an acrostic poem (Prov 31:10-31; Sir 51:13-30). Following Sirach's introductory hymn is a twenty-two-line poem (the number of letters in the Hebrew alphabet) which, with the final twenty-three-line acrostic poem, forms a kind of *inclusio*, evidence of the canonical unity of the book.

Ben Sira used most of the literary forms associated with the wisdom tradition. For example: proverb *(19:12);* hymn of praise (1:1-10); prayer of petition (22:27—23:6); autobiographical narrative (33:16—18); onomasticon (42:15—43:33); and didactic narrative (44:1—50:24; see Skehan and Di Lella, 1987:21–30). He also used macarisms (14:1, 2, 20; 25:8, 9; 26:1; 28:19; 31:8; 34:17; 48:11; 50:28) and woes (2:12, 13, 14; 41:8) in his exhortations, and "better . . . than" comparisons (19:24; 40:18-27) in his instructions.

The actual structure of the book of Sirach is not so easily determined. While most scholars agree that the eulogy of the heroes of Israel (44:1—50:24) is a discrete unit and that the final section (50:25—51:30) consists of an epilogue along with the acrostic poem, they agree little about how the greater part of the book should be divided. Many commentators simply regard the material as a collection of various unrelated instructions (MacKenzie, 1983:5–9; Skehan and Di Lella, 1987:4–6; Murphy, 1990:70f.). Some consider chapters 1–23 and 24–43 as distinct sections, each beginning with a hymn to Woman Wisdom (Di Lella, 1992:936–38; Gammie, 1990:356, with modifications, the arrangement adopted here; Roth, 1980, yet another arrangement). Others divide the book into three sections, 1–24; 25–43; 44–51, each ending with some kind of a poem: 24:1-34, a hymn of Woman Wisdom's self-praise; 42:15—43:33, a hymn in praise of the Creator; 51:13-30, a description of Ben Sira's search for wisdom (Jacob, 1978:254; Perdue, 1994:247).

The Book

My Grandfather

The grandson's preface provides historical information about his own translation, insight into the character of his grandfather's instructions, and a description of the canonical organization of the biblical material that was current at the time. He states that he translated the work during the "thirty-eighth year of the reign of King Euergetes," or 132 B.C.E. Three times he refers to a tripartite Bible, "the law, the prophets, and later authors/the rest of the books." This suggests two very important points: (1) that as early as the second half of the second century B.C.E., the First Testament had basically the tripartite form it has today; and (2) that this Bible was revered as both formative and normative sacred teaching, despite the limitations of the Septuagint (Greek) version. The grandson further claims, and the text of the book itself demonstrates, that Ben Sira was familiar with and cites or alludes to most of the books of our present-day First Testament of the Bible.

The grandson is clearly speaking to diaspora Jews, for he insists that his readers should praise Israel for preserving and handing down the religious truths. His insistence suggests that there is some difference between Israel and his audience. Furthermore, he invites them to read his grandfather's instruction in his own Greek translation, inadequate as this may be compared to the original Hebrew version. Finally, he identifies his audience as those who are living abroad, presumably beyond the confines of the land of Israel. His concern for members of the diaspora community and his translation into the Greek language highlight two very important theological issues: (1) the enduring significance of the Jewish tradition; and (2) the inherent merit of another culture as the matrix within which the revelation of the God of Israel can take root and flourish.

Creation, Wisdom, and the Fear of the Lord

The first part of the book (chapters 1–23) opens with a hymn extolling the virtues of wisdom (1:1-10). This is followed by a poem that links wisdom with the "fear of the Lord" (1:11-30). The remainder of the first part (chapters 2–23) consists of instructions about various aspects of life demonstrating how the "fear of the Lord" is a manifestation of or the way to wisdom. These instructions are found in a series of exhortations to righteous living that includes teachings about: one's duties toward God and toward one's parents (2:1—3:16); humility, social responsibility, and the benefits of wisdom (3:17—4:19); appropriate speech, authentic reputation, choosing friends, seeking wisdom and avoiding evil (4:20—7:17); domestic, religious, and social obligations (7:18—8:19); relationships with women, acquaintances, and rulers (9:1—10:5); pride, honor, and humility (10:6—11:6); the need for careful discernment (11:7—14:19); the blessings of wisdom and freedom, and the punishment of sinners (14:20—16:23); the Creator's wisdom and compassion (16:24—18:14); social virtues and vices (18:15—23:15); and sexual propriety (23:16-27).

Wisdom and the fear of the Lord are intimately associated in this first chapter (Perdue, 1994:251–54) and in other poems throughout this section of the book. Some of these poems are primarily concerned with aspects of wisdom itself, while others focus on the human attitude of fear of the Lord. This study will examine the poems that praise wisdom before the theme of fear of the Lord is addressed.

The introductory hymn (1:1-10) sets the context for understanding the various themes and teachings contained within the first section of the book. First, it places Wisdom, personified as a woman, in the beginning of God's creative activity, at the heart of creation. Next, it describes Woman Wisdom as coming *from God*, being *with God*, and fully comprehended *only by God*. Then it states that God bestowed Wisdom first on all of God's works, then on all human beings, finally lavishing her on those who love God. In other words, all of creation is somehow permeated with Wisdom. The hymn borrows from earlier Israelite characterizations of wisdom, combining Proverbs' testimony to Woman Wisdom's cosmic origin (Prov 8:22-31) with Job's account of the inaccessibility of wisdom to humans (Job 28). The image of Wisdom sketched here is clearly of Israelite origin, although it enjoys its own unique contours.

A second poem describes Woman Wisdom as actively involved in the lives of human beings, "her children" (4:11-19). It claims that, though grasped fully only by God, the intimate relationship that she enjoys with God benefits others as well. She is accessible to those who sincerely search for her. God blesses those who love her and obey her, for service of Wisdom is considered service of the Lord. But the special favors of Wisdom are not easily secured. Wisdom tests her children before she reveals her secrets, and her discipline is rigorous. If they pass the test, they are rewarded; if they prove unfaithful, she will withdraw from them.

A third poem praising Woman Wisdom (6:18-37) urges the Jewish reader to strive mightily for her. The structure of this poem is quite interesting. The twenty-two nonalphabetic lines are divided into three parts by the typical wisdom address "child" (vv. 18, 23, 32). The hardships involved in the pursuit of Wisdom are first described in imagery from agriculture (vv. 18-22). Plowing, sowing, and harvesting are demanding, but their yield is well worth the effort. Fools may not have the will needed for the task, and they will abandon the undertaking, but those who persevere will be rewarded. A second image is taken from the experience of capturing an animal (vv. 23-31). Wisdom's discipline fetters and collars those who seek to enjoy her. When they have withstood Wisdom's testing, the shackles that once confined them become glorious adornment. The third part of this poem (vv. 32-37) does not contain the kind of comparisons found in the previous two parts. It is straightforward advice. The "child" is directed to listen to the teachings of the elders and to observe their behavior in order to imitate it. Through this kind of apprenticeship, the "child" will gain the Wisdom he or she seeks.

In the very first chapter, after he praises the Wisdom that stands with God, Ben Sira turns to its human counterpart, fear of the Lord (1:11-30). As Wisdom belongs to God, so fear of the Lord is the hallmark of the truly wise person. Its intimate relationship with Wisdom and the fulfillment and happiness it confers make this a most desirable virtue. For human beings the fear of the Lord is, in fact, both the beginning and the fullness of Wisdom (1:14, 16).

This particular poem is programmatic for understanding the instructions in the second section of the book, evidence of the canonical unity of the book. Its first half (vv. 11-21) extols the marvels of fear of the Lord, a major theme of the first part of the book. Fear of the Lord brings joy and happiness (vv. 11-13) and is the way to Wisdom (vv. 14-21). It gives the faithful access to Wisdom from the time they were in the womb, throughout their lives, and down through the generations of their descendants.

The second half of the poem (vv. 22-30) provides instruction as to what kind of behavior to pursue and what to avoid. Such instruction is the major focus of the teachings of this section. The wise know how to control their anger and to act prudently, thus escaping ruin. Ben Sira teaches that observing the commandments pleases God and will assure one of wisdom. He warns against disobedience, hypocrisy, and pride. The poem begins with a tribute to the fear of the Lord (v. 11) and ends with a condemnation of those whose hearts lack such fear.

The importance of fear of the Lord is stated again and again in the instructions that follow. The "child/children" to whom the teaching is directed (2:1; cf. 3:1, 12, 17; 4:1; 6:18, 23, 32; 10:28; 11:10; 14:11; 16:24; 18:15; 21:1; 23:7) are also referred to as "you who fear the Lord." They are challenged to trust God and to hope for God's blessing (2:7-9), and further advised that "those who fear the Lord" are careful about the friendships they form (6:16f.), and respect religious leaders (7:29f.). Most significantly, Ben Sira identifies fear of the Lord with observance of the law (2:15-17; 10:19; 15:1, 13, 19; 19:20; 21:6, 11; 32:14-17), thereby teaching the importance of fidelity to the traditions of the ancestors.

Honor, the reputation that one enjoys within the community, and its opposite, shame, are of great concern to Ben Sira. Normally one is honored because of one's lineage, one's accomplishments, and the integrity of one's family. Ben Sira distrusts such grounds for evaluation, holding that the person who fears the Lord is the one worthy of honor (10:19-31).

A well-crafted two-stanza poem describes the blessedness of the one who aspires to Woman Wisdom (14:20—15:10). The first stanza (14:20—27) is a macarism ("happy is . . .") consisting of a series of characterizations of the one who seeks her, characterizations that stem from colorful images of Wisdom herself. It scrutinizes Wisdom's ways, considers her dwelling the most desirable place for others to reside, and seeks her gracious protection. The second stanza (15:1-10) relates the blessings granted the one who fears the Lord and obeys the law. For the righteous, Wisdom will provide motherly nurture and the welcome embrace of a bride. She will be a support and an advocate, the source of joy and gladness. To the impious, she is inaccessible.

Ben Sira marvels at the wisdom of the creator as manifested in the created world (16:24—17:11). Not only does it reveal order and harmony but it is replete with myriads of marvelous living things (cf. 13:15-19), unique among which are human beings (cf. 15:14). Though finite and mortal (10:9-11; 17:27-32), they are made in God's image, given responsibility for the other creatures (cf. Gen 1:26-28), and endowed with intelligence and fear of the Lord. Fear of the Lord recalls the earlier hymn in praise of Wisdom (1:1-10). As wonderful as humankind may be, it is still bound by limitations (18:1-12). Only God is incomparable in majesty. No one can duplicate God's works or even comprehend God's ways (20:9-12). It is precisely because of human finitude that God's justice is matched by God's mercy and compassion (18:11-14; cf. 2:18; 17:29f.).

Insistence on God's compassion tempers the idea of strict retribution, which plays a very important role in the teaching of this book (16:1-23; 21:1-10), as it does in the entire wisdom tradition. While righteousness according to law and custom is the primary criterion by which the appropriateness of behavior is normally judged, the admonitions of Ben Sira are particularly concerned with virtues such as: trust in God (2:6-10); humility (3:17-29; 7:4-6; 10:6—11:6); care for the poor (4:1-10); prudence in speech (4:20-31; 19:4-17; 20:1-8, 18-20), in one's choice of friends (6:5-17), and in the use of material resources (14:3-19); good social relations (7:18—10:5; 11:29—14:2); careful discernment (11:7-9); and self-control (18:19—19:3).

The first part of the book of Sirach closes with traditional wisdom teaching: fear the Lord and obey the commandments (23:27; cf. Eccl 12:13). Beginning with praise of Woman Wisdom (1:1-10) and an exhortation to fear the Lord so that she can be enjoyed (1:11-30), it ends with a warning about the foolish woman whose enjoyment leads to destruction (23:22-27). There is no doubt about which woman Ben Sira would have one pursue; his teaching is quite clear. Choose Woman Wisdom!

Creation, Wisdom, and the Law

The second major division of the book (24–43) opens, as did the first, with a hymn in praise of Woman Wisdom (24:1-33). Unlike the earlier hymn, this one is self-descriptive. Wisdom sings her own praises. A lengthy hymn celebrating the magnificent works of God in creation (42:15—43:34) closes the division. Between these two hymns is a collection of instructions dealing with various aspects of life: its joys (25:1-12; 40:18-27) and its sorrows (26:28; 40:1-11, 28-30); wicked and virtuous women (25:13—26:27); honesty, trustworthiness and self-control (26:29—28:26); the right attitude toward riches (29:1-20; 31:1-11) and the care of property and servants (33:20-33); hospitality, child-rearing, and proper etiquette (29:21—30:25; 31:12—32:13); true and false hope, authentic worship, and prayer (34:1-8, 14—36:22); proper discernment (36:23—38:23) and worthwhile occupations (34:9-13; 38:24—39:11); the fate of the wicked (40:12-17; 41:5-13); and true and false shame (41:15—42:14). There is also a poem that extols the law (32:14—33:19) and a hymn that praises the creative ingenuity of God (39:12-35).

Along with the same wisdom teaching devices used in the first section of the book, Ben Sira employs numerical proverbs, a wisdom form that groups very different things together because they have one thing in common; for example: things beautiful in the sight of God (25:1); kinds of hateful people (25:2). He uses the x, x + 1 pattern to name things that frighten him (26:5f.) and those that offend him (26:28). He combines this form of the proverb with the macarism when he lists those people whom he considers blessed or happy (25:7-10).

In both structure (thirty-five lines) and content (cosmic origin and role in human history), the opening hymn resembles Proverbs 8 (Skehan, 1979; Skehan and Di Lella, 1987:327–42; Perdue, 1994:264–72). A short introduction (vv. 1-2) states the theme of Woman Wisdom's twenty-two line address (vv. 3-22). Following this first-person speech, Ben Sira identifies Wisdom with the law that Israel received from God through Moses, and then he traces his own teaching back to this source of life (for an allusion to this same identification found in Deut 5:4-8, see Sheppard, 1980:63–71). The Wisdom that comes from God is, in reality, the law that is the basis of the teaching of Ben Sira. This is a very bold statement.

Wisdom states that she came forth from God (cf. 1:1-10). In the beginning, she acted in the way a deity would act, enthroned on a pillar of clouds (24:4), exercising some form of dominion over heaven, earth, the sea, and all nations (vv. 5-7; cf. Camp, 1985; Lang, 1986). Then she sought a dwelling place. Would it be with the gods in the heavens? in the cosmic sea? or would she establish herself in the midst of the human community? Although Wisdom was the one seeking a place to settle, it was the Creator-God who decided where she would abide, and God decided in favor of Israel (vv. 8-12). Establishing the proper place for each marvel of creation was not a divine afterthought, it was actually part of primordial creation itself (cf. Pss 74:13-17; 89:9-14). One can conclude from this that the establishment of cosmic Wisdom in the midst of Israel, decided as it was in the primordial realm, is here seen as part of the very structure of the created cosmos. Wisdom was there from the beginning, ministering to God, waiting to be revealed to the children of Israel.

After her dwelling place was chosen, Wisdom pitched her tent (v. 8) in the same city where the tent of God had been set up, and in this divine tent she ministered before God. She was established not merely in the midst of the people of Israel or in its land; she made her place in its very heart, in Jerusalem its capital, in the temple. The connections here are not coincidental. Ben Sira was intent on upholding the claim of Jerusalem's special election by God. At an earlier time in Israel's history partiality toward the city of David may have been a central principle of royal theology. Here it is a sign of ethnic favoritism, namely, the choice of Israel over all other nations.

There is another bias behind this statement: Ben Sira's interest in things priestly. Wisdom herself states that she is not just in Jerusalem, she is in the temple ministering before God. In the first section of the book, fear of the Lord is likened to respect for the priest (7:29-31). This same priestly bias occurs later in the praise of the heroes (chapters 44–50), which sketches the history of Israel in such a way as to show that its ultimate goal was Second-Temple Judaism as lived at the time of Simon son of Onias.

The poem continues describing how Wisdom matured and bore fruit in Israel (vv. 13-17). Several images of superabundance characterize the splendor into which it grew. She is compared to the mighty cedar, the elegant cypress, the graceful palm, and the luxuriant terebinth, as well as to beautiful flowers, fragrant plants, and fertile vines. Wisdom flourished, but it was the soil of Israel that provided the means for such extraordinary flowering. Once again the uniqueness of Israel is underscored.

Wisdom closes her speech with an invitation: come and enjoy my fruits (cf. Prov 8:32-36; 9:5f.; Isa 55:1-3). Although she claims to be sweet to the taste, she also admits that having once tasted her pleasures, one will never be completely satisfied. A taste for her makes one desire even more. This implies that the search for Wisdom is a lifelong search and suggests that Wisdom is not a fixed commodity that, once possessed, will last forever. Nor will it even remain unchanged.

With the conclusion of Woman Wisdom's self-praise, Ben Sira speaks. Quoting Deuteronomy (33:4), he identifies Wisdom with "the book of the covenant," the Deuteronomic term for the law (cf. 2 Kgs 22:8). He then turns to images reflective of the myth of the garden in Eden out of which flowed rivers that watered the entire world (cf. Gen 2:10-14). With these images he implies that as these rivers were the source of primordial life and fertility, so wisdom is the source of continued life for the faithful. To the paradisiacal Pishon, Gihon, Tigris, and Euphrates, Ben Sira adds the Jordan and the Nile, rivers that represent the nations of Israel and Egypt respectively. Every good thing for which these rivers came to be known is here applied to the law, which he has identified with Wisdom. His mention of the primal man's inability to fully comprehend wisdom does not refer to the sinful attempt to snatch or claim the wisdom that belongs to God (Gen 3:5; Ezek 28:6); rather, it acknowledges human limitation. Only God can fully comprehend wisdom.

Ben Sira develops the water image into a description of his own participation in the dissemination of Wisdom. As a student of wisdom, he filled his own life with its invigorating power. As a teacher of wisdom, he became a conduit of this life-giving water, channeling it to the lives of others. Convinced that his wisdom is as inspired as was the prophecy of old, Ben Sira set out to teach it to all who would listen and learn. Herein lies the reason for his grandson's translation into another language. Both believed in the lasting value of this instruction.

Much of the teaching that follows this hymn to Wisdom resembles that in the first section of the book. The teacher instructs the "child" (31:22; 37:27; 38:9, 16; 40:28; 41:14) about prudent living (for example, 29:21-28; 30:18-25), social conformity (32:14—33:3) and family stability (25:1). Fear of the Lord is a virtue held up for emulation (25:6, 10f.; 32:16; 33:1; 40:27), and there is a promise that it will be richly rewarded (34:14-20).

Other teaching in this part of the book has a slightly different emphasis. Although he advocates enjoyment of life to the extent that one is able (30:18-25; 40:18-27), Ben Sira does not ignore life's hardships (40:1-11). In fact, at times his observations resemble those of the author of the book of Job (cf. Job 7:1-6; 13:28—14:1,6,14). Acknowledging that humankind has been molded by the divine potter out of the stuff of the earth (33:10-13; cf. Gen 2:7), he speaks of the reality of death (41:1-4, 11-13) and offers directions on the proper way to mourn the death of another and to prepare the body for burial (38:16-23).

He insists that, under normal circumstances, wisdom is found with the aged and so they should be accorded special respect (25:3-6; 32:3-9). Experience and travel, such as he himself enjoyed, is another avenue for gaining wisdom (34:9-13). Furthermore, certain tasks demand special training (38:25-34). He held the medical profession in high regard, for, with the help of God, physicians are able to work wonders (38:1-15). No occupation compares, however, with that of the scribe (38:34c—39:11). The scribe studies and teaches others, prays and offers counsel. The scribe is directed by the Lord and is filled with the spirit of understanding (Harrington, 1980:181–88). According to Ben Sira, this is truly the noblest of professions.

In a patriarchal society, the honor of a man is often judged by his ability to keep the women of his household under control. Ben Sira expounds extensively on the dangers of an unruly woman (25:16-26; 26:5-12, 19-27). She can entice a man away from his duty, make his family life unbearable, and shame him before the community. On the other hand, a good woman is a delight to her husband and an asset to the family (26:1-4, 13-18; 36:26-31). Daughters are of particular concern to their fathers. Their fecundity must be assured and guarded, and they must be properly trained in household skills. According to Ben Sira, as important as they may be, women are the source of great anxiety. A wise man must learn how to keep those under his charge in order.

This second part of the book contains some very interesting teaching about creation. In one poem, Ben Sira addresses the polarities found in creation (33:7-15). He asks: If all daylight comes from the sun, why are some days sacred and others profane (vv. 7-9)? His answer: because that is the way God distinguished them. In similar manner, all human beings come from the ground, yet some are raised up and others are not (vv. 10-13). What does this preference mean? Most commentators consider Ben Sira's explanation an ethnic or cultic preference rather than moral predestination (see Skehan and Di Lella, 1987:399f.; Perdue, 1994:272–74). The poem ends with the statement of what seems to be a general principle. All of reality is balanced in these fundamental contrasting opposites: good and evil; life and death; the pious and sinners (vv. 14f.; cf. Eccl 3:1-8). This may be Ben Sira's way of handling the question of theodicy, the righteousness of God in the face of injustice in the world.

As part of his praise of the skills of the physician, Ben Sira briefly describes the healing powers of certain natural substances (38:4-8). Thus he points to the common link joining various facets of the natural world. Earth medicines can heal the human body because both they and it are made of the same substance. There is a natural link and an interdependence at play in the material world.

In a rather long hymn, Ben Sira exalts the goodness and value of creation and praises God as Creator and wise Sustainer (39:12-35). Characterizing himself as a full moon radiating brightness, he calls upon his sons (students?) to be open to his teaching. Then, like well-cultivated flowers, they will be able to spread their fragrance and their beauty abroad. He summons these "sons" to praise God and even tells them for what to be thankful: all the works of the Lord are good; and everything has a purpose.

Again and again the hymn acclaims the goodness of creation (vv. 16, 18, 33) and the providence of God in caring for it. God has made everything in order and provides for every need at the proper time (vv. 21, 31, 33f.; cf. Eccl 1:1-8, 11). Having made everything, God knows everything and exercises saving power over all. Divine providence sees to it that the good works of creation effect blessings for the righteous and misfortune for the ungodly (vv. 22-35; cf. the syncrises in Wis 11:2—19:22). In fact, it is through the natural world itself that God administers justice (vv. 28-31; cf. Wis 5:16b-23). After discussing the dual function of creation, Ben Sira ends the hymn as he began it, with a call to sing praise to God.

The last and longest hymn to the God of creation (42:15—43:33) also closes the second part of the book. Its form and content are reminiscent of the onomasticon of Egypt, a listing of natural phenomena (cf. Job 36:27—37:13; 38–41). It opens with a declaration of remembrance of the works of the Lord (42:15-17). Ordinarily this phrase refers to the mighty acts of God in Israel's history. Here it refers the wonders of creation that Ben Sira himself has observed, wonders that were created effortlessly by the divine word (cf. Gen 1) and that manifest the glory of God (vv. 16f.).

In the priestly tradition, "glory of God" refers to the divine self-manifestation in the cloud (Exod 16:10) or in the tabernacle (Exod 40:34); it is usually associated with some form of revelation. It should be noted that here revelation takes place in created phenomena rather than historical events. Ben Sira maintains that the wonders of creation are so magnificent that not even heavenly beings can adequately recount them. Only God can reveal them or proclaim them, for only the God who created them can comprehend them (vv. 18-21). Nonetheless, certain aspects of creation can be grasped by human beings (vv. 22-25), specifically, its beauty, its purposefulness, and the fact that it appears to be perfectly balanced in opposing pairs (cf. 33:15).

Ben Sira praises the splendor and order of the heavens and the moisture that falls from it, as well as the roles that these natural phenomena play in the arrangement of the universe (43:1-22; cf. Gen 1:14-19; Job 38:4-38). The sun burns with such force that it both illumines the sky and, at times, parches the earth. The moon marks the seasons and festivals, waxing and waning in a regular pattern. In addition to these major celestial bodies, the sky is further adorned with myriads of stars and, on occasion, a glorious rainbow. This tribute to the rainbow leads into praise of the various forms of moisture that the heavens bestow upon the earth. These include frost and snow and hailstones, wind and thunder and lightning, clouds and dew. The imagery used in this testimonial is some of the most vibrant in the book. This theophanic hymn depicts elements in nature as instruments of God's blessing and judgment. Nature is not passive when it comes to God's justice.

Just as God created and rules over the heavens and the earth, so the realm of the cosmic deep complies with the divine plan (43:23-26; cf. Job 9:13; 26:12; Isa 27:1; 51:9; Pss 89:9f.; 104:25f.). This control is particularly significant because having authority over the cosmic sea means being victorious over cosmic chaos. It is a way of acclaiming not only the universal but also the undisputed authority of God.

The final stanza of the hymn (vv. 27-35) corresponds to the opening stanza (42:15-18). It repeatedly praises the unparalleled majesty of God, whose works are incomparable and whose ways are unfathomable. Yet even these wonders cannot capture the awesomeness of the creator. Although human praise will always fall short of what God deserves, Ben Sira calls for praise nonetheless. Both the hymn and the second section of the book end with mention of the pious to whom God has given wisdom. The final verse prepares for the following hymn in praise of the ancestors of Israel.

This second section of the book takes the earlier themes of creation, wisdom, and the fear of the Lord and associates them with the special privilege that Israel claimed. In identifying Wisdom with the law of Israel, it brings obedience to that law into the cosmic realm. Subtle as this may seem, Ben Sira is insisting on the superiority of the religious tradition of Israel. This ethnocentric assertion is quite significant because the audience to which it is addressed is the diaspora in a Hellenistic setting.

Praise of the Ancestors of Old

The final part of the book (44:1—50:24) is the most unified. It is a hymn praising some of the heroes of Israel, men who manifested in their lives evidence that Wisdom had taken up her abode in that privileged nation. Ben Sira is the first wisdom writer to celebrate figures in Israel's saving history. Still, it is important to note that this is not like any other historical recounting. Ben Sira begins with the cosmic origin of Wisdom and then turns to the effects of her dwelling in Israel. He moves from cosmology to history. Unlike the other hymns in the book, this one praises men rather than God or Wisdom. Although it exalts the ancestors of the Jewish people, it follows the form of the Greek encomium, a commemorative speech that praises persons and institutions that embody certain cultural ideals, or a speech of high praise. This classical form of oration belongs to the category of epi-deictic literature, literature that sought to impress the audience rather than persuade it (Lee, 1986:81–103).

The hymn begins with an introduction followed by a series of poetic units of unequal length extolling select Israelite heroes. The reason for the praise provides insight into the specific character of the encomium. With one or two exceptions, these men are remembered because of the way they exemplify the cultural values that Ben Sira wishes to promote rather than because of their contribution to Israel's history. What may be startling to some is the evaluation accorded Solomon. His early years may have been marked by wisdom (47:14-18; cf. 1 Kgs 3:10-12), but the indiscretion of his latter years, a time when he should have excelled in good judgment, along with the folly of his son Rehoboam, are blamed for the division of the Davidic monarchy into two separate kingdoms (47:19-25; cf. 1 Kgs 11-12).

The introduction (44:1-15) consists of a list of twelve categories of memorable ancestors. Although the men included in the hymn were those who had been honored in their own generations and, in Ben Sira's judgment, should be remembered in later ones, the primary focus seems to be the categories rather than the individuals within them. The categories include rulers (David and Solomon), heroes (Joshua, Caleb, and the judges), royal counselors (Nathan, Isaiah, and Jeremiah), prophets (Samuel, Elijah, Elisha, Isaiah, Jeremiah, Ezekiel, and minor prophets), governors (Joseph), lawgivers (Moses), sages (Solomon and Job), framers of proverbs (Solomon), musicians (David), poets (Solomon and Hezekiah), rich householders (Abraham, Isaac, and Jacob), men of peace (Job; cf. Skehan and Di Lella, 1987:500f.; for a slightly different classification, see Lee, 1986:224–26). Besides those explicitly named, there were many whose deeds were remembered but whose names have been lost except to their own descendants, who have inherited their wealth as well as their commitment to the covenant.

There is a general pattern in the profile of these heroes: (1) a designation of office; (2) mention of divine election; (3) reference to covenant; (4) mention of the individual's piety; (5) account of deeds; (6) historical data; (7) mention of rewards (Mack, 1985:18–26). These profiles are not randomly arranged. Rather, an underlying movement appears in their order, and it is not the mere unfolding of the history of Israel. Each event describes a moment invested with the glory of divine purpose and accomplishment. Together they move through Israel's history to a final manifestation of God's purpose, namely, Judaism in the form in which it existed at the time of Simon the high priest. In other words, the hymn retells history in such a way as to show that the contemporary form of Second-Temple Judaism is the appropriate climax to Israel's covenantal history. Every ancient figure both excelled in a cultural value Ben Sira deemed important for his time and moved the religious tradition to its full realization, second-century B.C.E. Judaism (Mack, 1985:37–65).

The poem's priestly bias is unmistakable (Martin, 1986:253–54). It shapes Israel's history as a history of the covenants that established Israel's cult. Beginning with Noah and the covenant made with all of creation (cf. Gen 9:9f.), the story speaks of Abraham and circumcision (cf. Gen 17:10-14), Moses and the law (the sign of this covenant is the Sabbath; cf. Exod 31:12-17). The longest acclamation belongs to Aaron (45:6-22). Following his praise of Phineas, priest-grandson of Aaron, Ben Sira directs his attention to the reigning high priest and prays that those who follow him will enjoy the glory that befits such an exalted state (45:6).

The remaining heroes, though not priests themselves, are somehow connected to Jerusalem, the temple, and its worship. David is hailed for his commitment to observance of the festivals and the musical contributions he made to cultic ceremonies and Solomon renowned for his wisdom, which was demonstrated in his building of the temple. Elijah and Elisha performed their remarkable feats in the face of the northern kings, who had dissociated themselves and their nation from Jerusalem. Hezekiah, Isaiah, Josiah, and all of the remaining worthies were committed to Jerusalem and the temple that was holy to the LORD.

All of this "history" culminates in the celebration of Simon son of Onias (50:1-21), the high priest at the time of Ben Sira himself. Simon was "the priest who presided over the sacred people in the holy city and the sacral ruler whose office made God present in the Temple and in the midst of the chosen" (Perdue, 1994:285). Clearly the temple pageantry made a deep impression on Ben Sira. His description of the high priest's exit from the Holy Place is a collage of brilliant nature comparisons. The vividness of the account of the ensuing ritual is remarkable in its detail and the concluding prayer for peace in Israel is quite pointed in its national partiality.

The guiding principle of this overview of Israel's history is the wisdom bestowed by God on the godly (43:33). Wisdom is the beginning and the end of history. Because of wisdom the men cited in the encomium excelled in the virtues for which they are remembered. The record of their virtue then becomes the incentive for the emulation of their descendants. Thus wisdom inspires history, and history becomes a wisdom lesson for others.

The remainder of the book consists of a numerical proverb decrying the hated Edomites, Philistines, and Samaritans (50:25f.), an epilogue wherein the author fully identifies himself and declares "blessed" those who follow his teachings (vv. 26-29), a prayer of thanksgiving (51:1-12), and an acrostic poem that recounts Ben Sira's search for Wisdom (vv. 13-30).

The final poem forms a kind of *inclusio* with the first poem (1:11-30). In this autobiographical account, Ben Sira portrays himself as one who from his youth was eager to gain Wisdom. He prayed for her, he listened for her in the instruction given him. Having received her, he resolved to live according to her designs. With understanding came the tongue to teach the lessons of wisdom to others. And so Ben Sira invites the uneducated to his school (51:23), to submit themselves to the discipline of Wisdom and, thereby, gain for themselves the riches that accompany her.

Rhetorical Function

The prologue to the Wisdom of Jesus Ben Sira lays out quite clearly the purpose and the content of both Ben Sira's message and that of his grandson. That purpose was to take the teachings found in the Law, the Prophets, and the Writings of Israel and recontextualize them so that a new generation of believers "who love learning might make even greater progress in living according to the law." Toward this end, Ben Sira reinterpreted the ancient traditions for his contemporaries (ca. 180 B.C.E.), and his grandson translated these teachings into Greek for the Hellenized people of his day (ca. 132 B.C.E.).

The book appears to be simply a compilation of essays of various lengths, arranged in a random fashion. Some topics are treated again and again, others only once. Despite this apparent lack of organization, the underlying argument of the collection of instructions is clear: While all people seek wisdom, it is only fully accessible to God. God bestows wisdom, however, on those who fear the Lord. The way to fear of the Lord leads one to and takes the form of observance of the law. Finally, Ben Sira's teaching is a trustworthy guide to this observance. Therefore, one can conclude that the way to wisdom is observance of the law. This is the fundamental message of Ben Sira, whether directed to his own compatriots or to the diaspora Jews of the time of his grandson.

This document is a fine example of teaching that has been recontextualized. First, traditions originate out of the experience of a particular believing community during a time in its history considered formative by a later generation. These traditions are then handed down and refashioned at another time for the descendants of these believers. Finally, they are translated for the sake of still another community within a very different culture at a much later time. The prologue states that they are handed down from one context to another because of the enduring importance of the original message. The uniqueness of each new context accounts for any possible variations in the teaching itself.

Both Ben Sira and his grandson were seasoned travelers and had learned much from their contact with other cultures (34:12f.; prologue). Although staunch advocates of the prominence of their own tradition, unlike Pseudo-

Solomon they never really condemned the beliefs or practices of others. Thus, this book functions less as a contentious polemic against another culture than as a persuasive argument in support of the superiority of Judaism. Because it contains so many allusions to Israel's religious history, it is clear that the teaching was meant for believers who were acquainted with the early traditions. That these Jews had to be reassured or convinced of the excellence of their own religion suggests that they were wavering in their faith and had to be reminded of the inestimable treasure that was theirs.

The teachings can be received in several different ways depending upon the perspective of the reader. Primarily intended for Hellenized Jews who were enthralled by the scope, depth, precision, and creativity of Greek thought, it speaks to those who had lost confidence in the value of their tradition of origin. Those who sought refinement and enlightenment are shown that, while real wisdom belongs to God alone, God prepared a special place for wisdom in Jerusalem, the heart of Israel. They learn further that only those who are devoted to the traditions of old, who model their lives after the example of the ancestors of Israel, can hope to enjoy the blessings that wisdom bestowed upon the faithful. The book intends to persuade the fallen away of the validity of this point of view, to call them back to fidelity. It maintains that if they seek true wisdom, they will find it in Israel; if they are truly wise, they will recognize the truth of this claim.

The fact that neither Ben Sira nor his grandson condemned the other cultures that they encountered but, in fact, were actually influenced by them, should be noted. This acculturation was not accidental; both men intended it in order to address what they considered to be the religious needs of "outsiders." In each case, the ancient traditions were expressed in new ways to new audiences. Furthermore, the prologue clearly states that Ben Sira added his own teachings to "the Law, the Prophets, and the other books of our ancestors," thus claiming for his work the authority enjoyed by the earlier traditions. His grandson followed his example, translating the work so that it might accompany the Greek version of the Bible (the Septuagint) and enjoy the authority accorded it.

The way both Ben Sira and his grandson recontextualized and reinterpreted their religious traditions in the face of new social or cultural realities should speak to traditionalists who might resist any change in teaching or practice. Accommodation to change does not necessarily mean that the traditions forfeit their religious relevance; quite the contrary. It is based on the conviction that the significance of the religious traditions far exceeds their specific cultural expression. Religion may transform the culture, but culture also reshapes religion. This is a lesson that strict traditionalists can learn from Ben Sira.

Finally, there are those within the believing community who share the perspective of Ben Sira and his grandson. Although they are open to cross-cultural enrichment, they are nonetheless convinced of the preeminence of their own religious heritage. Their ethnocentricity may not be contentious, but it still exists and it influences the way they judge the religious integrity of others. Those who have strayed are encouraged to return, because their defection has made them foolish and wicked. There is both concern for the "outsiders" and hope that they might embrace the religion of the author/translator. The possibility that the perspective of the "outsider" might have merit is never considered. Only Israel enjoys the truth; only Israel can boast of wisdom.

Unmasking the Powers

The ethnocentricity of this teaching may be noncontentious, but it is biased nonetheless. Its chauvinism is first evident in the prologue's concern to "help the outsider." At first glance such behavior may appear to be magnanimous, but a closer look will reveal its patronizing attitude. It does not even entertain the possibility that the outsider might have something of value to teach, and this despite the fact that both Ben Sira and his grandson did indeed learn from the culture that they encountered. They seem to have appropriated ideas and patterns of expression from the other culture and then used them to praise their own accomplishments with no thought of their dependence on that culture.

The book depicts Israel as God's favorite nation (17:17; 36:1-17) and the divinely chosen dwelling place of cosmic wisdom (24:8-12, 23). Because the underlying theme of this book is the desirability of wisdom, a declaration that asserts Israel's distinctiveness in this area supports its claim of superiority. The denunciation of Israel's political rivals (50:25f.) and the character of the portrayal of its heroes further demonstrate the scope and significance of wisdom's presence in Israel's life. No other people enjoy such integrity and possess such religious insight. No other nation can boast a history of such discretion, valor, and nobility. Not only is Ben Sira biased in favor of his own people, but he maintains that God is as well.

The basis of this uniqueness is the covenant. Much of the teaching of the book extols a distinctive relationship between God and this chosen people (17:12; 44:12; 45:15). It also applauds the special covenants made with Noah (44:18), with Abraham (44:20, 23), with Aaron (45:7, 15), with Phineas (45:24), and with David (45:25; 47:11), all of whom are considered Israelite heroes. Ben Sira's instruction exhorts the believers to commit themselves to the covenantal law (9:15; 15:15; 17:11; 19:17; 28:6f.; 29:1, 9, 11; 32:15, 23f.; 33:2f.; 35:1, 5; 37:12; 40:14; 41:8; 42:2). It links observance of this law to both the fear of the Lord (2:16; 19:24; 23:27) and the acquisition of wisdom (1:26; 6:37; 15:1; 19:20; 21:11; 34:8; 39:1, 8). Finally, it credits fidelity to the law for the blessings bestowed on the heroes of the past (44:20; 45:5, 17; 46:14; 49:4). The covenant and its law are both a sign of God's partiality and the way that Israel lives out this privilege.

The bias in Israel's favor is undeniable. If the fear of the Lord is the way that human beings enter into the realm of wisdom, and if obedience to the law is the path to the fear of the Lord, then it is clear why Ben Sira teaches that only through submission to the demands of covenant law can one approach the throne of wisdom. In fact, he goes so far as to identify the law of the covenant with the wisdom from on high (24:23), thus setting Israel's religious tradition far above the way of life of any other people. According to Ben Sira, the life that issues from compliance to the law is in a class of its own, with no peer, no rival, and no comparison.

Besides the ethnic favoritism, an equally obvious class bias exists. Material prosperity and the security that comes with it are perceived as the reward for fidelity and the fruits of the virtue of the fear of the Lord (1:16-18; 2:9; 4:15). The kind of liturgical sacrifice that is advocated by this author requires economic resources in order for people to participate (34:21-27; 35:1-13). Other admonitions also presume financial security and social privilege. They advocate proper attitudes toward possessions (7:22; 11:4; 14:3-10; 21:4; 29:1-7, 14-20; 31:1-11; 33:20; 40:18) and appropriate social etiquette (8:1f., 8, 12f.; 13:2, 9-11; 22:23; 31:12-18; 37:29-31). Even the prospect of death is viewed differently by those of dissimilar class status. Death is bitter to the prosperous who are at peace in their possessions but a welcome release for those whose life is beset with trouble (41:1f.).

On the other hand, Ben Sira does teach that privilege carries with it certain responsibilities. He admonishes his students to be sympathetic toward the needy (4:1-6, 8-10) and to give alms to the poor (3:30; 4:31; 7:10, 32; 12:3-7; 17:22; 29:8, 12; 40:17, 24). He offers direction for giving due respect to public officials to whom the advantaged presumably have access (7:31), for handling household servants (6:11; 7:20f.; 33:25-33), and for fostering a healthy attitude toward wealth (5:1, 8; 18:25, 32; 19:1; 29:9-13), and he tells his students not to aspire to high places that might be within their reach (7:4-7, 14) but to be humble. This may all be seen as a form of training in attitudes of sensitivity, but it is still clearly advice that one would give to those with financial means and social status within the community rather than to those who are underprivileged or marginal.

The ethnocentricity and class bias here do not differ greatly from what is present in other books that make up Israel's wisdom tradition. Ben Sira's gender prejudice is more straightforward and harsher than what is found elsewhere, however. First, as is the case in Proverbs, the instruction is handed down from father to son (3:1; 7:3; 39:13; cf. Prov 1:8, 10, 15; 2:1; 3:1, 11, 21; 4:1, 10, 20; 5:1, 7, 20; 6:1, 3, 20; 7:1, 24; 8:32). Whether this bond is natural, one of relationship between teacher and student, or merely a metaphorical technique, the gender bias is clear. All of the teaching here is androcentric, using male references (6:36; 9:17—10:5) for the sake of instruction of the male student (30:1-13). This gender bias is also evident in the historical summary, where the heroes remembered are exclusively male and only their male descendants merit mention by the author (45:13, 15, 25; 47:12).

More specifically, Ben Sira considers women a constant temptation to men, enticing them, even physically weakening them. In his vituperation against them, he attacks women from various social settings within the community: married women, virgins, and women unattached to traditional households (9:1-9; 19:2; 41:20-22). His disdain for women is relentless and all-encompassing. He goes so far as to state that nothing is as base as a woman (25:13-26). Finally, he lays the guilt of sin on the woman's shoulders, contending that it was because of the first woman that sin came into the world, and as a consequence of her depravity we must now all die (25:24).

Ben Sira is especially solicitous about and skeptical of the virtue of women within the patriarchal household, in particular that of the wives and the daughters. Even a cursory glance will show that the marriage contract, as he perceives it, is not one of equal reciprocity. Rather, in order to guarantee the legitimacy of patrilineal inheritance, a wife must be faithful to her husband (23:22-27). Yet he does not insist that marital fidelity be mutual. A wife must be respected by her children (3:2-11; 7:27; 23:14; 41:17), but not necessarily by her husband.

A wife who is judged to be virtuous or wise is considered primarily to enhance the status of the husband (7:19; 25:8). By contrast, a mean and scandalous wife disgraces him (26:5-9). This reflects the honor-shame code of the ancient society, which publicly judges a man by his ability to control his private life according to accepted societal norms. Ben Sira does not accord women any personal worth. Instead, he believes that their value lies in their ability to contribute to the androcentric concerns of their patriarchal society. Their worth is measured by their husbands' enjoyment of them or of their talents and abilities (7:26; 26:1-4, 13-27; 36:26-31; 40:19, 23; 42:6). Whether or not women suffer or are in any way deprived in the marriage appears to be of no consequence.

Ben Sira's misogyny is glaring in his attitude toward daughters. Unabashedly, he deems their birth a loss (22:3). Regardless of the nature of their personalities and the quality of their characters, they are always a great concern to their fathers (7:24f.; 22:4f.; 42:9f.). Apparently this paternal anxiety escalated when a daughter was independent-minded (26:10f.; 42:11-14), because independence in a woman was not prized. Daughters were suspected of indecency, perhaps even promiscuity (26:12). Because of their potential for immorality (26:12), they required careful oversight, first in their families of origin and then in the families of the men who married them. If daughters are held in such contempt, it is understandable that wives are disdained.

Finally, when Ben Sira describes the happiness that one will enjoy in the possession of Wisdom, he uses two female images, mother and bride (15:1-6). Although the description intends to conjure up a picture of a kind of utopian experience, the gender bias is obvious. Like a mother, Wisdom serves the man hand and foot, meeting his every possible need or wish with no intermission and no thought of recompense. She is also compared to a young bride, whose only concern is to provide pleasure for her groom. While these characterizations may signal Wisdom's dedication to her devotees and the delight that she brings, they also lay bare the prejudicial attitude toward women that is part of this author's worldview.

Into the Looking Glass

The advocacy stand sensitive to questions of race or ethnic origin, class, and gender has uncovered the biases that underlie the worldview of Ben Sira. At issue now is the nature and scope of the revelatory potential of this teaching. How can this biblical message, which has functioned as a mirror, now act as a doorway through which to pass into a world with new transformative possibilities?

Without denying Ben Sira's ethnic bias, it is important to highlight his dependence on the very culture that he seems to be scorning. Besides the proverbs, the "better . . . than" statements, the prayers and hymns, and the meditations that Ben Sira inherited from his own Israelite literary tradition, he also made use of the encomium (chapters 44–51), a form of praise borrowed from Greek culture. He is quite adroit in his use of several rhetorical devices found in the encomium. The skill with which he employed this form is evidence of the level of his acculturation into the literary world of the Greeks.

The grandson's accommodation to a foreign culture is obvious in his eagerness to translate the teachings of his grandfather into Greek, the lingua franca of his day. His prologue is quite telling in this regard. Acknowledging the limitations of any translation, he never suggests that the biblical message cannot be communicated in a language other than the original. On the contrary, he simply states that the new translation may not have exactly the same meaning, but it will still provide direction for those inclined to "live according to the law."

While he is chiefly concerned with the instruction and subsequent covenantal commitment of Israelites living in the Hellenistic diaspora, he did not limit the scope of his audience to his own religious group. It is his stated hope that these very compatriots, through both the spoken and the written word, will share the riches of their tradition with those in their society who do not belong to the community of believers. Whether or not he intended that this sharing be a form of proselytizing is not clear, but the prologue does not explicitly indicate that such was his hope. Therefore, one can conclude that the grandson entertained an open frame of mind toward the people among whom his compatriots lived. The grandson's ethnic bias did not really exclude the outsider, nor did it require that the outsider move into the community of faith.

Ben Sira's perspective may be biased in favor of the religious traditions of Israel, but it does not repudiate other cultures, as does the teaching found in the Wisdom of Solomon. On the contrary, the very first hymn in praise of Wisdom states that God pours Wisdom out upon *all* of God's works, upon *all* the living, upon *all* who love God (1:10). At the beginning she held sway over *every* people and nation (24:6). There is a fundamental universality in this picture. Wisdom encompasses all, and all have equal access to her influence. Even when wisdom is ensconced in Israel, her blessings flow out of it to all corners of the world as did the life-giving rivers in Eden. Wisdom may have a unique relationship with Israel but it does not prohibit another kind of relationship with another nation.

A similar openness to the "other" is evident in Ben Sira's concise version of the creation of human beings (17:1-17). This poetic account reveals an anthropology devoid of ethnic differentiation, much less explicit bias. Made in the image of God, all people have the same origin, are granted the same abilities, and struggle with the same human limitations. The poem recalls that God established a covenant with all flesh (cf. Gen 9:9-17) and eventually appointed a ruler for every nation. According to this author, Israel's special appointment as the chosen of the Lord does not seem to have abrogated any of what was described earlier in the poem. Israel may be preferred, but the nations are nonetheless guided by the Creator-God and by God's Wisdom.

The class bias observed in the teaching of Ben Sira is not ubiquitous. In fact, it is tempered by statements that either voice a disregard for class distinctions or declare God's preference for those disadvantaged by such distinctions. The inclusive anthropological perspective discussed above in relation to ethnic differences holds true in regard to class distinction as well

(17:1-17). All people, regardless of social or economic class, were created the same and enjoy the same providential care. Ben Sira further declares that hard work and anxiety over possible suffering and eventual death are the lot of every human being, rich or poor, ruler or beggar (40:1-9, cf. Job 7:1f.). Certain aspects of life know no class discrimination.

In those areas of life in which social or economic distinctions exist, Ben Sira's observations and subsequent admonitions are sometimes contradictory. At times he deplores the life of the disadvantaged (29:21-28; 40:28-30); at other times he seems to prefer it (10:14-17; 11:5f., 12). His apparent inconsistency may simply be his way of dealing with the manifest paradoxes of life (20:9-17; 39:27). But he is convinced beyond doubt that both prosperity and need come from the hand of God (11:14) and that God can reverse fortunes, raising up the lowly and bringing down the mighty (11:21). In Ben Sira's view, righteousness rather than apparent good or poor fortune is the real determining factor (10:22-24; 35:16; 40:18). In this, there is no class preference.

As has been the case throughout this study of the wisdom tradition, the gender bias of the author(s) is the most difficult to address. Ben Sira's attitude toward women is, as stated above, acrimonious and prejudicial. He not only tacitly excludes them from his concern, he explicitly disdains them. In his eyes they are more than worthless, they are a liability. A daughter is always a source of anxiety. More likely than not, her lascivious inclinations will bring shame on the household, which, in its turn, will lessen her marriageability, resulting in financial setback. A wife's petulant dispositions can make her husband's life miserable. Rather than being an asset and a comfort, she can become a handicap and a source of affliction.

Without minimizing the bigotry in all of this, there are elements in the book that suggest a new way of interpreting the material. First, the structure of the book sets up a literary context within which the depiction of women might be interpreted. The two sections of instruction, chapters 1–23 and chapters 24–43, each begin with a poem praising Woman Wisdom, and the entire book ends with a similar poem (51:13-30). Perhaps this extraordinary figure does not define the character of human women, but it does color the way they are perceived, since the vehicle and tenor of a metaphor are mutually interpretive. This being the case, the dominant female characterization of the book and the setting within which actual women are described are both complimentary and can enhance the image of women that the book creates.

The importance of the characterization of Woman Wisdom cannot be underestimated. Whether Ben Sira inherited this figure from his Israelite tradition (Prov 8) or from the Greek representation of Isis (Wis 7), he portrays her in language and imagery normally reserved for God. She is resplendent in demeanor, awe-inspiring in her proficiency, unlimited in her influence, the desire of all flesh, and the darling of God. Ben Sira is clearly enthralled with this female character.

Clearly, the household organization that the author presumes is patriarchal and the point of view that he advances is androcentric. His male students are exhorted, however, to respect their mothers as well as their fathers (3:2-16; 7:27). Mention of mothers may here be merely a fiction of parallel construction and not to be construed as actual instruction. There is, however, no parallel construction in which the student is told that when in public he should remember the kind of training he received at home (23:14), or that he should be ashamed of his sexual immorality before both parents (41:17). Both parents are to be respected (3:7; 7:28).

While women generally and daughters and wives specifically are not held in high regard, mothers certainly are. This may well be a common feature of patriarchal societies, wherein mothers are the primary nurturers of the male children until they reach puberty. It is clear in other places of the tradition, however, that this respect does not diminish when the son leaves the domain of the mother's influence. Instead, it continues and frequently even grows stronger. Perhaps this is because sons are convinced of their mothers' total commitment to them, a devotion that they may not be able to expect from their sisters and later from their wives. This commitment probably includes a certain degree of self-interest on the part of the woman, for if and when she is widowed, a mother will be dependent upon her son for support, care, and legal protection.

As was true in both Proverbs and the Wisdom of Solomon, the profiles of human women are reciprocally conditioned by the metaphorical characterization of Woman Wisdom (Camp, 1985:71–77). Women may be portrayed here in well-defined cultural roles, but the metaphor of Woman Wisdom challenges the restrictive contours of the stereotypes (McFague, 1982). The image of Woman Wisdom tempers the bigotry of the author and offers contemporary interpreters an avenue for reinterpretation.

Last but not least is a consideration of the cosmological perspective underlying the entire book. As has been seen in other books of the wisdom tradition, cosmology is not merely one aspect among many but the context within which all else is found. This can be seen first in the book's basic literary structure. Poems praising creation frame whatever else is being taught. Two of the three major sections (chapters 1–23 and 24–43) begin with a poem describing the intimate relationship between Wisdom and creation. Each of these poems sets the mood for understanding what follows. The third section (chapters 44–51) follows a poem that exalts the glories of creation. If the praise of the ancestors is in fact an addition to an earlier well-organized treatise of exhortation, as many commentators believe (Mack, 1985; Lee, 1986), then this last poem along with the opening one functions as a kind of *inclusio* (Perdue, 1994:248), bracketing Ben Sira's early treatise within a creation framework.

The first poem (1:1-10) praises Wisdom's primordial origin. There she is described as having been created before the rest of the universe, and her incomprehensibility is compared to the unimaginable scope and wonder of the cosmos. This metaphorical comparison celebrates both Wisdom and the created world, for the splendor of one serves to describe the marvels of the other. The first part of the second poem (24:1-7) recounts anew Wisdom's beginnings and then depicts her as holding sway over the heights, the depths, and all the earth. Once again, the author has employed the wonders of creation in order to sketch the glories of Wisdom. The lengthy poem that forms the second half of the *inclusio* (42:15—43:33) is longer than the others and far more lyrical. It leaves the believer standing in awe of the wondrous yet mysterious works of God in creation. These works somehow originated in Wisdom, remain established through Wisdom, and point to the incomprehensibility of both Wisdom and the Creator-God.

There is no doubt about Ben Sira's desire to demonstrate the superiority of Israelite religious tradition. His identification of Wisdom with the book of the covenant, the law (24:23), offers evidence of this. What makes this such a special privilege for Israel, however, is the cosmic character of this Wisdom. She is not merely the Sophia of Greek philosophy but the mist that emanated from the mouth of the Most High, the one who dwelt in the highest heavens, whose throne was in a pillar of cloud, who compassed the vault of heaven and traversed the depths of the abyss (24:3-5). This is cosmic Wisdom. Were she not the foundation of all of creation, her lodging in Israel would not be as momentous as it is. The grandeur of Wisdom and the privilege accorded Israel that flows from this grandeur are rooted in Wisdom's primordial cosmic origin.

To the Godly God Has Given Wisdom

This phrase contains the basis of Ben Sira's teaching. It clearly states that Wisdom is God's to give, and it identifies those to whom God gives Wisdom. Like every good proverbial statement, it describes one facet of life in such a way as to encourage people to act in the manner recounted so that they can enjoy the ensuing consequences. This phrase teaches a very important lesson: if you want Wisdom, act in a godly manner. For Ben Sira and for his grandson, this godly manner was none other than faithful observance of the laws and customs of Israel.

While the essence of their teaching boasts continuity with the traditions of the ancestors, the manner of expression demonstrates a certain degree of discontinuity. Ben Sira's account of the history of several Israelite heroes differs from that found in earlier accounts, and his grandson admits that his translation does not carry exactly the same sense as that found in the Hebrew. Something of the original connotation may be lost when a tradition is recontextualized, but something else is gained from the new context. The fact that a religious insight can have meaning in more than one cultural situation is evidence of its enduring revelatory value and relevance.

Both Ben Sira and his grandson faced a very serious challenge. The philosophical excellence of Greek thought rivaled the seemingly unsophisticated beliefs of Judaism. Each man, in his own day, took upon himself the task of convincing first his compatriots, and then anyone else who would listen, of the superiority of the religious traditions of Israel. They believed that the law of the covenant provided a way of life that was pleasing to God, and that those who feared the Lord would follow this way. In fact, "the fear of the Lord is the beginning of wisdom" (1:14).

Acknowledging the limitations of Ben Sira's point of view, his ethnocentricity, his class bias, and his gender prejudice, the statement "to the godly God has given Wisdom" is as relevant for others as it was at the time of the original author. Following the example of both Ben Sira and his grandson, believers of every generation have had to look anew at what they consider faithfulness to be. This entailed a knowledge and appreciation of the religious tradition received and insight into their own contemporary situations. Only then were they in a position to recontextualize in a manner faithful to the past as well as to the present. The challenge for us today is no less demanding, and the reward is no less sublime: To the godly God will give Wisdom.

Works Consulted

Camp, Claudia V. 1985. *Wisdom and the Feminine in the Book of Proverbs*. Sheffield: Almond Press.

Di Lella, Alexander. 1987. *The Wisdom of Ben Sira*. The Anchor Bible. New York: Doubleday.

_____. 1992. "Wisdom of Ben Sira." In *The Anchor Bible Dictionary*, volume 6. Edited by David Noel Freedman. New York: Doubleday.

Gammie, John G. 1990. "The Sage in Sirach." In *The Sage in Israel and the Ancient Near East*. Edited by John G. Gammie and Leo G. Perdue. Winona Lake, Ind.: Eisenbrauns.

Harrington, Daniel J. 1980. "The Wisdom of the Scribe according to Ben Sira." In *Ideal Figures in Ancient Israel*. Edited by George W. E. Nickelsburg and John J. Collins. Chico, Calif.: Scholars Press.

Jacob, Edmond. 1978. "Wisdom and Religion in Sirach." In *Israelite Wisdom: Theological and Literary Essays in Honor of Samuel Terrien.* Edited by John G. Gammie, Walter A. Brueggemann, W. Lee Humphreys, and James M. Ward. Missoula, Mont.: Scholars Press.

Lang, Bernhard. 1986. *Wisdom and the Book of Proverbs: An Israelite Goddess Redefined.* New York: Pilgrim Press.

Lee, Thomas R. 1986. *Studies in the Form of Sirach 44–50.* Society of Biblical Literature Dissertation Series 75. Atlanta: Scholars Press.

McFague, Sallie. 1982. *Metaphorical Theology.* Philadelphia: Fortress Press.

Mack, Burton L. 1985. *Wisdom and the Hebrew Epic: Ben Sira's Hymn in Praise of the Fathers.* Chicago: University of Chicago Press.

MacKenzie, R. A. F. 1983. *Sirach.* Old Testament Message. Wilmington, Del.: Michael Glazier.

Martin, James D. 1986. "Ben Sira—A Child of His Time." In *A Word in Season: Essays in Honor of William McKane.* Journal for the Study of Old Testament Supplement Series 42. Edited by James D. Martin and Philip R. Davies. Sheffield: University of Sheffield Press.

Murphy, Roland E. 1990. *The Tree of Life: An Exploration of Biblical Wisdom Literature.* Anchor Bible Reference Library. New York: Doubleday.

Perdue, Leo G. 1994. *Wisdom and Creation: The Theology of Wisdom Literature.* Nashville: Abingdon Press.

Roth, Wolfgang. 1980. "On the Gnomic-Discursive Wisdom of Jesus Ben Sirach." *Semeia* 17:59–79.

Sheppard, Gerald T. 1980. *Wisdom as a Hermeneutical Construct: A Study in the Sapientializing of the Old Testament.* Beihefte zur Zeitschrift für die alttestamentliche Wissenschaft 151. Berlin: Walter de Gruyter.

Skehan, Patrick W. 1979. "Structures in Poems on Wisdom: Proverbs 8 and Sirach 24." *Catholic Biblical Quarterly:*41: 365–79.

Skehan, Patrick W., and Alexander A. Di Lella. 1987. *The Wisdom of Ben Sira.* The Anchor Bible. New York: Doubleday.

Index

193